CAMPFIRES
AND
GAME TRAILS

Hunting North American Big Game

Craig Boddington

SAFARI PRESS
(An Imprint of The Woodbine Publishing Co.)
P. O. Box 3095, Long Beach, CA 90803, USA

To my parents, Jeanne and Bud Boddington,
who inspired, instructed, supported—
and most of all encouraged.

CAMPFIRES AND GAME TRAILS. Published by Safari Press (an imprint of The Woodbine Publishing Co.).

Boddington, Craig

ISBN 0-940143-31-3

1989, Long Beach, California

10 9 8 7 6 5 4 3 2 1

Readers wishing to receive the Safari Press catalog featuring many fine books on hunting big game all over the world should write to: Safari Press, P. O. Box 3095, Long Beach, CA 90803; or call: in USA (except CA) 800-451-4788; in CANADA 800-848-5649; in CALIFORNIA & WORLDWIDE 213-430-3693; FAX 213-596-4267.

Contents

Foreword

A refreshing aspect of this book is the attitude of the author. He is enthusiastic, interested and engaging in all his hunting experiences. He shares with the reader the spontaneity, the thrills and the satisfaction of a long stalk and a good killing shot. His hunting experience has been broad and he writes of none of the 27 species of North American game that he has not brought to bag. A number of similar books on hunting all our game give a sketchy treatment to those species which the author has not hunted. Not so Boddington.

The various species of our deer are given a fulsome treatment. It is obvious that the author is conducting a love affair with this most common of our big game animals. And rightly it should be so. Literally millions of American big game sportsmen never quest for any game except the whitetail deer. To have given the longest chapter to this species shows, I think, a fine and sensitive understanding. I applaud his lengthy dissertation. It is obvious he has shot a good many deer and his observations and more particularly his recommendations are remarkably sound.

Not in any case does Boddington recommend rifles and calibers that are most surely inadequate for the game being hunted. You will find no offerings of the .270 Winchester for moose, grizzly and Alaska brown bear. We have had pundits in the past who would have us believe that the .270 was right next to nuclear reaction in its lethality.

It appeals to me after a close reading of this tome that our author is somewhat of a big bore/heavy bullet *aficionado*. When in doubt, he invariably goes for such rounds as the .338 and the .340 Weatherby. I approved of this. It may be that he hunted too long with Elmer Keith.

An invaluable portion of this text, and it is notable throughout every chapter, is the recommendation of specific areas for specific game animals. This data is fresh and vital, established after very recent hunting expeditions and may be depended on. Again, Boddington often speaks of the guide or the guide/outfitter with whom he hunted and this is extremely worthwhile. It has been my long experience that the very most satisfactory way to organize a wholly productive big game expedition is to listen to the advice of the fellow who has just been over the ground. The Boddington opus is most worthwhile in this regard.

This is an enthralling book, a captivating portrayal of the sportsman who is never so happy as when he is high in the Mackenzies, adrift on an ice floe off Banks Island in the Arctic, or breasting 10-foot snow drifts in the Selway-Bitterroot of Idaho. His contagion is spontaneous and it bubbles forth in his writing as he responds to those old challenges.

Colonel Charles Askins
San Antonio, Texas

Chapter 1
North American Big Game

North American hunters are blessed with some of the finest and most varied hunting on the globe. In terms of quantity and quality of game species—and availability of good hunting country—most of us have no idea how fortunate we are. In the midst of heavy industrialization and burgeoning human populations, the Europeans have maintained amazingly excellent hunting, but they have learned to pay for it. To those few who can, our concept of free, albeit regulated, hunting on public lands is totally foreign.

The vast continent of Asia holds many remarkable game species, but changing politics and loss of habitat have wreaked havoc on wildlife. Few areas in all of Asia remain open to hunting, and fewer still retain high concentrations of wildlife. South America was never blessed with the variety of game found on our continent, and much of what was originally present is in trouble today. The South Pacific, most notably Australia and New Zealand, does offer some fine hunting, but almost none of it is for native species. Rather, hunting "down under" is for species introduced during the pioneer era, since almost no native game could truly be classed as 'big game.'

What of Africa? The African continent contains an incredible number of big game species, more than 150, and many of them are of great interest to the sportsman. The "Dark Continent" offers some of the world's best hunting, and the concentrations of game in some areas are second to none on the globe. But it's a big continent, and fully half of it is virtually devoid of wildlife. Of the remainder, some nations offer hunting and some do not. With the exception of a few southern countries, the wildlife is on the decline throughout Africa.

Contrast all this with North America. From the outskirts of our eastern metropolitan areas to the very city limits of Los Angeles, and from the jungles of Yucatan to the polar ice cap, we have dynamic, viable wildlife populations, and we have good hunting. Every Canadian province, every U.S. and Mexican state offer hunting of some type, and almost all offer some species of big game.

Like all the other continents, we went through the ravages of our settlement era, when little thought was given to tomorrow. Less than a century ago our wildlife populations bottomed out and the long road back began.

Today we've come a long distance on that road. Changing land use has brought some species, such as the whitetail deer, to levels of plenty never seen before. Other game animals, such as the bison and grizzly, will never again be as abundant as they once were. But it's interesting to note that, during the excesses of earlier days, North America was far

Only a couple of truly free-ranging bison herds exist in the world today, but fortunately there are many private-land herds on large enough acreage to offer a good hunting experience. (Photo by Bob Robb)

Few animals in the world capture the imagination to the extent of the grizzly. He has made no concessions to man—certainly his undoing and the reason he has been pushed into the deepest wilderness today—but probably also why we admire him so much. (Photo by William D. Phifer)

more fortunate than other lands—not a single species of large mammal was lost to extinction. The native game we hunt in North America today is comprised of the same species that were present in Lewis and Clark's day, in Columbus' day, and for many thousands of years before the birth of Christ.

This is not to say that man has had no effect on North American wildlife; of course we have, and continue to have. For the first few hundred years of modern man's involvement on this continent the impact was disastrous. We did lose several races and subspecies of our big game animals, but fortunately all of our large mammals occupied a wide enough range so that no species were lost. Animals such as the bison and pronghorn could easily have been wiped out totally, but last minute protective measures saved the day. Our last few decades have

Mule deer have the reputation for being easier quarry than whitetails. They do prefer more open country, but today a big muley is a hard-won prize, maybe just as tough to come by as a nice whitetail.

seen regulated hunting used as a tool of modern game management, enlightened game management that has brought North American hunters a wealth of wildlife and hunting experiences unmatched Earth. The beginning of this century was the first great turning point

Caribou are the most accessible of our northern game. Depending on which authority you adhere to, there are five or six caribou subspecies ranging from the Atlantic to the Pacific. Caribou grow the most antler in relation to body size of any of the world's deer. (Photo by William D. Phifer)

for our wildlife, when pioneer hunter-conservationists such as Theodore Roosevelt and William T. Hornaday checked the decline and started our wildlife on the road back.

The next turning point lies ahead, perhaps in the not too distant future. Expanding land use and mineral exploration are the next threats to this continent's wildlife, perhaps an even more serious threat than the market hunters of a century ago. Chances are we will always have our more adaptable species such as whitetail deer and black bear, but other animals—our great bears and our nomadic caribou—are incapable of living with Man, and must have the wilderness. Man, it seems, must also have the wilderness for his mineral wealth and energy-producing potential. Our game managers, financed mostly through hunters' dollars, are winning today, but great battles lie ahead.

For the moment, however, the picture has never been brighter for the North American hunter. With only a couple of exceptions, all of our big game species are available for hunting today, and without exception all

Moose are the largest members of the deer family; a big Alaskan bull can weigh a ton! Like many animals, they lose much of their caution during the rut. There are many tales of bull moose attacking cars, packstrings, even locomotives—and the tales are true. (Photo by William D. Phifer)

of our big game exists in huntable numbers both now and for the immediate future. In the following chapters we will look at North American big game, as it is today and as it is hunted today. The scientific data will be as accurate as I can make it, but it must be remembered that this is a hunting book, not a book of natural history.

It has long been accepted that we have 27 species of North American big game. This is not a figure that either scientists or hunters are in agreement on; the hunter's classification separates some subspecies, overlooks others, and creates a few categories that have no actual basis in taxonomy. The late Grancel Fitz, great hunter and naturalist and long-time scion of the Boone and Crockett Club, is believed to be the first man to collect all 27 species of North American big game, a feat that very few have duplicated. The figure "27" dates from Fitz' time, and is probably not complete, or at least not up to date.

The desert bighorn is one of North America's most difficult trophies today. Hunting is tightly controlled, and most permits allocated are filled, but those permits are very hard to obtain. Fortunately, most desert sheep herds are on the increase today. The number of permits should grow a bit each year. (Photo by Dr. Loren Lutz)

If there were 27, they would include four deer—whitetail, mule, blacktail and Coues, the elk, the pronghorn, four bears—black, grizzly, polar and Alaskan brown, four caribou—woodland, barren ground, mountain and Quebec Labrador, three moose—Canadian, Shiras and Alaska Yukon, four sheep—Dall, Stone, Rocky Mountain bighorn and desert bighorn, Rocky Mountain goat, walrus, muskox, cougar, jaguar and bison. Today we recognize additional categories for caribou—Peary and Central Canadian barren ground, an additional elk—the Roosevelt and an additional deer—the Sitka blacktail. Some record-keeping organizations even recognize an additional moose, two muskox subspecies and two walrus.

I haven't attempted to enumerate exactly how many big game species we have, nor have I attempted to follow either taxonomic or geographic guidelines in the writing of this book. Instead, I have grouped

Wild sheep are gregarious animals, even the biggest rams are rarely found alone, but are usually accompanied by a few lesser rams. Herd animals are always harder to stalk, especially such sharp-eyed creatures as wild sheep. At least one ram is almost always posted as "sentinel" and even if he isn't the one you want, he's the one you must watch for as you work in close. (Photo by William D. Phifer)

our big game as they appear to me as a hunter. Arctic game, though quite diverse, appears together in one chapter, likewise the grizzly and brown bear. In the former case, the hunting is fairly similar and the country identical; the grouping seemed natural. In the latter, the animals are nearly identical, but the hunting totally different—the contrast alone seemed to have the makings for an interesting chapter. Our four sheep and one goat, arguably classed as "mountain game" in this book, are quite different in appearance, but throughout their vast range the hunting is so similar as to require discussion within one chapter. And so it goes.

To the accepted native big game species I have added one more, the javelina, and I have paired him with a naturalized citizen, the wild boar. No picture of modern big game hunting in North America could be complete without mention of our non-native big game, and the wild boar is just one of many introduced species. These animals have added new opportunities for American hunters, and require a chapter for themselves.

The Rocky Mountain goat is another animal that is increasing in population and expanding its range. This fine billy weighed 300 pounds and sported 10-inch horns—excellent anywhere, but especially excellent for Montana, where it was taken. (Photo by Jack Atcheson Sr.)

The mountain lion remains very plentiful across much of western North America. An extremely shy, wary animal, he will be seen by very few humans without the aid of good dogs. (Photo by Denise Hendershot)

There are, in addition to the clearly recognizable "big game" animals, a variety of other game species that, variously classed as big game, small game, varmints and furbearers, are fine trophies in their own right and add immeasurably to the varied excitement of hunting on this continent. An incomplete list would include the wolf, coyote, fox, wolverine, lynx, bobcat, ocelot and coati mundi. These animals do not have their own chapter, although perhaps they deserve one. Some of them are mentioned specifically along with the major species they co-exist with, and others may not be mentioned again throughout this book—but they shouldn't be forgotten. Collectively, this class of "trophy varmints" adds much to big game hunting, and some member of this group is found in all of North America's hunting country.

In general, North American hunting is fairly specialized. One might conceivably leave camp in the morning and hope to encounter one or two, perhaps even three species. Even though our total game list is extensive, our habitat is such that traditionally we hunt for one (or at the most two or three) animals. Usually we hunt hard, for in addition to plentiful game, we must contend with plentiful hunting pressure in the more accessible areas. In our true wilderness we hunt doubly hard,

The jaguar is probably our most limited game species, and certainly one of the most difficult—if not *the* most difficult—trophies to obtain. This huge specimen was taken in the jungle region of southern Mexico. (Photo by Rick Furniss)

Javelina are extremely abundant across much of Texas and southern Arizona. Whether they're our biggest small game or our smallest big game, they offer enjoyable hunting.

for there's usually a good reason why it's still wilderness—it will be remote and rugged, country that gives the advantage to the animal.

Our continent offers some of the world's most rewarding hunting, especially to a North American hunter. We've grown up dreaming of a great ram or a big grizzly, and we've grown up being outwitted by big bucks. When we turn those dreams into realities, we can feel an enormous sense of accomplishment. The huge bucks, heavy-horned rams and great bears are still there. Right now in the 1980s—and almost certainly into the 1990s and beyond—the record books are being, and will continue to be, rewritten. The hunting isn't getting any easier, but trophy quality is undiminished virtually across the board, and is improving in many categories.

Although North American hunting is rarely easy, it's exciting, rewarding, and often carried out in some of the world's most beautiful country. Whether whitetail hunting in the Appalachian autumn, taking a packstring into the Rockies, or pussyfooting along an Alaskan salmon stream, it's all North American hunting for North American game, and the vast majority of the land is ours to hunt in accordance with the game regulations we have insisted on. Our campfires may be set from the Atlantic to the Pacific, from Mexico to the Arctic, and we may follow game trails virtually anywhere in this continent.

Chapter 2
Deer

For most of us, there is simply no thrill that can match the sight of a big buck, be he whitetail, blacktail, muley or Coues deer. American hunters love their deer, and for plenty of good reasons. Our deer are the most populous and most popular game animals in the entire world as well as in North America. Deer hunting introduces most of us to big game hunting and it's a kind of hunting we always go back to. Few things on Earth equal the enjoyment of a good deer hunt, and that's a statement hunters who have hunted throughout the world will generally agree to. There are certainly more exotic North American game species, such as the muskox or caribou, more dangerous species, such as the grizzly bear and jaguar, and more beautiful trophies, such as our wild sheep, but for out-and-out smarts, nothing beats a big, mature buck deer—regardless of species. Only the elk matches him on this continent.

In our deer species, game is plentiful and available, yet offers a true challenge to the hunter. Although our deer may be overshadowed, antler-wise, by elk, caribou and moose, there's nothing wrong with a big buck deer of any type. In fact, in most trophy rooms across North America, you'll find shoulder-mounts of deer in places of honor mixed in with African, Asian, European and other domestic game. That applies only if the hunter has actually taken good specimens of our deer—and many experienced hunters have not. Through the aid of guided hunts, controlled permits, private land hunts, and with plenty

In so much whitetail hunting this is all there is—a flash of a running buck. Such shots are always extremely difficult, but more so if you're looking for a trophy and must take a snap-judgement as to spread, number of points and length of tines.

of dollars, it is possible to collect good specimens of most big game species within a short period of time. Not so with deer. The big trophies almost never come easily, but instead are the product of research and often long seasons of hard hunting. A good buck is earned, and is awarded a place of honor in the hunter's den regardless of how many seemingly more important trophies surround it.

Our deer are our most democratic game, favoring not the wealthy nor the influential—only the dedicated, persistent, highly skilled hunter. Perhaps that's why we all come back to deer hunting. It's not only what we were all raised with, but on this continent, it's the test of a true hunter.

American hunters have come to identify, at least for record-keeping purposes, four classes of North American deer. As is often the case, hunters' classifications and scientific thinking don't exactly coincide.

Technically speaking, caribou, moose and elk are also deer in the sense that they're antlered game, but this chapter will concentrate only on members of the *Odocoileus* subfamily. The various mule (and black-tail) deer are classed as *Odocoileus hemionus*, while the whitetails are classed as *Odocoileus virginianus*. In other words, regardless of how many classifications hunters create for deer, there are only two species of North American deer—the mule deer group and the whitetail group.

These species obviously cover vast areas, and there are significant regional differences in both body size and antler development within both groups. The blacktail, a subspecies of mule deer, has long been considered separately; likewise the Coues deer, a whitetail subspecies once thought to be a totally separate species. The four categories for North American deer make lots of sense—at least until examined from the scientist's viewpoint.

A wildlife biologist would be quick to point out that between seven and 10 mule deer subspecies exist in North America, plus a full 30 whitetail subspecies, not counting eight more whitetail subspecies in South America. So hunters have distilled some 45 biologically distinct subspecies into four categories. A few subspecies probably could be considered separately. One, the Sitka blacktail, has already been awarded its own record book category, and there are a few others that are easily enough distinguished to rate separate treatment. What follows is an overview of the four North American deer.

Whitetail Deer

The whitetail deer, *Odocoileus virginianus*, is perhaps the most populous big game animal on Earth. From South America north almost to the Arctic Circle, its 38 subspecies number close to 20 million animals. In the United States, it is found in every state excluding California, Nevada and Utah—an exclusion that probably won't last much longer, as the whitetail is on the move today rapidly expanding its range, particularly in the Northwest. In Montana, Alberta, Idaho, British Columbia and Washington, the whitetail population is spilling over into areas long considered mule deer-only habitat, and throughout this region trophy size seems to be increasing annually. In the long run this could bode ill for mule deer in this region, but in the meantime it's good news for whitetail hunters.

The good news on whitetails isn't confined to the Northwest. Throughout much of the U.S., the herds are approaching, at, or above carrying capacity, and each year sees record deer harvests, lengthened seasons, and increased hunting opportunity.

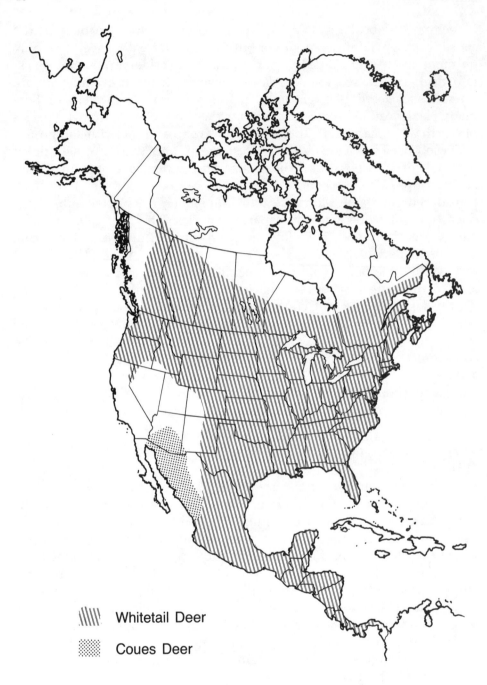

||||| Whitetail Deer

::::: Coues Deer

WHITETAIL DEER RANGE

It wasn't always that way. It's an oft-repeated homily that "we have more deer today than in Columbus' time." Probably true, but nobody can speak accurately of Columbus' day. We *can* go back to the beginning of this century, when only a half-million or so whitetail existed from coast to coast. Obviously, modern management has worked a miracle in this century.

I grew up in eastern Kansas, prime whitetail habitat, but we had almost no deer when I was a boy. In my Boy Scout days the very sight of a deer was red-letter experience, and a mighty rare one. Our first deer season in modern times wasn't held until 1965, and permits were tightly limited. Today Kansas deer permits are still limited, but there are more each year and today whitetail deer are a common sight in woodlots that were devoid of deer just 25 years ago.

Of course, Kansas is a poor example; it has.some good whitetail habitat, but much of it is marginal. To put things more in perspective, consider that today at least 13 states have herds that exceed the half-million mark—that was once our total population! These states include Alabama, Florida, Georgia, Michigan, Minnesota, Mississippi, New

Relatively few whitetail seasons correspond with the rut, but those that do offer the best chance for a real trophy buck. Across whitetail range the rut may vary from October through January, and in a given area it may vary by a week or two from one year to the next.

Much Eastern whitetail hunting is a waiting game, with the bucks going to the most patient hunters. The axiom is "he who can sit longest gets the deer." In hard-hunted woods where less patient hunters will move game, the saying is often true.

York, Pennsylvania, of course Texas, both Virginia and West Virginia, and Wisconsin.

Generally speaking, the seasons and bag limits are most liberal in the Deep South. South Carolina, for example, has a six-month deer season with a buck-per-day bag limit. Mind boggling as it sounds, it's a safe bet for the state. Overall hunter success is fairly low throughout the South, so unsuccessful hunters more than make up for the highly skilled few who take a half-dozen or more bucks in a season. Also to be kept in perspective are three other factors. First, the deer herd throughout most of the South is at or above carrying capacity, and a high harvest is needed annually. Second, human populations are relatively low, hence the required harvest can be divided up among fewer hunters. And third, in the timber, swamps, and heavy cover of the South's best whitetail habitat, all the advantages are on the deer's side.

It takes a long season for a significant harvest, plus the skilled hunters (who do most of the harvesting) need the legal authorization to take deer, since nobody else would.

In states such as Pennsylvania, Michigan, Wisconsin and Minnesota, the problem is just the opposite. There are plenty of deer, but also plenty of hunters. Seasons must be short and bag limits restrictive lest the harvest be too large for the local deer herd to support. Seasons also tend to be quite short throughout most of the Midwest, where the bulk of the country is in agriculture—excellent for the deer that are present, but without the ability to support a large population.

There are still other far-Western states in which whitetails and mule deer co-exist. In rare cases they're managed separately, but if the two are found in the same area, the bulk of the hunting pressure almost always goes on the mule deer; he's larger in terms of providing venison, and typically somewhat easier to hunt. Under such circumstances the serious whitetail hunter may have a short season or a long one, but he'll have the whitetail habitat all to himself. Montana has gained some well-deserved notoriety as a top whitetail state, but Idaho, Wyoming, Washington and Oregon have produced some super bucks, and eastern Colorado has some untapped whitetail potential. Throughout this region the mule deer is king, and a whitetail hunter can have an open field.

Hunters speak simply of "whitetail deer," and that's the entry you read in the record books. Beneath that there will probably be a tagline something like "*Odocoileus virginianus virgininanus* and certain related subspecies." That tagline actually says a mouthful; *O. v. virgininanus*, the typical subspecies, is found only from Virginia west through Kentucky and Tennessee and south through the Carolinas, Georgia, Alabama and Louisiana. Throughout the United States, Mexico and Central America a full 29 more whitetail subspecies are believed to be present, and neither you nor I could reliably tell them apart.

To be sure, at the extremes of the range, differences would be noted. Whitetails do follow the biological principle which states that within a given species, the farther north (or south) of the Equator, the larger the body size. The theory is that in warmer climates, closer to the Equator, a smaller overall body size will have a relatively larger surface area for heat dissipation. The ears will tend to be larger for the same reason. Farther from the Equator, the body size increases, but the surface area does not increase at the same rate, allowing better heat retention in colder climates. Thus the southern whitetail subspecies are a good deal smaller in body than the northern. Few of us could tell *O. v. texanus*, the Texas whitetail, from *O. v. macrourus*, the Kansas whitetail, or either from the Virginia whitetail or *O. v. seminolus*, the Florida whitetail. But we would most certainly see the difference between a north-ernmost subspecies, either the Dakota or northern woodland (*dacotensis* or *borealis*), and a southern subspecies, whether a Texas, Florida, Coues, or even a Central American whitetail.The most striking differ-ence would be size, but the ears, tail and pelage would also show some differences.

The size difference is considerable. A whitetail taken in Alberta may well weigh in excess of 300 pounds *field-dressed*, while a deer that dresses out at 125 pounds is quite normal across most whitetail range. The overall size difference does to some degree explain the difference in antler size. The northern subspecies have a most definite edge, and it shows up quite clearly in the record book. However, the difference in antler size is generally not nearly as pronounced as the difference in body size. Why this is, I can't say.

Fortunately for those of us involved in various recordkeeping sys-tems, hunters have not yet demanded separate categories for the vari-ous whitetail subspecies. For now, and throughout our hunting history, a whitetail is a whitetail is a whitetail, except when he happens to be a Coues deer. While the separation of *O. v. couesi* may not be any more justified than the separation of any other whitetail subspecies would be, it's valid for two reasons—it's traditional, and the subspecies is isolated from other whitetail subspecies, at least in the United States. In any case, Coues deer do have a separate category, and they'll be treated accordingly elsewhere in this chapter.

The only other differentiation made among the whitetail subspecies in the major record-keeping systems is in Safari Club International's *Record Book of Trophy Animals* which, as a worldwide system, awards a separate category to "Tropical Whitetail Deer," defined as all whitetails found from the southern extent of *couesi* and *texanus* southward. For SCI, with international application, the category is certainly valid; white-tails from the interior of Mexico (not northern Mexico) and points southward are quite small.

Whitetail hunting is very much a regional sport, steeped in tradition and ritual. Across the incredibly wide range occupied by these deer the terrain and vegetation differ tremendously. Hunting situations differ, too, and these have combined to dictate the hunting methods that are most prevalent in one region or another. Some of the methods that will be mentioned may seem unsportsmanlike or even downright danger-ous, but judgements cannot be made until you've been there; there's generally a pretty good reason for a hunting technique's ascendancy in one region or another. I've been fortunate to hunt whitetails from Wyoming to Virginia and Montana to Texas. They might be the same

Texas outfitter Robert Rogers rattled up this South Texas beauty. Rattling works, no doubt about it, but you must be in the right place at the right time. (Photo by Robert Rogers)

deer, but the country isn't the same and therefore the deer aren't hunted in the same way.

Take hunting deer with dogs, for example. Illegal in most of the U.S. and Canada, it's *the* way to hunt deer in much of the Deep South, and I believe it's also practiced in parts of eastern Canada. It sounds a bit strange, and is certainly the source of many campfire arguments—if not fistfights. But you have to look at the country. Hound hunting is mostly practiced in low-lying coastal regions, swampy ground filled with impenetrable vegetation. A man could get through that kind of country perhaps, but he couldn't stillhunt through it. He could put a stand on the edges, but only on the edges. So the hunter and some of his buddies take up positions along one or two sides of a particularly thick piece of swamp, and the dogs are turned loose on the other side. In essence, it's no different than the deer drives practiced in so many parts of the country except the drivers are canine instead of human.

I have seen dogs used in Arkansas, but all I'd gotten out of the experience was a feeling that the distant yapping messed up a perfectly

This Montana whitetail is about as good as they get—a heavy-horned 10-pointer with a wide spread. (Photo by Bob Robb)

nice, quiet day in the woods. But near North Carolina's Lake Matta-muskeet, I discovered the attraction hound hunting holds for so many deer hunters. I was on a levee facing an incredibly dense section of swamp, a mile or more across. In theory the dogs had been released on the far side and would push game my direction. So far nothing had happened, and it was getting toward mid-morning. Then, far out in the swamp, I could hear the dogs in full cry. It *was* exciting, especially when it got closer and I knew for certain the commotion was heading my way.

There was a belt of waterlogged country directly in front of me, and I suppose the dogs lost the scent on the far side of that. The cry of the dogs stopped, but I heard the unmistakeable splashing of a large animal. Deer, bear, or boar? It seemed far too much noise for a deer, but in a moment I saw antlers floating above a patch of low huckleberry. I shot the buck when he made his move, and he's still on my wall. It wasn't a hunt in terms of planning or stalking, nor was the shot particularly difficult. But those last few moments, when the baying was so close— and then stopped—were tense and full of excitement. I'm not sure I'd personally care to hunt deer that way again, but I can understand those who choose to. It's something you can't knock until you've tried it, and in that kind of country it's one of the few hunting techniques that make sense.

Deer drives with human drivers are practiced across much of the country. They may be used in conjunction with tree stands or established stands, or, in farm country, from one woodlot to another. Deer drives, too, are steeped in tradition and are often orchestrated with the precision of a military operation. They can be formal or informal; two or three hunters can have a very effective mini-drive, but I've also been on some drives in Pennsylvania that took more than a dozen hunters. Drives of the latter magnitude scare me because I wasn't raised with

Alberta had an amazing whitetail season in 1984, with several Boone and Crockett bucks taken. This one, taken by Mike Szydlik, left, guided by Russell Thornberry, right, doesn't quite make it but it's an *eight-point* buck that scores just two points out, an amazing deer. (Photo by Russel Thornberry)

that hunting method. If I had been, I'm sure I'd figure it was *the* way to hunt deer!

The idea behind a drive is quite obvious. Standers or blockers are positioned on likely escape routes while drivers push through a likely patch of cover. The standers get the best opportunity, but the drivers may have a shot as deer attempt to break back. It's an effective way to get venison, but in my opinion not a good way to trophy hunt. The best bucks didn't get that way by being dumb, and most deer drives in most parts of the country follow traditional routes so most mature bucks have been driven time and again, and know exactly how to escape. Like hound hunting, it's also a method that doesn't give you much time when you see antlers. No careful sizing of racks—just see horns and let 'er rip!

For safety's sake, everybody must know where everyone else is at all times, and if I were driving deer I'd pick the folks I hunted with very carefully. Two- or three-man drives through very small patches of cover can be surprisingly productive, and are much safer and easier to arrange. A friend of mine has recently combined deer drives with portable tree stands—pure dynamite. The standers are not only up where they're safe, they're up where they can *see*. He and his party have filled out with this combo for the last two or three seasons.

Stillhunting is perhaps the most difficult hunting technique, especially for whitetails. To stillhunt effectively, you must be sneakier than the game you're after—and almost nothing is sneakier than a whitetail in close cover! I'll admit that I'm not good at it. Like 99 percent of us, I move far too fast and not quietly enough, in spite of the fact that I know I'm doing it while I'm doing it. Stillhunting, properly done, means being still while you move very slowly through likely cover. A few hundred feet an hour may be too fast, and you must constantly look, *search*, for deer. A horizontal line in vertical brush, the twitch of an ear, a patch of off-color, the successful stillhunter will see such things. Me, I was raised in open country and I get claustrophobic in heavy cover. I love to *attempt* to stillhunt whitetails, but I'm not very good at it.

Variations on the theme usually involve a couple of hunters working along set patterns. One man, a hundred yards or so behind the other, working into the wind, can be quite effective; a wary buck may well circle the first man unseen to catch his scent and give the second man a shot.

Wind is, of course, of primary importance in almost all whitetail hunting techniques, but most particularly in stillhunting. Low sun behind can also be helpful, giving you better light and just perhaps giving an extra split-second when and if you spot a deer. The idea is to move very, very slowly, take just a few steps, then pause and look. *Really look*. It's the rare man who can outwit a big whitetail in this manner, but it can be done.

While most whitetail hunters attempt stillhunting to some degree, I suspect that more whitetails are taken by standhunting than any other method—and perhaps all other methods combined. The premise is simple. You can't move as quietly as a deer, but a deer will move, usually, along habitual routes. The idea is to find a vantage point, get the wind right, and let him come to you.

Standhunting doesn't always work, but it is unquestionably the most consistent technique. It takes patience, especially in crowded deer woods where hunter movement causes deer movement. It's an oft-repeated saying that he who sits longest brings home the buck. If you choose your site well, sooner or later you should have a chance—if you stick it out!

This young 8-point (Eastern count) whitetail is very typical of the Texas Hill Country bucks. There are literally loads of whitetails, and plenty of average bucks like this—but finding a monster is unlikely.

Depending on the weather, terrain and time of year, there are innumerable good places to take a stand. Well-used trails, feeding areas, adjacent to heavy cover, watering spots, scrapes (during the rut)—you name it. The idea is to scout out a spot, situate your stand to give you all the advantages possible, and then stay with it until you connect or you're certain you need to look for a new spot.

It's true that peak deer movement occurs morning and evening, but there is movement at midday especially when the deer have been subjected to the bulk of the hunting pressure early and late. I was on a ranch in south Texas just last year where, customarily, hunters were on stand early and late but back at camp at midday. Not much was happening, so we changed the pattern. I saw more deer movement at high noon than I'd seen on the whole hunt.

The current rage is elevated stands, and although I'm terrified of heights, they're the way to go. In most cover it helps to get a few feet above the brushline for better visibility, but there are other benefits. It's safer, for one thing. Your shot will go into the ground, and nobody else's shot should come high enough to cause you problems. The height also helps with your scent, or so it's said. It might help a little, but I'd still use plenty of a good scent mask.

Stillhunting, standhunting, and driving are the principal whitetail hunting techniques, but everyone wants to know about horn rattling. It works—no question about it. However, it's a method best suited to the hunter who lives in close proximity to good whitetail country. First of all, it will only work during the actual rut. Second, it seems that it is unlikely to work unless there is a rather high buck/doe ratio. And third, you have to know the country well enough to suspect that there will be a buck close enough to hear you clash the horns.

That first qualifier lets me out. I live a couple thousand miles from good whitetail country, and I spent four seasons trying to time the rut "just right." Never made it on time. On the other hand, my colleague John Wootters, perhaps the nation's most knowledgeable whitetail hunter, lives in good whitetail country. He's out there most of the deer season, but he's able to time the rut and hunt full-bore when it's at its peak. A nonresident is hard-pressed to do that. And so is the hunter who lives in a short-season state. If your regular deer season is only 10 days or two weeks long, and many are shorter than that, then regardless of the timing of the season, you'll be lucky to catch the rut 25 percent of the time. But make no mistake—horn rattling works, and it can work in any area if the conditions are right. It's also an exciting enough hunting method that it's well worth taking a long shot on!

Available options may be to consider any special bow or muzzle-loader seasons in your area, even if that particular arm doesn't interest you. It may cost some extra practice, but catching the rut with a legal hunting season on is one of the big keys to success. When the rut comes in, the big bucks literally come out of the woodwork and regardless of which hunting method you prefer, the rut evens the odds just a bit for the bigger bucks.

Good whitetails are available across the species' entire range, although some regions are certainly a great deal better than others. There are very few states or provinces that have never produced a Boone and Crockett whitetail—typical, nontypical, or both. The nature of the beast is such that the nonresident hunter is always at a complete disadvantage; it's nearly impossible to time the hunt exactly right, plus there's the problem of learning new country. A guided hunt may simplify things, but not as much as with other species.Whitetail hunters may want to journey far afield to see what other areas have to offer or to hunt a different whitetail in different country, but in most cases, if you live in good whitetail country your chances at a big buck are best close to home. Provided, of course, that you can spend the time needed to scout, and then the time required to hunt properly.

If you can't, or if you don't live in whitetail country, then you need to do some research. The record books are a good source, but even better (because it's more up-to-date) is the Boone and Crockett Club's *18th Big Game Awards 1980-1982*, compiling all the Boone and Crockett listings for that period. It's an eye-opener; 110 typical deer and 70 nontypical deer made the book during those three years. They came from 32 states and provinces, including one from Mexico. The entries were spread out, but some states had an amazing number. *O. v. borealis*, the northwoods whitetail, came out the clear winner in the antler race. Wisconsin led with 23 Boone and Crockett entries, and Minnesota was a close second with 20. In that region, and representing that subspecies, Maine had 11, while Michigan and Ohio had nine each. It's worth mentioning that Michigan's harvest is about three times that of Ohio.

Alberta did very well with 10 entries. Alberta's whitetails have received quite a lot of publicity in recent years, and with good reason. They're in a building situation, and while neither overall numbers nor harvests figures are impressive, the bucks are. In the 1984 rifle season typical and non-typical records for the province were broken, plus the bow typical record. Texas also did well with nine entries, but it must be remembered that Texas has something like 3½ million deer! Missouri also had nine entries, but their harvest is usually around 60,000—one-fifth that of Texas!

Some other sleepers, states with modest harvests but more than their share of book entries, are Iowa (five entries, but a harvest of less than

30,000); Kentucky, with eight entries and a very modest harvest of under 30,000; Illinois with six and an annual harvest of 25,000; Nebraska with four record deer and a harvest of about 20,000; and Maryland, four entries with an annual harvest of about 17,000.

Obviously, the record book deer are spread out, and the very best odds available for them are about one in 15,000. Aside from the astronomical odds, the truth is that a Boone and Crockett whitetail is so good and so perfect that it has become a nearly unreachable goal. Few hunters give the book serious consideration, though perhaps they should. A place that will produce an inordinate number of record book deer will produce an even greater number of wall-hangers. And most of us would be quite happy with a buck that missed the book by several points.

The Boone and Crockett system takes into account beam length and circumference, inside spread, point length, number of points, and symmetry. The Safari Club book sets a slightly more reachable goal based on similar, but not identical, measurements. Exact judging in accordance with either system's point tally "on the hoof" is impossible, although experienced whitetail fanatics can come close. More important

These shed horns were found in the spring of '84 in north-central Manitoba. Most serious whitetail hunters would agree that there are bigger bucks out there than have *ever* been taken!

than the record book score is the mass and the length of the fighting tines, and a lot of personal preference is involved when judging deer antlers. Some hunters prefer a wide spread, while the mass is more important to others. Some look for number of points, while others would gladly trade a spindly-antlered 12-pointer for a massive eight-pointer. Nobody is either right or wrong, and part of the fun of deer hunting is that no two racks are exactly alike. If it looks good to you, take it; if not, pass and hope a better one comes along.

If you live in whitetail country and have done your scouting, then you know what the score is. You know what you can pass up and what you can't, and if you do pass a buck, you should know what your odds are of seeing another. The nonresident hunter, even if he's guided, is at a terrible disadvantage. He *should* know what he's looking at and what he's looking for, but often he doesn't. Every good whitetail guide has a story about the dude who walked into camp demanding to shoot a Boone and Crockett whitetail; they rarely do. Over the years Texas has produced a lot of book deer, but very, very few of them, if any, have been taken by guided nonresidents. The game doesn't work that way, and Lady Luck isn't that generous.

There are lots of places to hunt whitetails, but darned few of them give the nonresident much of a chance. If he can buy a license—and in many cases he can't—he'll find that there are no guides, no access, limited public land, and a very short season in which to put it all together. If you have friends or connections, great. But if you don't, there are only three places right now where the nonresident has a fair shake, and where the seasons are long enough and the hunter success high enough to be worth taking a gamble. They are Montana, Texas and Alberta.

Obviously that's a gross oversimplification. Many good places exist where you can hunt whitetails, and a good whitetail hunter would probably do well in any of them, given a place to hunt and a few days to become acclimated. But even in states with more than a million whitetails, the hunter success is usually well below 25 percent. Even though the hunting is excellent, the nonresident beginning whitetail hunter is wasting his time charging into the Maine or Minnesota woods or the Deep South's timber country. If you know somebody, or can find a good guide, it might be a different story. But I would still look at the three areas I've just mentioned.

Right now Alberta offers the best chance for a record-class whitetail. Few hunters will take or even see such a buck, but there are plenty of dandies up there. The herd is still building, but the genetics are there, and hunting pressure on the whitetails is fairly light. Nonresident non-Canadians must be guided, but Alberta has several good whitetail guides. It's tough hunting, and success will not be more than 60 percent or so, but the big bucks are certainly there.

Eastern Montana has an exploding whitetail population. At present only one buck is allowed, but an additional license is available that allows the hunter to take several does—and it isn't difficult to find landowners who are happy to get rid of some deer! With a building population based on the genetics of the large Dakota subspecies, Montana has excellent potential for the trophy hunter. Only a couple of Boone and Crockett bucks have been taken there in recent seasons, and that's surprising. They should be there. Much of the whitetail habitat is riverbottoms, where "normal" whitetail techniques can be employed, plus the country is open enough to allow glassing early and late. Some good guides are available, but eastern Montana can be hunted successfully unguided, provided the hunters are willing to spend some time and knock on a few doors.

Texas is in a world all its own when it comes to deer hunting. The state contains about 3.2 million deer. The season is long, a multiple-deer limit is in effect, and the overall hunter success is quite high. The big catch is that 98 percent of the entire state is private land. There is *no* public land for deer hunting. Private landowners have become well aware of the potential value of a whitetail buck and while access to private land is quite available, it's rarely free. On the other hand, a deer hunt in Texas is worth every penny just for the experience. A well-managed private ranch in good Texas deer country is quite an eye-opener. On the last day of the 1983-84 season, Robert Rogers and I saw over 50 eight-point-or-better bucks on a ranch north of McAllen, Texas. We didn't see exactly what we were looking for, but with average-to-good deer all over the place, it never got boring!

There may not be much chance of taking a record-book whitetail in Texas, but the odds are excellent for a very nice, respectable, wall-hanging buck. Typically the deer hunting can be divided into two classes—trophy hunting in the Brush Country of South Texas, and Hill Country hunts. The Hill Country has lots of deer, and the country is open enough to allow glassing. However, really large bucks are few and far between; it's more of a fun hunt, while farther south it's serious business. The Brush Country of South Texas (this also applies to adjacent northern Mexico) is tough country to hunt. It's characterized by a wall of black brush stretching from horizon to horizon. You can't hunt in it, so you must catch the deer crossing *senderos*, rattle them up, or simply waylay them along a trail. There aren't nearly as many deer in the Brush Country, and the chances for success are much lower—but there are some monsters. To the north of the Brush Country proper, a transitional zone offers excellent hunting. Likewise to the east, the brush thins out but the trophy quality diminishes very little.

There's nothing magical about the three areas I've just mentioned;

Treestands are extremely popular in many parts of the country, especially with handy portable models readily available today. In many kinds of brush they give the hunter better visibility, plus get human scent up off the ground. (Photo by Durwood Hollis)

many other good places to hunt whitetails exist, depending on how much time and effort you're willing to put in. Big whitetails are simply where you find them. I've seen the best whitetails of my life along Nebraska's Platte River during a very short bird hunt. On the other hand, the eighth-ranked typical whitetail in the current Boone and Crockett book was taken on a farm in northeastern Kansas where three generations of Boddingtons have hunted quail—and as far as I know none of us ever saw a deer on the place!

Coues Deer

The little whitetail of our arid Southwest, *O. v. couesi*, is the only whitetail subspecies singled out for separate categorization in the record books. This probably started back in the nineteenth century when Army quartermaster Lt. Elliot Coues studied and identified a hitherto-unknown deer; for decades the Coues deer was considered a totally separate species. Today it is accepted for what it is, a subspecies of the amazingly adaptable whitetail, yet its separate classification continues.

I agree for several reasons. First, while the Coues deer's range does border that of tropical whitetail subspecies deep in Mexico, in the

Some of the best Coues deer habitat is best reached on foot. Their prime country is simply too rough to get riding stock into!

United States the subspecies is totally isolated, untrue of other white-tail subspecies that have broad intergrade areas between. Second, the Coues deer is truly tiny; its live weight rarely exceeds 110 pounds, and the antlers, though whitetail through and through, are miniaturized. The current Boone and Crockett record whitetail (typical) is 206⅛ points; for Coues deer it's 143. The new world record whitetail for non-typical antlers scores a whopping 333⅞; the Coues deer non-typical record is 151⅘. The minimum scores are 170 for typical whitetail and 195 for nontypical; 110 for typical Coues deer and 120 for nontypical. It can be argued that several states have never produced a record white-tail, but getting a "regular" whitetail from anywhere that exceeds the minimums for Coues deer is no great trick. Getting a Coues deer that meets the minimum, on the other hand, is quite a chore.

Although size is the greatest difference, appearance also differs con-siderably. The ears and tail are somewhat outsized, probably to aid in heat dissipation, and the color is a striking iron-gray. They're quite beautiful and one of my favorite game animals.

They are also one of North America's least-known game animals, and

If Coues deer were as big as elk, most hunters would think twice about hunting them on foot! Fortunately even a big buck makes a possible load for one hunter and a light load for two hunters with pack frames.

one of the least written-about. I've seen several books on deer hunting that dismissed the Coues deer in a few paragraphs or less. That's justifiable, since they are whitetails of a kind, but it's unfortunate since it discounts both a great trophy animal and a unique kind of deer hunting.

It's my understanding that Elliot Coues pronounced his name "cows," but he isn't around to swear to it. You'll hear the Coues deer called "cows" as in barnyard and "cooz" as in pigeons—sometimes both ways in the same sentence. Neither is necessarily right or wrong, so take your pick.

The Coues deer is extremely limited both in range and population. Arizona probably has the most, with current estimates placing the herd at about 40,000. The greatest population is in the southeast corner of the state, but in pockets of suitable habitat, Coues deer may be found clear to the Mogollon Rim to the north and all the way to the Colorado River on the east. Their range just barely spills over into southwestern New Mexico. No firm population figures are available, but New Mexico's population must be much less than 10,000. The remainder are found in Mexico, where they occupy quite a wide range in Sonora and on down the Sierra Madres to Sinaloa. Although they remain plentiful in a few places in Mexico, the total world population is probably less than 75,000.

The Coues deer, considered desert game, is not a creature of the desert floor. Rather he is found in isolated mountain ranges offering browse and a little water. Most Coues deer live in elevations between 4,000 and 8,000 feet, in a vegetation belt where there is some cactus, but also scrub oak, manzanita, mountain mahogany and desert grasses.

They're scattered very thinly over a vast range, and nowhere are they particularly abundant. Arizona offers perhaps the best, or at least the most accessible and most easily arranged, hunting, but some nice heads come out of New Mexico and Mexico every year. Less important than where you hunt is how you hunt, for hunting Coues deer is much like looking for a needle in a very big haystack.

In hunting eastern whitetail, glassing can be a part of virtually any of the methods discussed. For Coues deer, glassing is the *only* method. Coues deer habitat is big country, rugged, unforgiving land studded with plants, and a few animals, that bite. However, it has plenty of relief and is well-suited to the skillful use of optics.

I was introduced to Coues deer by the writings of Jack O'Connor. The little desert whitetail was one of his favorite animals, and he made it sound like a kind of hunting I just had to try. Marvin and Warner Glenn, a father-son guiding team out of Douglas, Arizona, began my

My best Coues deer was taken in the Catalina Mountains just north of Tucson. Heavy-antlered with a wide spread, a Coues deer like is a superb trophy, although it appears small by Eastern whitetail standards.

education in these deer. They hunt on tough riding mules, a good choice in that harsh country, and they use the mules to get beyond where foot hunters will penetrate. From there it's a glassing game early and late. Coues deer tend to move around quite a lot in the mornings and afternoons, perhaps because they must move to find food, or perhaps because, deep in the mountains, there is no hunting pressure by normal standards.

During the midday hours, we'll occasionally push canyons, perhaps putting a stationary gun at a likely saddle and using the mules (if we have them) or driving on foot. Once in a while you can get a shot in that manner, but the country is really too big with too many unseen escape routes. It must be remembered that, while the country may resemble a lunar scene to an Eastern whitetail hunter, these deer are still whitetails, and under pressure they have the same instincts for avoiding danger.

If the Glenns began my Coues deer education, then I have to give Duwane Adams and Frank Morales from San Manuel, Arizona credit for advanced studies. Duwane wrote a letter to me several years ago, stating that he liked a story written about Coues deer hunting, but he reckoned he could find me a bigger buck than I'd taken. I took him up on it, and we've been hunting together ever since. These guys do nothing but glass until a suitable buck is spotted. We'll often leave camp four hours ahead of daylight and hike back into the mountains with flashlights—a thorny, dangerous business, but necessary. Daybreak will find us on a ridge overlooking a grassy basin or oak-studded hillside. Duwane and Frank unlimber their tripod-mounted 15x60 Zeiss binoculars, and the search begins.

Coues deer are amazingly hard to see. They blend in better than any other animal I know, plus the country is huge and the deer are tiny. Part of the secret, I think, is believing that they're there, and looking until you see them. Duwane and I glassed 14 bucks from one ridge one morning, selected the biggest one, made a long stalk, and got him. The next season, Frank, Bruce Wolf and I hiked into the same canyon, set up on the same ridge and glassed about 60 deer in a couple of hours. We saw no monsters that day, but took a pretty fair buck. All that makes it sound easy, but it's far from that. To get into a concentration of Coues deer like that, first you have to get there. Much of the country, like that canyon, is far too rough and steep for riding stock. To get there we'd left camp at 2 A.M. and had climbed steadily uphill for several hours, arriving on our ridge just at dawn. There's a lot of easier country, but few places have that many deer.

By and large, a half-dozen to a dozen Coues deer is a lot to see in a full day's hunting. However, that isn't the whole story. Across much of their range they're actually underharvested, and the buck/doe ratio is quite high. You might see only a half-dozen deer, but chances are that two or three of them will be bucks. Surprisingly, they're also not as spooky as one might expect. The real problem is finding a buck, but once that is done a stalk is usually possible.

Although Arizona is on an across-the-board permit drawing for deer licenses, resident interest in Coues deer is so low that obtaining permits is usually no problem. Neither Mexico nor New Mexico limit their deer permits. Most of the mountain ranges throughout southeastern Arizona, adjacent New Mexico, and the lower Sierra Madres of Sonora have produced good Coues deer. The Santa Ritas, Chiricahuas, Dragoons, Peloncillos, Canelo Hills, Catalinas, Galiuros are all good. The idea is to get well back into the mountains, hunt hard, and know what you're looking for.

This last is one of the toughest parts, especially for a hunter accustomed to "normal" whitetails. If he looks big, he's probably huge, and

Careful glassing is the key to much deer hunting in the West. Duwane Adams uses his tripod-mounted 15x60 Zeiss glasses to scan some Coues deer habitat.

if you can see antlers with your eyes beyond 150 yards, he's probably a shootable buck. A typical Coues buck has a normal whitetail rack, usually three points per side plus eyeguards for a total of eight points, eastern count. Ten-pointers do occur but aren't as common as with other whitetail subspecies. Nontypicals also occur very infrequently. In most Coues deer range, the buck/doe ratio and the longevity of the deer are such that a respectable eight-pointer of 70 Boone and Crockett points or so is possible. Such a buck will have a spread of 12 to 14 inches, and is really a very acceptable Coues deer. An eight-pointer with good mass, long points, and an outside spread of 16 to 18 inches is borderline Boone and Crockett material, depending on symmetry. That may not sound like much of a buck, but don't knock 'em 'til you've tried 'em. Good things come in small packages, and this classy little deer is one of the best packages this continent has to offer.

Mule Deer

The mule deer of the American West hasn't captured the admiration of modern hunters to the same degree the whitetail has. He isn't a cult object among any groups of hunters that I know of, nor are there specific organizations devoted to him, nor are there displays and exhibits of nationwide interest that specialize in mule deer and mule deer hunting. There are a couple of good books on mule deer and mule deer hunting, but nothing like the huge body of sporting literature that the whitetail has evoked. The whitetail *aficionados*, perhaps today's largest group of "specialist hunters," seem to have relegated the mule deer to the same status as the stereotypical dumb blonde—pretty, but not to be taken seriously.

If a mule deer must be judged in relation to a whitetail, then there is some justification for this attitude. By habit and habitat he prefers more open country, and that does indeed make him more vulnerable to the rifle-toting modern hunter. For the hunter preferring primitive arms, though, the situation is reversed—the mule deer is more difficult to obtain. Here's an interesting comparison. The Pope and Young Club, which maintains bowhunting records using essentially the same scoring method as Boone and Crockett, establishes minimum scores that are justifiably lower than those for Boone and Crockett. The current (1981) edition of *Bowhunting Big Game Records of North America* lists only one typical mule deer and one non-typical mule deer that would have made the Boone and Crockett book. The same edition lists 35 typical whitetails and 23 non-typical whitetails that meet the rifleman's minimum score. Of course, the mule deer is not a whitetail, and it's ridiculous to judge it by the same criteria. Like all of North America's diverse game species, it should be judged on its own merits.

Mule deer habitat encompasses a wide variety of terrain, from prairie to desert and from foothill to timberline. It is regarded, somewhat incorrectly, as a creature of the western mountains, but mountain hunting is the most common mule deer hunting. The typical mule deer subspecies, *Odocoileus hemionus hemionus*—the Rocky Mountain mule deer—is the largest of the muleys in both body and antler development. A fully mature buck should weigh in the neighborhood of 225 pounds, although very large Rocky Mountain bucks in the 300-pound class aren't that unusual. The Rocky Mountain muley by far the most numerous and widespread subspecies, is found from the Great Plains of central Kansas, Nebraska and the Dakotas west to the crest of the Sierras and from southern Arizona north through southwestern Saskatchewan, Alberta and British Columbia almost to the Northwest Territories border.

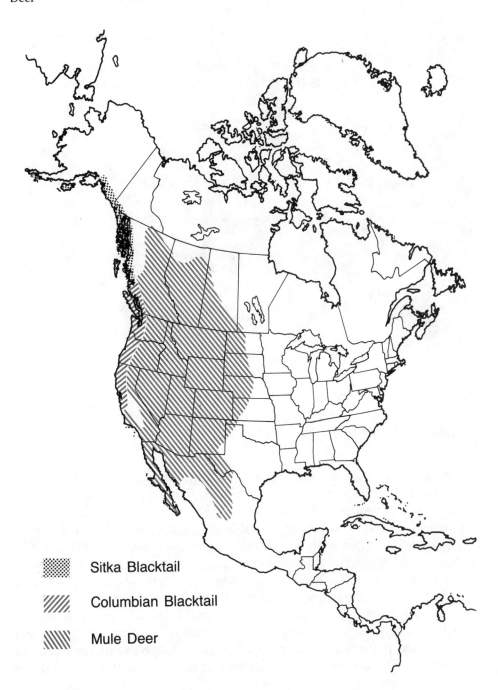

Sitka Blacktail

Columbian Blacktail

Mule Deer

BLACKTAIL AND MULE DEER RANGE

This high-horned Rocky Mountain mule deer is a beauty, a perfectly acceptable trophy to most hunters but he's a long ways short of record proportions. (Photo by Bob Robb)

Current taxonomical thinking is in agreement on six other mule deer subspecies in addition to *O. h. hemionus.* Two of these, *O. h. columbianus,* the Columbian blacktail, and *O. h. sitkensis,* the Sitka blacktail, are considered separately for record-keeping purposes. The other four are lumped together with the Rocky Mountain subspecies. This is understandable, since the differences are slight and hunting opportunities limited for these subspecies, but unfortunate since only the large Rocky Mountain subspecies has a reasonable chance of growing antlers of record book dimensions. All of the mule and blacktail deer have antlers which bifurcate, that is, the main beam forks, then that fork also forks for a typical pattern of four points per side. Brow points may also be present, but the brow tines are usually not as prominent as on whitetail and may be absent even on quite large muleys. The smaller subspecies, though they have the potential to develop four-by-four antlers, often stop at three or even two points per side.

In southwest Texas, southern Arizona and New Mexico, and deep into Sonora and Chihuahua ranges the desert mule deer, *O. h. crooki.*

In the late Fifties and early Sixties mule deer populations were at an all-time high and hunting pressure was still modest. Meat poles like this were common in deer camps across Utah and Colorado—and most would hold a couple of real monsters. (Photo by Bob Tatsch)

Slightly smaller, lighter in color and more uniformly gray-brown in facial markings, the desert mule deer has adapted to life in much more arid climes. A very few exceptional desert bucks have reached record-class proportions, but their habitat and appearance is so distinctive that trophy hunters regard them as a different deer despite the record book.

The California mule deer, *O. h. californicus*, is found only in California, roughly from Lake Tahoe southwest to just south of Los Angeles. This is a still-smaller mule deer subspecies, virtually indistinguishable

Montana's Missouri Breaks are traditional mule deer haunts, but in recent years this rugged country has become home to some superb whitetail bucks as well. (Photo by Bob Robb)

from Rocky Mountain deer except for size. There are broad intergrade areas between California mule deer and Columbian blacktail along California's central coast, resulting in a bastard strain of deer that defy classification as either mule deer or blacktail. Even where pure, California mule deer rarely attain trophy proportions today.

Farther south, from California's Orange County below Los Angeles to halfway down the Baja Peninsula are southern mule deer, *O. h. fuliginatus*. Although small, with big bucks rarely exceeding 130 pounds, the southern mule deer are interesting in appearance. They're decidedly blocky of build and have extremely short facial structure. Like all the mule deer, they will develop the typical four-by-four-plus eyeguards antler structure, but spreads in excess of 20 to 22 inches are rare. From central Baja south to the tip of the peninsula is *O. h. peninsulae*, the peninsular mule deer. Another small muley subspecies, they are not plentiful and are certainly our least-known mule deer.

Mule deer have not learned to live in close proximity to man nearly

Colorado outfitter Jerry Hughes and I both look pleased with this Nevada muley. No record, it has good conformation and a spread of about 29 inches, a nice buck on today's market.

California hunter Bill Sims shows an outstanding southern mule deer, subspecies *O.h. fuliginatus*. These little deer are found only in southern California and northern Baja.

as well as the whitetail. Their senses are just as acute; excellent hearing and sense of smell, and superb eyesight. But unlike the whitetail which depends heavily upon its nose, the mule deer places more reliance on

This lovely four-by-four muley came off Colorado's Ute Indian Reservation, a traditional hotspot for big bucks. (Photo by Bob Tatsch)

its eyesight. It prefers big, more open country, where it can put that eyesight to better use in avoiding danger.

The mule deer is less a creature of habit than the whitetail. It may use the same bedding and feeding grounds for extended periods of time, but is less likely to move along established trails. Isolated patches of cover and timbered canyons can occasionally be driven with good results, but mule deer hunting is primarily a game of stillhunting, glassing and stalking.

In low country, most mule deer populations are fairly resident, but in the high country mule deer do migrate from summer alpine pasture to lower wintering grounds. Later hunts, when available, are often the most productive. A good snowstorm in late October or November, once it subsides, will often bring on the rut, and it will certainly cause more daylight movement and create good tracking conditions. On several occasions I've had hard hunting for days, with few deer seen and decent bucks seemingly nonexistent. Then comes a snowfall, and mule deer seem to come out of the woodwork. I would guess that most big bucks are taken in snow conditions, if not during the rut itself.

Of course, snows are impossible to plan and the rut is totally unreliable. In dry, warm, early season conditions, hunting is often tough—days afoot or in the saddle, and endless hours of painstaking glassing. While glassing and stalking is the classic mule deer technique, under such difficult conditions drives through quakie patches and mountain mahogany or scrub oak hillsides and canyons can be the best, and perhaps only, solution.

After days of trying everything else, we used a series of drives in Nevada's Monitor Peak range to take a couple of super bucks in the eleventh hour of the hunt. But given a choice (which isn't always available), I'd take a late hunt every time and hope for some snow. My first real trophy mule deer came that way, in Montana years ago. We'd hunted for days and seen precious little, but it was the right time of year and the snow finally came. The morning dawned crystal clear, and hungry deer were on the move. We picked up some tracks at timber's edge and followed them down into some low sagebrush draws, surprising a nice swollen-necked buck and his does in their beds.

There really aren't any special tactics or tricks for taking big mule deer, except to hunt long and hard in good country. But my old friend Jerry Hughes, a fine Nevada outfitter, has come up with a new wrinkle that's worth mentioning. He hunts mule deer in big, tough country—huge quakie patches and impenetrable mountain mahogany thickets. When he's certain the rut is on, he quits hunting bucks. Instead he hunts for small herds of the less wary does. When he finds a group, he stays with them and watches them, sometimes for days. Sooner or

This buck's neck is swollen with the rut—that's the time to get the big ones. (Photo by Bob Robb)

later, a big buck will come out of the thick stuff and join the does, just as sure as clockwork. I haven't tried this technique myself, but if Jerry says it works, then it works, but the conditions must be right.

In the early Sixties mule deer populations were at an all-time high and hunting pressure was very light throughout the West. In those days trophy mule deer were indeed fairly easy to come by, and although those days are long gone, their legacy persists in the widespread belief that big muleys are pushovers. They aren't, not anymore. A four-point (western count) buck with a 22- to 24-inch spread isn't difficult to find in much mule deer range, but the same can be said of a basket-racked average eight-point whitetail across much whitetail range. A mossy-horned muley with heavy antlers, long tines and a spread approaching 30 inches is a whole different kettle of fish.

In real numbers, many more record-class whitetails are taken than record-class mule deer. Of course, that's not a fair comparison since there are a great many more whitetails than muleys. Statistically, I would have to concede that a record-class mule deer is more common than a record-class whitetail—but on the ground, one is just about as hard to find as another. Make no mistake, trophy hunters have learned that the easy pickings are over for big muleys. As with whitetails, the outfitter with a good track record on big mule deer can virtually name his price.

Fortunately, mule deer are democratic animals. An outfitted hunt might increase the odds a bit, that's natural, but guides are not necessary in most areas, nor are they needed for good hunters in good condition who are willing to put in the time to research a good area and then to spend the time required to hunt that area properly.

What are some good areas? The central Rockies have historically produced the most and the best, with western Colorado remaining the odds-on choice. Boone and Crockett's *18th Big Game Awards 1980-1982* recognized a total of 55 typical and non-typical record muleys. Sixteen came from Colorado, with Eagle County producing half of these. Surprisingly, Idaho came in second with eight entries; southeastern Idaho in particular is superb country for big muleys. Wyoming and Utah had six each. Arizona's Kaibab is back as a top mule deer area, and if a

Deer drives can sometimes work even for big muleys. Colorado outfitter Alan Baier orchestrated a drive along a juniper ridge, and this buck made a fatal mistake.

permit can be drawn it's good country, but very tough to hunt. Of course, the record book is only part of the story. As with record whitetails, a record muley is so huge as to be unbelievable, and few hunters would consider turning down a buck of significantly smaller proportions. For trophy-class, wall-hanging muleys, all of the Rocky Mountain states offer good potential. Area wildlife biologists in these states are good sources of information, and the aim should be to pinpoint areas that have trophy potential but also aren't overrun with hunters, a problem in many of the traditional trophy hotspots.

What constitutes a good muley today? A heavy-horned four-by-four with a 30-inch spread has always been the trophy hunter's goal, and that remains in effect today. Depending on point length and mass, such a buck may or may not make the record book minimum, but it will be a super buck and hard to find, perhaps impossible in many areas. A representative buck will be a four-by-four with some mass and a spread in the neighborhood of 24 inches. That's actually a pretty good mule deer today, although an attainable goal in most good habi-

It's hard to say who came out on the worst end of this bargain—the hunter, the horse, or the deer. Good mule deer come hard today, and you have to be willing to work for them.

tat. Anything above 26 or 28 inches in spread, especially with some mass and point length, is getting into the rarified air of exceptional quality. I've talked to too many first-time mule deer hunters who fully expect to take their pick of 30-inch-plus bucks. Even 20 years ago bucks like that didn't grow on trees. Today such expectations are unrealistic except for the hunter in outstanding physical condition who is perfectly willing to go home empty-handed unless he finds exactly what he's looking for. Me, sure I'd like to get a better muley than I've gotten before, and if I stay at it I probably will, but to me the main attraction is hunting them in the clean, clear air of their high country haunts, and the experience alone is worth more than getting wrapped up in the presence or absence of a couple extra inches of antler.

Blacktail Deer

The Columbian blacktail of the Pacific Coast and the smaller Sitka blacktail of southeast Alaska have historically been lumped together in the record books, discounting the fact that Sitka deer almost never attain the minimum score established for blacktails. That has changed now. The Pope and Young and Safari Club International record books have recognized categories for Sitka deer for several years, and in December, 1983 the Boone and Crockett Club, certainly our most conservative record-keeping organization, authorized a new category for Sitka deer. I suspect interest in hunting these little deer will increase substantially now that recognition is available for superlative trophies.

Blacktail deer are subspecies of the mule deer, differentiated by much smaller size and a tail that is fully striped with black on the upper surface as opposed to the mule deer's black-tipped tail. They react basically the same and are hunted in the same manner, depending on the terrain.

Much of California's blacktail range is virtually indistinguishable from mule deer habitat—rolling, semi-open country where glassing and stalking are practical. In the dense, near-rain forest habitat of coastal Oregon, Washington and southern British Columbia, the close cover changes things dramatically. Here the hunting is more closely akin to hunting whitetails in the eastern timber; trail-watching and very careful stillhunting are the only viable techniques. Much blacktail habitat is characterized by patches of close cover and driving is a very effective technique. In California, where I do most of my blacktail hunting, we drive poison-oak choked canyons with one hunter in the bottom and one or two hunters up high on adjacent ridges—fast action, but often productive.

The various record-keeping systems vary somewhat as to the exact

The Sitka blacktail is a fascinating deer. In good feed conditions they can grow quite large in the body, but the antlers are very small; four points per side are possible, but many bucks never go beyond a fork-horn with eyeguards. This buck is a four-by-two with eyeguards; odd configurations like that are fairly common. (Photo by Bob Tatsch)

boundaries between mule deer and Columbian blacktail, *O. h. columbianus*. There are broad intergrade areas, particularly in central California. Generally speaking, it's safe to say that true blacktail deer start at
about Monterey Bay and run north along the west side of the Sierras
along the coast all the way to Alaska. Bella Coola, along the north-
central British Columbian coast, is considered to be the dividing line
between Columbian blacktail and Sitka blacktail, *O. h. sitkensis*. The
Boone and Crockett Club establishes the most stringent boundaries;
SCI the most lenient. The latter organization requires photographic
evidence of blacktails taken in marginal areas.

In terms of numbers of deer harvested in relation to record book
entries, the blacktail deer is probably our easiest deer to put in the
record book, but it's a tough chore. California dominates the record
books, both in terms of historical and recent entries. Oregon is a close
second, with Washington lagging behind. Very few record blacktails
have been taken in British Columbia.

This Columbian blacktail was taken in northern California's lava country.
Blacktail inhabit a wide variety of terrain, from coastal jungles to alpine
meadows, but in most areas a three-by-three such as this is a normal
mature buck.

It takes a good man to pack a blacktail whole, but it can be done; dressed out the weight of even a good throphy buck won't exceed 100 pounds. On a big muley, though, good luck! (Photo by Mike Ballew)

This California blacktail is truly exceptional; few bucks ever reach the classic four-by-four-with-eyeguards configuration, and fewer still achieve spreads that go outside the ears. (Photo by Mike Ballew)

For the person living far from blacktail country, this little deer poses a problem in that, throughout their range, there are just a handful of outfitters offering guided hunts. I've hunted them in Oregon, and can vouch for the dense vegetation making hunting extremely tough for the outsider. Some of the more open alpine habitat in the high country of California's Shasta, Humboldt and Mendocino Counties are better places for the beginning blacktail hunter, with wilderness areas such as the Trinity Alps excellent for the tough backpacking hunter.

The Sitka deer is best hunted in southeast Alaska, and particularly on some of the offshore islands. Kodiak is excellent and Afognak quite good. Although much smaller in the antlers, these deer grow to hefty body size. Two hundred-pound deer are quite possible on Kodiak. Seasons are long and bag limits liberal. A separate tag must be purchased for each deer, but the limit is five in most areas. The deer are underhunted so the hunting is very productive and enjoyable. Guides are not required, and several air taxi services in towns such as Juneau and Kodiak will ferry hunters into good deer country. One note of caution—the Sitka deer share their habitat with Alaskan brown bears, and the cover is often quite dense. Utmost caution is essential while hunting and especially while handling meat.

The blacktail deer is the only deer recognized in just one category, "blacktail deer," with no typical and non-typical category. Blacktail deer do occasionally grow non-typical antlers, but they are so unusual that no category is established for them. Typical of a trophy blacktail is a miniature mule deer rack, four points per side plus eyeguards, and an outside spread of 18 to 22 inches. Now, that's a good blacktail, and such a buck should make the book. Many blacktails are three-by-three when mature, and the lower portion of the book has numerous three-pointers plus eyeguards.

We're not certain how big or how small the Sitka blacktails are, but it's a sure thing that a four-point buck is most unusual. I recently studied a number of deer from Kodiak Island, and one characteristic showed up continually—the racks were very similar to an eight-point

The petite blacktail is simply a miniaturized mule deer; it has the same bifurcated antlers, but a fully mature buck will almost never exceed 130 pounds. The tail striped by a broad black band from top to bottom is a giveaway. (Photo by Mike Ballew)

whitetail rack, with little apparent bifurcation. The tines tended to come up off the main beam without forking, and if I hadn't known where the deer had come from, I'd have said they were whitetails. The racks aren't large, but they develop a fair amount of mass and a four-point buck, though rare, is possible. Their population seems to be exploding, particularly on Kodiak, which is a transplanted herd. It will be interesting to see what the future holds for these little deer.

Notes on Deer Rifles

Every hunter has his or her own idea about what constitutes the perfect deer rifle. Nobody is either right or wrong, for there are literally dozens of perfectly good rifle/cartridge combos well-suited to all types of deer hunting, and quite a few more specialized rigs to fit certain regional situations.

In many states the various .22 centerfires are legal for deer; I've shot deer with a .22-250 with lightning bolt results, and based on that I'll concede that the hot .22s are fine on our smaller deer under circumstances that permit exact shot placement. But for most deer hunting, I feel a rifle with much more punch is called for. A deer rifle must be relied upon to place a fatal shot from nearly any angle, and from the shooting distances expected where you are hunting.

In much of the country, that makes a .243 or 6mm Remington with a low or medium-powered scope a fine choice. However, there are circumstances where a bit more gun is called for. A typical southern whitetail at 140 pounds live weight, for example, is a much different animal from a Montana or Alberta whitetail that might top 350 pounds, or a Rocky Mountain mule deer in the same weight class.

For all-around deer hunting, accurate scoped rifles in chamberings such as .25-06, .270, .280, .30-06 and .308 are excellent choices. They'll do what needs to be done on any deer, whether in close or at extreme range. While the belted magnums certainly aren't needed, there's nothing wrong with the .240, .257, and .270 Weatherby cartridges, the .264 Winchester Magnum, and the various 7mm and .300 magnums.

What about the brush rifles—the traditional .30-30 carbine or the .35 Remington, .444 Marlin and other large-caliber, low-velocity numbers? Even in areas where the use of such cartridges is long-standing tradition, the flat-shooting scope-sighted turnbolt rifle is gradually taking over. The reason is versatility. The .30-30 and .35 Remington are traditional deer-getters, and their ability to function as such cannot be questioned. Likewise such big bore cartridges as the .348 and .375 Winchester, the .444 Marlin and the great .45-70. The problem is that

Rimrock country is always a good place to look for any of the mule deer subspecies. They like to bed where they can use their eyes as well as their other senses to detect danger.

occasional clearing; the traditional open sights and the arcing trajectory of these cartridges make such shots more difficult than they need be. Nor do they "bust brush" any better than more modern high-velocity cartridges. The truth is no cartridge is reliable in brush, but a spitzer at high velocity is just as likely to get through as a round-nose that's twice as heavy and traveling half the speed.

In some situations, such as ultra-dense timber and perhaps swamp, where it's essential to drop an animal quickly to avoid loss, the big bores have their place. Although on deer-sized animals, their edge over higher-velocity rifles which shoot quick-expanding round-nosed bullets might be questionable. But if the possibility of a longer shot exists, there's no reason to handicap yourself. Good "compromise" cartridges are available, such as the .358 Winchester in Browning's lever action, or the new .356 Winchester in Winchester and Marlin lever actions. Both

This Colorado muley was bedded at long range, then taken after a lengthy waiting game. On today's market I feel it's a toss-up as to which of our deer are most difficult to trophy hunt.

cartridges will do just fine out to 200 yards, but hit hard up close as well.

Much of our deer hunting, some of the best, is limited by local law to shotguns-only. Most shotgun zones require slugs, but a few stipulate buckshot and some leave a choice. If there's a choice, there's no choice. Slugs are incredibly more efficient than buckshot, and can actually be very efficient deer getters out to a surprising distance.

The slug gun must be equipped with sights and be sighted in. A slug barrel might shoot better than a standard barrel, but it might not. Before investing in a slug gun or slug barrel for your present gun, try several brands of slugs. With rifle sights, preferably a scope, the accuracy should be available to make a 12-gauge slug a 100-yard deer cartridge.

A last word on scopes. Everybody shoots better with a scope than they do without, and that includes up close, on running game, whatever. You see better with a scope, and you must focus only on the target and superimpose your reticle on that target. With iron sights, your eye must shift from rear sight to front sight to target and get them all in proper alignment. In close cover, a 1.5X, 2X, or 3X scope is plenty. For general use, a 4X is about right, and for wide-open country

A high-country mule deer camp offers some of the continent's most majestic scenery coupled with clean air and usually pleasant fall weather.

a 6X is plenty. I use open sights, particularly an aperture (peep) sight in close cover, and I like them. I'm not a bowhunter or blackpowder enthusiast. For me, an open-sighted rifle is my concession to tradition, a primitive arm, if you will. But if I want venison, give me a scope every time.

Incidentally, fanciers of true primitive arms—bows, muzzleloaders, and crossbows in an increasing number of states—are offered some very attractive special seasons, and these seasons can offer an exceptional opportunity to make even the most dedicated rifleman want to change his or her luck. Such arms, and the handgun as well, require a special commitment in the extra time required to master them, but the rewards can certainly be worth the effort.

Chapter 3
Elk

The wapiti of the American West may well be the grandest game this continent has to offer. Few animals on Earth are as majestic as a good six-by-six bull elk, and few animals are as hard-won. Elk country, too, is breathtakingly beautiful, and a hunt for these animals in the typical weather and color of autumn in the Rockies is a matchless experience.

The problem with elk hunting is that the animals are so numerous and the hunting so accessible that most hunters expect elk hunting to be easier than it is, and then are disappointed when they find out the truth. The truth is that elk hunting, particularly on the public lands that make up most of the elk range, is perhaps the toughest hunting in North America, and a true trophy-class bull elk is the most difficult trophy to obtain.

An elk hunt is often a hunter's first out-of-state hunt or first hunt involving any major expenditure. Since elk are plentiful and, after all, only big deer, hunters expect that they can go to the Rockies and bust a good one.

It rarely works that way. Elk are crafty in the way that a big whitetail is crafty, and they live in tough, unforgiving, big country where a man is at a decided disadvantage. Current management for maximum yield rather than trophy quality has rendered it ever more difficult to find a big bull. In many areas true trophy-class elk represent less than five percent of the population. And it's a sure thing that what big bulls remain didn't get big by being stupid.

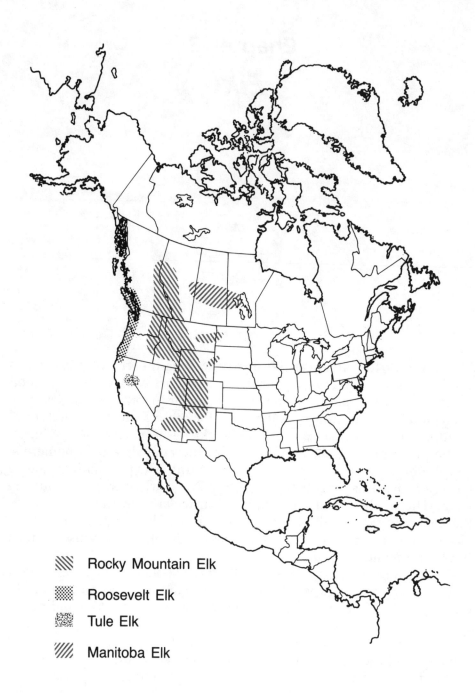

▧ Rocky Mountain Elk

▨ Roosevelt Elk

▨ Tule Elk

▨ Manitoba Elk

ELK RANGE

My old friend Jack Atcheson, the Butte, Montana booking agent, taxidermist and elk-hunting enthusiast, has lived in elk country all his life. I would guess that he's arranged more elk hunts for more people than anyone else in the country. He feels that a really big bull elk is the toughest trophy, and elk hunts are the bane of his existence since it seems impossible to convince hunters what they're up against. Elk hunts probably have the lowest hunter success rate of any hunting on the continent.

Most good sheep outfitters can consistently deliver at least 75 percent of the time. Many do better, and those who do worse simply won't stay in business. Eighty to 90 percent is pretty good for brown bear, and perhaps 60 percent is acceptable for grizzly. Most decent moose hunts are well above 50 percent, and many are closer to 100 percent. You can hit a bad year on caribou, but in a good year a perfect 100 percent season isn't unusual. Guided deer hunts, whether for mule deer or whitetail, are usually well above the 50 percent mark, and in many areas much better than that.

Ah, but elk hunts. In a bulls-only area, any outfitter who hits 50 percent has done well, real well. Once in a while weather conditions may allow 75 percent success, but that is nearly unheard of. There just aren't any perfect 100 percent seasons with elk. It simply doesn't happen except in unusual or controlled circumstances, and it doesn't matter how good the outfitter, guide, or hunter, elk are just plain hard to come by.

If you question that, take a look at the hunter success ratios from the best elk states. In management circles, time has proven that 10 to 15 percent hunter success is pretty good and that's in states where deer success is well over 50 percent statewide! Our top elk-producing states are Montana, Wyoming, Idaho, Washington, Colorado, and Oregon, not necessarily in that order. Only Wyoming consistently tops 25 percent hunter success for its general elk season. Arizona, with tightly controlled permits, also does very well, approaching 25 percent success. New Mexico, too, has a pretty good success percentage, probably because of their system of private land permits in addition to public permits.

Elk hunting may be tough, but it's also rewarding. If you want to *hunt*, elk hunting is a great game. But if the most important thing is to shoot a trophy, then you'd be better off planning to hunt caribou, moose, bear—even sheep! Your chances of filling your license would probably be better. Of course, you wouldn't have been elk hunting— and that's an experience no hunter should miss.

An elk hunt in the Rockies must be one of the world's finest experi-

A big bull elk is one of the world's most majestic animals—and also one of the hunter's toughest prizes. (Photo by Bob Robb)

ences. The quarry will exact the utmost from a hunter in terms of hunting skill, physical effort, and patience. Aside from the elk itself, much of the magic in elk hunting lies with its habitat. To hunt elk in the fall, you must journey into some beautiful wilderness regions at the loveliest time of the year. You'll see the crimson and gold of the turning leaves as autumn descends on the mountains. Early you'll be treated to the bugling of rutting bulls, perhaps the eeriest sound in nature. Late you'll probably catch the first storms of winter and watch the mountains be enveloped in a clean, white unbroken blanket. You may or may not get a trophy bull, or any elk, no matter how hard you hunt or how badly you want one. But taking an elk is only part of the experience, perhaps a small part, of hunting these animals. You may come home without rack or meat, but you won't come home empty-handed. Only the most unimaginative person could come home without being richer for the experience.

The American elk, perhaps more properly called by his Shawnee Indian name "wapiti," is a very large deer, the largest representative of the round-antlered deer family, *Cervus*. A mature bull will usually weigh from 600 to 800 pounds. The former figure is fairly average for the Rocky Mountain elk, while the Roosevelt subspecies of the Pacific Northwest is a bit larger, averaging close to the latter figure. Exceptional individuals will top these figures. Roosevelt elk have occasionally gone over 1,000 pounds, and the transplanted Roosevelt elk on Alaska's Afognak Island are huge, perhaps because of the absence of normal elk parasites. Afognak elk have *dressed out* over 1,000 pounds!

Body color is usually a pale buff, often appearing yellowish-tan on a distant hillside. Legs and underparts are darker, and head and neck are deep chestnut, with a neck ruff of fairly long hair. Elk have a rump patch that's very bright buff and quite distinctive at a distance.

Of course, the elk's lovely antlers are the hunter's prize. A mature bull will typically have long main beams with five forward-jutting points plus the main beam tip curving back, for a total of six points per side. Seven points per side is occasionally seen, and Roosevelt elk have a tendency for additional points at the main beam tip on exceptional specimens.

The American elk is actually not a distinct species. It is a subspecies of the *Cervus elaphus* which circumnavigates the globe in the northern hemisphere. Scientists accept the fact that elk crossed to North America via the Siberian land bridge at some time in the distant past. There are "elk" in Asia, ranging from Mongolia up through Siberia, that are virtually indistinguishable from our elk. In these regions, trophy hunters know them by their local term "maral stag," but on a wall the mounted head is hard to tell from an elk.

An elk hunt in the western mountains may not be the best way to fill a freezer, but it is a most memorable experience. The clean, chill air of the high elk country and the warmth of a good fire are the stuff memories are made of.

Farther east, the various *Cervus elaphus* species are called red deer or red stags. From the Soviet Union westward they get progressively smaller, with stags from Scotland and Spain only a bit larger than a big mule deer. Many of the red deer from all parts of Europe have antlers that are decidedly elk-like, though smaller. However, the typical red deer antler conformation has distinct "crowning" on the upper antlers, a cluster of additional points where the last point (except the main beam tip) would grow on our North American elk. This crowning continues eastward, occurring to a lesser degree on the Asian maral stags, to still a lesser degree on Roosevelt elk. It is almost never seen on a Rocky Mountain elk. Of course, all of these animals are biologically of the same species, and will interbreed freely given a chance.

In North America, the elk was once found from the Atlantic to the Pacific and from Mexico to Alaska. It probably had the widest distribution of any deer species on the continent. At one time we had fully 10 subspecies of *Cervus elaphus*, but three became extinct in prehistoric times and left only fossil evidence. Man, modern man to be more

A cold spike camp on a mountainside is familiar to most serious elk hunters. Sometimes the only way to have a chance is to literally sleep with the elk.

precise, eradicated three other subspecies during the exploration and settling of North America. The Eastern elk, once fairly common in the Northeast, disappeared in the early nineteenth century. Another subspecies in southern California also vanished, and the Merriam's elk of Arizona, New Mexico, and Mexico became extinct around 1900.

From this it's obvious that the elk was not originally a creature of the high mountains, but instead a highly adaptable animal that flourished over a broad range of this continent's terrain and climatic conditions. In the days of Lewis and Clark, elk were quite abundant in the northern Great Plains, and virtually everywhere in the West. But during our westward expansion the elk were pushed into the most remote mountain regions, and by the turn of the century only a remnant population survived. In the last 80 years modern game management has brought them back to a remarkable degree, but with few exceptions they are creatures of the mountains and remote wilderness today.

Of the 10 original subspecies believed to once inhabit North America, four remain today. By far the most abundant, and the one most commonly hunted today, is the Rocky Mountain elk, *C. e. nelsoni*. This elk ranges from northern British Columbia down through the Rockies to northern Arizona and New Mexico, and from eastern Oregon and Washington east to the Black Hills. Rocky Mountain elk have also been introduced into former Merriam's elk range in New Mexico and Arizona where they have done quite well. Introduced populations have also done well in such diverse places as Michigan's Upper Peninsula, Pennsylvania, and Virginia.

The big Roosevelt's elk, *C. e. roosevelti*, is the second most numerous elk. Distinguished primarily by larger body size and the occasional crowning of better bulls, it lives in the dense vegetation of the Pacific Northwest from northern California through Washington and Oregon to southern British Columbia. Roosevelt elk have also been introduced to Alaska's Afognak and Raspberry Islands, and to California's Santa Rosa Island. They've done fairly well in Alaska, and extremely well on Santa Rosa. For trophy records, the Boone and Crockett Club used to consider all elk in the same category, but in 1980 they created a separate category for Roosevelt elk. Both the Safari Club and Pope and Young (for bowhunting records) have long had a separate category for Roosevelt elk.

The Manitoba elk, *C. e. manitobensis*, is considered together with Rocky Mountain elk by all record-keeping organizations, and in fact is so similar that this is undoubtedly the wisest course. The Manitoba elk exists in very modest numbers in southwestern Manitoba on through Saskatchewan into eastern Alberta. Probably the largest herd is in the Duck and Riding Mountains of Manitoba. This elk is virtually identical

A typical six-by-six like this one represents a very small percentage of most elk herds today. Such bulls do exist throughout elk range, but they're getting harder to come by every year. (Photo by Bob Tatsch)

to the Rocky Mountain elk, but averages just a bit larger, about midway between the Rocky Mountain and Roosevelt subspecies.

These are the only huntable subspecies today, but there is a fourth, the little Tule elk (*C. e. nannodes*) of west-central California. Often called dwarf elk, the Tule elk is quite small. A mature bull will average only 400 pounds, about the same as Spanish red deer or really large muleys. The Tule elk were badly depleted during the settling of California. A modest herd exists in the Owens Valley, and the California Game Department has reintroduced them in several areas. The last legal hunt was held in the early Sixties, but it is quite possible that Tule elk will be hunted again at some time in the future. I've observed Tule elk on a couple of state refuges, and it's worth noting that these little elk seem to have a strong tendency, even stronger than the Roosevelt elk, to develop crown points.

Aspen thickets, called quakies, are favorite elk haunts, but they're an elk hunter's nightmare before snow falls. Too thick to offer visibility, the fallen leaves make them noisy to walk through. In good country, elk will be in them—but the chances of digging one out are slim.

It's relatively simple to judge trophy quality on an elk, although the common tendency is to simply count points. Most hunters talk about a six-by-six—called a royal elk—as their goal, but a very few have a seven-by-seven rack—an imperial elk—in mind. The truth is that number of points is only one consideration, and it may not be the most important. Record book measurements combine main beam length, mass, point lengths and number of points to achieve an aggregate score. Boone and Crockett also considers maximum *inside* spread and makes deductions for any lack of symmetry between left and right antler.

With elk, a spike is normal for the first set of antlers. Beyond that, feed and genetics come into play. Under the best conditions, a five-by-five or spindly six-point rack is quite possible for the second set. From there it's a progression of mass and beam length. Some elk will never become seven-pointers, and a few never go beyond five even at full maturity. An odd conformation such as spindly three- or four-point racks is not normal under most conditions, and could reflect poor feed, a bad winter, a dry spring, or a gene pool that isn't producing good racks. To make the Boone and Crockett book, an elk will have massive main beams that approach 60 inches, at least six long points, and will be evenly matched on both sides.

Of course, we're talking in superlative terms. Unless you're perfectly willing to go home empty-handed, you simply don't pass up a mature bull on most elk range today. In fact, sad to say, in many areas *any* bull elk is a good elk. In the pages of most hunting and outdoor magazines, and in the pictures in this book, you'll see nothing but six-pointers or better, maybe the occasional five-pointer. The inference is that *everybody* takes elk like that. It just isn't so. When conditions are perfect—a late migration, or an early bugling season—a hunter might see enough elk to get real picky. But by and large, chances at bull elk are hard-won and few and far between. Any elk taken in fair chase is an animal to be proud of, and an elk with some mass and five or six points per side is well worth putting on the wall. There's certainly nothing wrong with hunting for, and passing up everything except, the very best—just so long as you know what the odds are.

In their *18th Big Game Awards*, for the period 1980–1982, Boone and Crockett recognized 14 Rocky Mountain elk taken in recent years. In the same period approximately 75 typical and 50 non-typical whitetails taken in recent seasons were recognized. Which is tougher? Statistically perhaps the whitetail, since the annual whitetail harvest nationwide is many times that for the elk. But in real terms, it could well take a lifetime of searching to find a "book" animal of either species.

Roosevelt elk tend to have thick antlers that are significantly shorter than those found on their Rocky Mountain cousins. Part of the Boone and Crockett Club's justification for a separate category is the fact that no Roosevelt elk has ever made the minimum score for inclusion into the book. The current Boone and Crockett minimum for Rocky Mountain (and Manitoba) elk is 375. The minimum for Roosevelt is 290, and the new world's record for Roosevelt elk is 356—19 points short of the Rocky Mountain minimum. Since Roosevelt elk is a new category, there is some catching up to do and there will probably be quite a few entries at first. But I suspect things will even out soon and a record-class Roosevelt elk will prove every bit as difficult to obtain as a Rocky Mountain record.

An elk that will go into the book may be an unrealistic goal on today's market, but most elk hunters are quite happy to settle for something less. That "something less"—a nice bull with some mass, fairly long beams, and from five to seven points per side—is certainly an attainable goal, but not one that will come easily. I've been fairly lucky in my elk hunting; to date I've scored exactly 50 percent. Each bull that I've taken I've worked for, usually pretty hard. However, I've probably worked harder for the elk that I didn't get. No matter how pretty the mountains are, they're tough to hunt day after day, and sometimes it seems like you're beating your head against a wall. You have to keep at it, because success could come just as easily on the last day as on the first, but after a 10 day (or longer) hunt with no shots fired, you'll really have earned that bull that you didn't collect.

To me, there are three distinct elk seasons: the early bugling season, the late season when snow is on the ground, and that indefinite period in between. Each time has its own advantages and disadvantages, and in many cases local seasons give you no choice. Let's look at each briefly.

Elk spend their summers fairly high, often above timberline. The mating season, mid-September through early October in most ranges, usually catches them far up in the high country. Getting to them at this time of year usually means a packtrip deep into the high country, a fine way to see the country and the classic way to hunt elk. The weather is usually pleasantly crisp in the mornings and comfortable at midday, but the bugling itself is the big attraction.

Like most animals, bull elk lose some of their caution during the mating season. They move a bit more, and are much easier to catch in the open. But the magic of the bugling season is *bugling*. The challenge of a bull elk is an incredible sound, a lilting, echoing trumpet that is bound to raise goosebumps on any hunter. To me, the bugle of a bull elk is the only sound in nature that equals the roaring of lions close at hand or the cacophony of sound that hyenas can produce.

It can be imitated quite easily, given a little practice. Commercial elk bugles are available that sound perfect, and instructional tapes are also available. Many hunters prefer to bugle with their mouths only, but I'll readily admit I can't do it. A far better bet, unless you happen to live in good elk country and can get in lots of practice, is to get a good commercial call and a tape or record and practice plenty. No two bulls sound exactly alike, and they have a fair amount of variance in their bugling—and so do most successful buglers.

The idea, of course, is to convince a rutting bull that an intruder has come into its territory, and get it to come to you to do battle. Usually you conduct a long-range bugling battle with the bull, fixing its location and working your way slowly toward it. At some point a decision must be reached—set up and let the elk come to you, or try to go on in after it. The former is much preferable, especially if you know how, and when, to bugle. But sometimes a bull simply won't come in, so you have to give it up or try to go get it.

Hunting the rut is probably the best time to have an opportunity at a

This big bull was taken with an 8mm Remington Magnum. Elk are among North America's toughest game to bring down. Strong, heavily muscled, and with massive shoulder bones, elk require a bullet designed to penetrate.

On foot, packing a bull elk is a serious chore. It's sure to take several trips, so the hunter must leave camp with the gear needed to field dress and perhaps quarter the carcass. Elk can sour quickly if not cooled out properly, and that's a shame—elk meat is second to nothing! (Photo by Bob Robb)

really good bull, but it has some limitations. For one thing, elk don't have calendars, so there is no exact time frame to catch the height of bugling activity. You can try, but if you should miss it you can have some tough hunting. Weather is also a big factor in any elk hunting, including the rut. At that time of year it can be cold one day and hot the next, and a few days of warm weather can shut down bugling activity like a faucet being turned off. Then there's the difficulty of finding an open season during the peak rutting period of late September. This last may take extra planning and may require some inconvenience, but it can be well worth it.

At this writing only Idaho and the Canadian provinces of Alberta and British Columbia open their general seasons early enough to catch the best bugling. But both Wyoming and Montana open some of their prime wilderness areas early in September, and Colorado, Arizona and New Mexico offer some special hunts. These hunts are often "special" in a true sense—a special opportunity at a big bull. They may require luck in a drawing, and they may even require some change in your customary hunting weapons. The bow season, for example, is often

Many special blackpowder and archery seasons are set during the rut. It might be worth a change in armament to take advantage of bugling season. The advantage of hunting the rut could well outweigh the disadvantage of using primitive arms. (Photo by Bob Robb)

held during the rut. A modern hunting bow with sharp broadheads is certainly adequate for elk, but only in skilled and well-practiced hands. I wouldn't recommend an elk hunt for a person's first bowhunt.

However, many of the special early hunts today are for muzzle-loaders, and these hunts might be well worth considering. A muzzle-loader of .50 or .54 caliber with one of today's conical bullets is quite adequate for elk, and the rifles are plenty accurate enough for use in conjunction with skillful bugling. Colorado's special early muzzleloader season has become incredibly popular, with permits fairly hard to draw. Smart hunters know that season offers perhaps the best chance at a big bull in that state!

The late season is totally different from the rut. What constitutes late hunting depends on the area, but I'm talking primarily about *winter* elk hunting, after the snow flies and is there to stay. Some states, including Montana, have general seasons that extend into this period, and other states, such as New Mexico, have special hunts that run into January. The rut controls elk movement during the early season, but the snow is in command during the late. Elk aren't migratory in the sense that caribou are, but they will move from summer pasture at high elevation to their wintering grounds when snow forces them to.

Elk are tough, and they like their high, wild places, especially the big bulls. But eventually they'll have to come down. The trick to late season hunting is knowing when they'll move and where they'll be.

As magnificent as a bugling hunt can be, I think I personally prefer the late season. The snow-covered mountains are majestic, and although it can be cold and miserable, the snow makes for quiet stalking and good tracking. There are a very few hunts in a very few areas that actually catch an elk migration. One of the best known is around Gardiner, Montana, where a special late hunt often catches the elk coming out of Yellowstone. It's a great place to get a big bull, if you can get a permit, but it's not much of an elk hunt in the traditional sense.

To me, late hunting is at its best when the snow is there to stay, but the elk haven't quite yet moved out. It's tough to get back into elk country at that time of year, and tougher still to hunt all day in knee-deep snow. But it's challenging hunting that offers excellent odds for success—as long as the elk are still there. They tend to move around quite a lot, digging for browse under the snow. Leaves are long since down offering the best visibility. I love the silence of the snow-covered mountains at that time of year, and I love reading the tales left in the snow.

I got my first introduction to elk hunting under such conditions. It was in the Pioneer Mountains of southwestern Montana, and I had the last 10 days of the general season to hunt, mid to late November. We

Relatively few general seasons catch the rut today, but if you can manage to hunt when elk are bugling, your chances for a good bull are at their peak and besides, you'll never forget the lilting wail of a bugling bull! (Photo by Bob Robb)

packed into camp in late fall, with just a few inches of snow cover. Eleven days later we packed back out in the dead of winter, with drifts piled over the horse trail and a pass to cross in the whiteout of a Montana blizzard.

The days in between brought some fresh snow, gradually piling up but leaving perfect tracking conditions in its wake. This was middle-elevation elk range; nothing above timberline, and rugged hills covered with conifers. A few openings and logged-over hillsides could be glassed, but the hunting was mainly by tracking and digging the elk out of the dense jackpines. It was quite an education. There were plenty of elk, but day after day they made fools of us in those dense jackpine jungles. We saw cows and calves aplenty, and one day stalked (stumbled might be a better term) into a bedded herd. Elk went everywhere, but all I could see was the bull sailing over a deadfall in one mighty leap before I could get my rifle up.

I was hunting with the late John Ward, an outfitter out of Sheridan, Montana. That year John had a moose tag, and I had no problems with him trying to fill it if we found a moose. With the season drawing to a close, we had agreed that he'd also take an elk if the opportunity arose.

On the day before Thanksgiving, after about seven days of hard hunting, we dropped down a couple thousand feet to check out some country we hadn't seen before. We saw nothing early, but hit a reasonably fresh moose track at midmorning. It was a cow, but with nothing else going on we tied the horses and followed the track for a while. After about an hour (with the track getting no fresher) we crossed fresh elk tracks, two bulls, traveling together, and heading straight up a long open ridge. John grinned at me and asked, "You want to hunt cow moose or bull elk?" And without waiting for an answer he turned uphill.

The snow got patchy on the open south slope, but we stayed with the elk and jumped them out of their beds right on top of the ridge. There was no shot when they jumped, but we ran and were lucky. On top of the slope was 100 yards of timber, then a logged-over slope. We caught the elk there and dumped two nice bulls—for John, his winter meat supply, for me, my first bull elk.

In hunting like that, persistence is worth a lot. Elk were all over the mountain, and it was probably just a matter of time before we got a shot. But with fresh tracks and elk spotted every day, it was no problem to keep hunting in spite of sore legs.

Late hunting can work the other way, too. If the snows come early, you can be hunting in country the elk have already abandoned, and few things are more hopeless. That happened the next year, at the same camp on the same mountain at exactly the same time. The snow was knee-deep when we started, waist-deep when we left. A few elk were seen during the first couple of days; the next couple of days just a scattering of tracks. And after that nothing at all. We should have packed up and headed for lower elevation—like the elk—but we didn't. Bob Reinick of Remington Arms was along on that hunt, and I well remember grinning at him every evening and saying, "We'll get 'em tomorrow!" We didn't, which is not unusual in elk hunting.

Between the rut and the late hunt, there's plenty of just plain old elk hunting. You don't have the advantage of bugling, nor the assurance of tracking snow. On the other hand, you don't have the risk of hot weather that might shut the rut down, nor the chance that the elk will have moved out. Mid-season hunting is tough. The timber can be dry and noisy, the elk scattered and unpredictable. And it's under these conditions that the majority of elk hunting is done. In alpine areas with

One of the rarest—and best—elk hunting conditions occurs when an early snowstorm coincides with the rut. That's the best of all worlds, impossible to plan on, but a real elk hunter's dream comes true when it happens. (Photo by Len Rue Jr.)

open meadows, glassing is possible early mornings and late evenings. Sometimes patches of timber or quakies can be driven. But most often, you have to stillhunt into the thick timber. With luck, you might get a bit of fresh snow and that's often exactly what is needed.

The most important thing about elk hunting is to plan enough time. Time to wait out the weather, time to figure out the area and the elk movement, and then time to hunt hard. My father, a couple of quail-hunting buddies and I made a drop-camp hunt near Durango, Colorado last year. It was a beautiful area, and although there was some hunting pressure it was far from crowded. We had a lovely camp alongside a babbling stream; it was as pleasant an experience as you could hope for. Except for sucess. It was the most unsuccessful hunt I've ever had. And it was our fault.

Plenty of elk were around, and although most of the sign was old, there was enough fresh sign to keep things interesting. But the weather was hot and dry. Stalking was like walking on popcorn, and the quakie patches, some as big as Los Angeles, had not dropped a single leaf. Neither Dad nor I ever saw an elk. Our two buddies, good Kansas squirrel and whitetail hunters, managed to sneak in on a couple bands of cows, but I have no idea how they did it under those conditions!

The traditional elk hunt is still by packstring into one of the wilderness regions of the Rockies, truly a great experience. (Photo by Bob Robb)

We did things dead wrong. We simply didn't plan enough time to wait out the weather. Sometimes there's just no way; the season ends before the break you need comes along. But not this time. The season still had several days to run, but we had commitments and had to leave. Elk hunting is elk hunting, and if it bothers you unduly to get skunked, you should hunt something else.

At hunters' gatherings, one of the most-asked questions is "where can I get a good bull elk?" There's no pat answer. With enough time to hunt—a minimum of seven days, but 10 is better and 14 better still—a hunter in good physical condition has a reasonable chance for an elk in almost all elk range. It takes a bit of luck, but a good friend of mine defines luck as "when preparation and opportunity meet."

Elk can certainly be hunted successfully unguided, but that requires a great deal more preparation and research. Carrying a bull out is a monumental task, and a man on foot must be in outstanding physical condition before he even contemplates such a task. The drop-camp is a good option for the man who doesn't want (or can't afford) a guided hunt. A drop-camp gets you into elk country, gives you a base of operations, and usually offers a plan to get your elk packed out. The actual hunting is up to you. The cost is usually minimal. On my elk trip to Colorado, I'm not sure we could have supplied our own camp for what the outfitter charged us.

Statistics do show that guided hunters are a great deal more success-ful than unguided ones, whether residents or nonresidents. The classic elk hunt is still a horseback hunt into remote country, and it's worth every penny just for the experience. But prospective elk hunters mustn't think that a guided elk hunt is a surefire means of getting a big bull. There is no surefire way to get a big bull!

Roosevelt elk hunting is probably the toughest nut to crack. These animals live in the dense vegetation of the Pacific Northwest, and they're damned hard to hunt. For an outsider unfamiliar with the country, a guided hunt is the only thing that makes sense but neither Washington nor Oregon have well-developed guiding industries.

Except for the residents of those two states, most elk hunters will go after the Rocky Mountain elk. If you live in elk country, you can probably find good hunting close to home, and can do the scouting needed to find them. Nonresidents have it tougher, and must pick a place to go. Statistically, Wyoming offers the best odds. Potential prob-lems are two-fold. First, Wyoming elk tags are getting harder to draw every year, and second, some of Wyoming's best areas require that nonresidents be guided.

Montana's elk hunting is just as good, actually leads the pack in Boone and Crockett bulls taken over the years. Idaho, too, offers some fine elk hunting. The licenses in both these states are limited quota, but are first-come, first-served.

Colorado is the top state in terms of total harvest, but hunting pressure is heavy and is compressed into a short season. There is some excellent elk hunting in this state, but the chances for a big bull are not good. On the other hand, for hunters in search of "any elk," this state might be a good choice.

Although drawing the permits requires luck, special hunts are available in most elk states. These may be special seasons or special areas, and they often really increase the odds. They're well worth looking into. If they're good opportunities, more often than not they're hard to draw, but you certainly won't draw if you don't apply.

Arizona is a sleeper; its elk herd is small, and permits few and hard to draw. On the other hand, this relatively small herd of elk has produced an inordinate number of huge bulls. I apply for elk in Arizona regularly, and when I draw I think I will get a super bull, but it might take years, and my name may never come up. Arizona also has a few Indian reservations with excellent elk herds. The White Mountain Apache reservations may well be the best place in the world to get a Boone and Crockett elk—but permits are extremely expensive.

Alberta, too, has produced an amazing number of huge elk, considering that this province only has 20,000 elk (Colorado has over 150,000). The hunting there is tough—rugged mountains with limited access. For the hunter willing to spend 14 or even 21 days, this province has excellent trophy potential, but only for the hunter with time, patience and persistence. Neighboring British Columbia also has a small herd of elk. Conditions in southern British Columbia are about the same as in Alberta. In northern British Columbia, in the Peace River region, a few outfitters have elk in their areas. These herds, totalling about 7,000, are hunted very little. Because they're at the extreme northern end of the elk range, trophy size is modest. However, a good-looking six-by-six isn't that hard to come by, and this area offers the unique opportunity to combine elk with such species as sheep, moose, goat, caribou and grizzly. Nonresidents must be guided in both provinces, and hunts cost a bit more than in the Rocky Mountain states.

On public land, New Mexico's potential is about the same as elsewhere—good, given the right conditions. In addition to public land permits, New Mexico has a system of landowner permits, whereby landowners in elk country are authorized a certain number of elk permits to do with as they see fit. Costs vary widely, ranging from simple trespass fees (plus the license fee) to fully guided and catered "luxury" hunts costing several thousand dollars. New Mexico doesn't usually

Much public land elk habitat is hunted hard today. It's possible to get good bulls, but you might have to go harder and farther than most hunters are willing or able. (Photo by Bob Robb)

have the largest bulls, but well-managed private land herds often have excellent bull/cow ratios, and may provide some of the best odds for mature, trophy-class bulls. The private land seasons are usually of short duration, and may not provide the total experience of a traditional pack-in hunt. In some cases they're actually quite easy, but the success is there. New Mexico, like Arizona, also has some Indian reservations that offer excellent elk hunting to non-tribal members. The Mescalero Apache Reservation is everything you've ever heard it is, and probably more. The Jicarilla also has some good elk hunting.

Rifles and cartridges for elk seem to be a big subject for campfire arguments, and I might as well get in my two cents. The great Jack O'Connor felt that the .270 was enough gun for elk. He knew more about elk hunting than I'll ever know, so I certainly wouldn't dispute that. However, I would say that cartridges on the order of the .270 Winchester are the absolute bottom end for elk hunting, and should be used only by good hunters who are willing to pick their shots.

Remington's Paul Spenard, guided by Arlys Kanseah, took this excellent bull on the Mescalero Reservation. Southern bulls tend to grow large in the body. This bull field-dressed over 700 pounds.

The elk is a huge deer, but it isn't even close to the moose in size. However, the elk is harder to put down. On quartering shots there's a lot of heavy bone and muscle to get through, and it takes a good bullet with adequate power to do the job.

I've done a fair amount of African hunting, and a question I get asked a lot goes something like this: "Are African animals really that much tougher than North American game?" On the small end, maybe. The greater prevalence of predators keeps African prey species keyed up at all times. But I think the elk is the toughest deer in the world. Hit badly, it'll go for miles. Hit solidly, it can go a surprising distance. Once we followed a rutting bull which had been shot through the lungs with an 8mm Remington Magnum. He was down in 125 yards—so far, no surprise. His head was still up, but that wasn't unusual. I saw the finisher go in right behind his shoulder. He got up, was knocked down, got up, was knocked down and finally required a spinal shot, in spite of four other close-range shots that were, or should have been, quite fatal. Bullet performance was perfect. The bull was just too full of adrenalin to stay down.

I wouldn't be afraid to hunt elk with a .270, .280, 7mm magnum, or .30-06. They're all good all-around big game cartridges, especially the latter two. But I'd have that nagging caution about quartering shots, and I wouldn't take a going-away shot. For me, a better bet would be one of the .300 magnums, whether H&H, Weatherby or Winchester, with a well-constructed 200-grain bullet. Better still are the "medium magnums." The 8mm Remington didn't sell well and was short-lived, but it's a great elk cartridge. The .338 Winchester Magnum and the .340 Weatherby are near-perfect for this kind of hunting; flat trajectory to reach out if needed, and the kind of punch that, if it doesn't anchor a bull, will at least cut down tracking distances. Even the big .375 H&H isn't out of place in an elk camp; I've taken elk with it. I've had built a .338, with a fiberglass stock. It's accurate, light, has a punch, and it's impervious to the elements—all the qualifications for an elk rifle.

Obviously, power is no substitute for shot placement. Elk must be hit right, regardless of what you hit them with, or you've got a big problem on your hands. A good elk hunt may well be this continent's ultimate hunting experience. The mountains, the colors, the clean air and the feel of a good horse underneath you all combine to make a special experience. But an elk hunt isn't just a ride in the backcountry, it's a search for a wary, crafty, tough animal. The object of an elk hunt is to find an elk. Today, the search is difficult and the chances are few and far between. When that chance comes, I want to make the shot as perfect as possible, but I also want to make it with a cartridge that I *know* will do the job!

Chapter 4
Pronghorn Antelope

It's a long drive from Kansas City to Douglas, Wyoming, but in those pre-55-mile-per-hour days you could make pretty good time. As I recall, we spent the night in a little town in Nebraska, then got up early and arrived in Douglas shortly after daybreak. Wyoming law said I had to be 14 to get an antelope license, so *of course* I was, but I wasn't doing any of the driving. My father and Henry Pohl were trading off, while I asked the endless questions that any youngster might on his first big game hunt.

I had seen pronghorns before. We had a few in Kansas even though we were a decade or more away from that state's first modern hunt. But I had seen them only from the Interstate, little white dots a tremendous distance away. As we drove through Nebraska, we saw the same little white dots. A few more than I'd seen on trips to western Kansas during pheasant season, to be sure, but I still didn't really know what a pronghorn looked like, and I could hardly believe that I was going to find out.

I don't know how many first-time pronghorn hunters have treated themselves to the drive from Douglas to Gillette on the way to that first hunt, or to any of several dozen Wyoming towns on the day before any antelope season. Most of us are accustomed to looking long and hard to see game—any game—let alone the kind of trophies we're looking for. That's not pronghorn hunting in good country. On that first drive from Douglas to Gillette, I lost count at about 500 animals—before we'd covered half the distance.

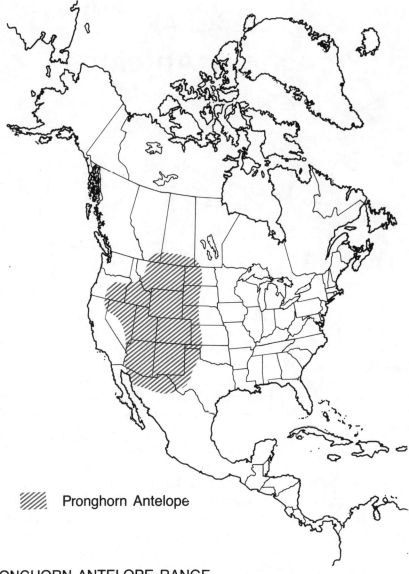

 Pronghorn Antelope

PRONGHORN ANTELOPE RANGE

Henry Pohl, of Bishop's Gunstock Company in Warsaw, Missouri, had done a lot of pronghorn hunting, but it was my father's first hunt as well as mine. It was exciting to see all those pronghorns along the highway, and for a youngster eager to take his first animal, it sure looked like it was going to be almost *too* easy. Of course, it wasn't.

Seeing pronghorns is rarely the problem when you're hunting this unique American animal, but finding a good trophy and getting close

enough for a decent shot can be difficult, and that's what makes hunting them the great sport that it is. On that first trip, Dad and I made
nearly every mistake in the book, from the planning stage onward. But
the three of us managed to bring home three pronghorns, and one of
them was a fairly decent buck. Just by chance it happened to be mine,
and it still hangs in the folks' den. Like I said, we did almost everything completely wrong and still managed to get our game. That
doesn't indicate that pronghorns are pushovers, but they are plentiful
and the ease with which they can be located on the Western plains
means that most pronghorn hunts will be successful.

Their sharp eyes, great speed and the wide open country they live in
makes hunting them a unique challenge, but hardly a difficult one.
Still, they are a beautiful big game species, and certainly one of the
most unique, having no close relatives anywhere else in the world.
And the plains habitat has its own stark beauty and lonely sense of
freedom. These factors combine to give pronghorn hunting its very
special attraction. I think it's one of the most pleasant hunts on this
continent and certainly one of my favorites.

One antelope isn't really an antelope at all, being very dissimilar to
the true antelopes of Africa and Asia. It's related much more closely to
the goat family, but biologically speaking occupies its own unique
genus, *Antilocapra*. There is only one species identified in this genus,
Antilocapra americana, and five subspecies—*americana*, *oregana* (in Oregon), *peninsularis* (in Baja California), *sonoriensis* and *mexicana*. The
americana subspecies is the one familiar to most hunters, and by far the
most numerous. The *mexicana* subspecies is found south of the border
and in a few places in Arizona and New Mexico, with the *sonoriensis*
subspecies to its west. Both the Peninsular and Sonoran subspecies are
considered endangered today. The differences between the five subspecies are slight and of little consequence to the hunter; no record-
keeping system has ever tried to differentiate between them.

The pronghorn is a relatively small animal, with a big buck rarely
weighing over 110 pounds or so. A seemingly blocky body is supported by surprisingly spindly legs, but the bones in those legs have
one of the highest tensile strengths in the animal kingdom and those
legs are capable of propelling the pronghorn at quite amazing speeds.
There's a lot of conjecture regarding the possible top end—50 to 60
miles per hour are common estimates. I wouldn't attempt to dispute
those estimates, or slightly higher ones. Of course, the top speed is for
short sprints. Even more amazing is the pronghorn's ability to maintain
nearly 40 miles per hour for *miles*. Suffice it to say that they're fast.

Apart from speed, the pronghorn's other outstanding attribute is its
eyesight. It's been likened to that of a man using 8X binoculars, al-

though I'm not sure there's any way to accurately measure the acuity of an animal's vision in human terms. But if you can see them, they have already seen you at virtually any range, and if you are perceived as a threat, the next step is to use those spindly legs to put some prairie between you and them. Another item worth noting regarding the pronghorn's eyes is that they are set very high in the skull and very far apart, giving the animal somewhat of a "bug-eyed" appearance and very close to 360-degree vision. If a pronghorn is in sight, you simply cannot approach closer without being seen, regardless of which way it's facing.

The pronghorn is a colorful animal, with a buff body, white under-parts, rump patch and throat markings, all offset by black nose and jet black horns. Those horns are the primary attraction for the trophy hunter, and for accuracy, it should be stated that they are in reality neither true horns nor true antlers. In fact, they're quite unique both in shape and composition. The outer "horn" with its distinctive pronged shape forms around a bony core, and this sheath is shed and grown new each year. The horn sheath is like solidified hair, primarily a protein composition, while the core it forms around is a bony mass about six inches long. These "horns" (we'll call them that for lack of a better word) are fairly fragile, and broken prongs and horn tips are common.

If symmetry is important to you, then you might remember to have a good look at both horns when you're sizing up a trophy head. More important, at least in terms of hunt planning, is the pronghorn's horn-shedding cycle. Most pronghorn seasons are held early enough that there is no problem, but be aware that the bucks will start shedding around the middle of November, sometimes a bit earlier. Some late seasons do run into this time frame, and occasionally you might find a pronghorn season open until early December, by which time the bucks will have dropped their horns.

In our pioneer days the pronghorn antelope was incredibly numer-ous and widespread west of the Mississippi. Some estimates place the pronghorn population in 1850 as higher than that for the bison, which may have reached 60 million animals! Whatever the figure, the plains in those days must have been a sight to behold. But the pronghorns vanished quickly, almost as quickly as the bison. By 1900, only a few thousand remained, and naturalists of the day felt their total extinction was a bygone conclusion. Obviously that didn't happen. Last minute protective measures saved the day, and hunters' dollars began paving the way for the long road back. Although tremendously affected by drought and severe winter, pronghorns are very prolific. Today they

This Montana pronghorn makes the book. The horns are 16⅞, the prongs are good, and it has nice mass. It's not a spectacular head in any dimension, but it has it all and both horns are in symmetry—a super trophy! (Photo by Jack Atcheson Sr.)

exist in huntable numbers in virtually every Western state, with a total population estimated to be well over 500,000.

Pronghorns are creatures of the unbroken prairies. They can survive around agriculture, though grudgingly, but they thrive in country that has never seen the plow. Occasionally you will find one in the willows along a creek bottom or on a cedar-studded hillside, but those are the exceptions. Our prairie goat much prefers to be out in the open where those amazing eyes can act as an early warning system, and where those seemingly-spindly legs can outdistance any predator.

Open range and available water seem to be among the most important factors governing pronghorn populations. Much of the American West is simply too dry, and this is particularly true of the Southwest, where the pronghorns could find all the open country their hearts desire. Conversely, pronghorns have literally been fenced out of much of their former habitat. These plains dwellers did not evolve without any obstacles in their paths, but they simply don't do well around fences. They *can* negotiate fences—their primary method is to go under

This is an exceptional New Mexico pronghorn, about 15½ inches in length with a nice shape. Remington's Paul Spenard took him with a 6mm Remington, a fine pronghorn rifle.

the bottom strand, but on a few occasions I've seen them go *over* three strands of barbed wire.

The problem isn't their physical inability to go under, over, around, or through barbed wire, but a seemingly stubborn reluctance to acknowledge its presence in their domain. For every pronghorn that will cross a fence, there are a dozen more that starve or die of thirst on one side when forage or water are available on the other side. Or they will let a blizzard drift them into a fenceline, where they'll be found piled up after the spring thaw. Just like the cowboys of old, our pronghorns are creatures of the open range.

In spite of all that, these hardy plains dwellers have managed to thrive and even continue to increase across much of western North America. In fact, in most areas where pronghorn seasons are held the animals are quite abundant. A bad winter or abnormally dry spring and summer can decimate a pronghorn herd, but under favorable conditions does will drop twins and can quickly build a herd up to the carrying capacity of the range. Hunting has two functions in pronghorn management. The obvious one is to keep the population in check (which often means harvesting does) and the other, in some cases, is to use hunting pressure to scatter a herd in the hopes of expanding their range into suitable habitat nearby.

For whatever reason, sound management has dictated that today we can hunt pronghorns in virtually every state west of the Mississippi, plus on the prairies of Canada, and that's very good news for any hunter. In general, pronghorn hunting today is by limited permits allocated by drawing. Some states offer their permits to residents only, while others have nonresident quotas. Like all permit drawings, the better—or better-known—areas are harder to draw to.

Obviously, some states have a great many more permits available than others, and some states have a great many more hunters trying for those permits! In California, where I now reside, we have quite a few permits available and some really excellent pronghorn hunting, but you're a lot luckier than I am if you're able to draw. If a Californian were to put in for a permit every year for seven or eight years, he (or she) would probably get a tag. Arizona, with a fairly modest herd but spectacular trophy quality, offers about the same odds for its residents and worse for nonresidents. Of course, you will most definitely never draw a tag if you don't apply, and every year I talk to hunters who beat the odds in permit drawings, often the first time they put in. So if there are pronghorn tags available in your state, regardless of how limited, by all means apply for them. You never know. But in the meantime, if you really want to hunt pronghorns you might think about getting a tag in one of the prime pronghorn states.

Of the western states, only Washington falls outside the pronghorn's range and only Washington and Oklahoma have no pronghorn season. With 15 states and the two provinces of Alberta and Saskatchewan all offering pronghorn hunting, it would seem that prospective pronghorn hunters have a bewildering choice of possible places to go. Actually, it's quite easy to pare that list down substantially. As mentioned, several states (and both provinces) offer permits to residents only. Kansas, the Dakotas, and California are included on this list and all are on the fringes of pronghorn habitat. If permits are reserved for residents, it's for a good reason, such as there aren't enough to go around. Oregon has a good herd of pronghorns, and some nice trophies. Between 1980 and 1982, six Oregon bucks qualified for the Boone and Crockett book. However, Oregon permits are hard to draw and this state attracts few nonresidents. Nevada has only recently offered nonresident permits. This arid state is marginal pronghorn habitat and the herd is small. However, that small herd produced nine B&C heads from 1980 to 1982, so it's a good place to trophy hunt if you don't mind long odds on the draw.

Arizona, of course, is famous for trophy pronghorns, but is one of the most difficult places to draw a tag. Utah's herd is quite small, but to the north Idaho has a surprisingly good herd, although the winters are too harsh for trophy quality to be outstanding. Few nonresidents travel to Idaho strictly for pronghorns, but hunting for them can often be done in conjunction with elk or deer hunting. On the east side, Nebraska offers a few hard-to-draw nonresident permits, but trophy quality is generally mediocre. A few decent bucks are taken in west Texas each year, although in that dry country trophy quality is usually poor.

The Lone Star State does offer the great advantage of landowner permits. Virtually all of Texas' pronghorns are on private land, and there is no drawing for private land permits; one must obtain them directly from the landowner. I have found it exceedingly difficult— almost impossible—to make hunting contacts of any kind in west Texas, but if you have them or can make them, there is no tag drawing!

If I seem to be working around the fringes of pronghorn country, I have been. But now let's get to the heart of the subject—the four states of Montana, Wyoming, Colorado, and New Mexico. Wyoming holds close to 50 percent of the nation's total pronghorn population. All tags are obtained by drawing, with applications made for a specific area. Some areas are tough to draw to, others are easy. Areas known to be top trophy areas are harder to draw. However, Wyoming has lots of antelope and allocates lots of permits. In most years buck licenses are left over in some areas after the draw, and many areas allow additional licenses for doe or fawn. There are always plenty of those tags left when the season opens. Wyoming is not known as a producer of record-class pronghorns. However, they're there. From 1980 to 1982 there were 98 pronghorns recorded that met the Boone and Crockett minimum of 82 points. Fifty-three of them came from Wyoming.

Montana, particularly the eastern portion, has a good pronghorn population; the second largest behind Wyoming. Because of the distance, few hunters travel to Montana for pronghorns only. However, the permits are not very hard to draw, and the pronghorn season runs concurrent with the deer and elk season. Right now eastern Montana offers perhaps the best mixed bag hunting in the United States, with whitetail, mule deer, pronghorn, wild turkey and several other species of gamebirds available on the same hunt.

Colorado has the fourth largest pronghorn herd, behind Wyoming, Montana, and South Dakota. Unlike South Dakota, though, Colorado offers nonresident hunting. Permits aren't easy to draw, but there are some dandy bucks on Colorado's plains.

Pronghorn have a ground-eating trot that seems effortless and fairly slow. They can eat up the ground at 35 or 40 miles per hour without getting out of first gear, and they can hold a pace like that for miles.

In terms of overall numbers of pronghorns, New Mexico is way down the list. However, the trophy quality available and the unique game regulations make New Mexico one of our best bets for pronghorns—in my judgement, second only to Wyoming, and just maybe second to none.

New Mexico has drawings for pronghorn permits on public land, as one might expect, but theirs is a "dual system" whereby the land-owners get private land permits to dispose of as they see fit (for a fee, one to a customer, of course). The seasons are very short, two or three days in a given area, and also very early, usually late August or September. Obviously, there are tremendous advantages to this system—no drawings to sweat out, and, since it's private land hunting, hunting pressure is tightly controlled. The big disadvantage is cost. Many of the larger ranches, and/or the better trophy ranches, have their permits guaranteed by outfitters so that the only way to gain access is through a guided hunt. In other cases the rancher will allocate the permits himself and charge a trespass fee. The New Mexico game department

Pronghorns are taken at longer ranges than most North American big game, but even at that most shots are exaggerated. This buck is well within 100 yards, and the average shot is probably not over 150 to 200 yards.

will provide a list of ranches that have private land permits, so it's quite possible to do some research and shop around. In any case, the New Mexico situation is tremendously convenient and a perfect situation for hunters short on time. The major drawback is that it will usually be a bit more expensive than pronghorn hunts in states where you must draw for a tag.

New Mexico has gained a well-earned reputation in recent years for producing exceptional pronghorns. From 1980 to 1982 only eight B&C heads came out of that state, but that's a significant number considering the low harvest and low population figures. In New Mexico one won't see as many antelope as in Wyoming, but you just might not have to look at as many to find a good one. This is basically true of all the southern or mild climate pronghorn areas, although New Mexico is the only such area with access readily available to nonresidents. Arizona, California, New Mexico, and Nevada all produce record or near-record heads at a disproportionately high number compared to the size of the herds.

It's my opinion that the reason for this is simply longevity. In the milder areas, pronghorns live long enough to reach trophy proportions. In 1978 my dad and I returned to the Campbell County, Wyoming ranch where we'd made our first pronghorn hunt more than ten years earlier. The ranch hadn't been hunted much, and the weather had been mild for a couple of years; we found a pronghorn hunter's paradise. There were literally dozens of bucks in the 14-inch class and several inching above 15. We took nice bucks—the best we've ever taken—but we'd been a bit too hasty. After we had our bucks down, I saw a couple that had to exceed 16 inches, with mass and prongs to match—I knew where I'd be on October 1st of '79.

The disastrous winter of 1978-79 was matched only by the winter of 1983-84. I was back on that ranch a couple of days ahead of the 1979 pronghorn season, looking for the monster bucks I knew to be there. Except they simply weren't there. Instead of quite respectable 14-inch bucks, most of the bucks had horns between 10 and 12 inches. We hunted hard, but the best we saw hardly reached 14 inches. What happened? Did the big bucks die, or did they finish the winter in such a depleted condition that they were unable to grow decent horns? Perhaps a combination of the two. Prolific though they are, pronghorns are subject to radical winterkills, and I believe that the older bucks, the trophies, are among the first to go.

Should you book a guided pronghorn hunt or do it yourself? That depends on several things—your experience and ability, the area you wish to hunt (or obtained a permit in), and the amount of time you want to spend.

Pronghorns, perhaps more so than any other North American big game animal, can be hunted sucessfully by the unguided first-time hunter. They're relatively easy to find and usually enough of them are around so that you can afford to make a few mistakes in the learning process. On private land in New Mexico, you will often be locked into a guided hunt. But over much of pronghorn country, the hunting is on public land with free access, and even on much private land access is available free or for a modest trespass fee. If you plan to hunt un-guided, you should make sure you have a place to hunt before you apply for a permit, but there really should be no problem finding one.

A couple of catches are associated with unguided pronghorn hunt-ing. First, pronghorns are difficult to judge. Unguided first-timers are unlikely to get as good a trophy as guided first-timers. Part of what you pay a guide for is to know what kind of quality the area you're in should produce, and then to recognize that quality when it appears. Second, pronghorn hunting, particularly on most public lands, de-pends heavily on careful pre-season scouting, or, for late-season hunts, on intimate knowledge of the terrain. These things are also part of what you pay a guide for.

If you plan to hunt unguided and don't have much experience with pronghorns, you should plan to spend several days before the season opens scouting and becoming familiar with the area. If you want to shoot a nice trophy, you should also do your homework, study photo-graphs and as many mounted heads as you can before you go, and of course try to make qualitative judgements while you're scouting. If time is as important as money, or if you want very badly to get a nice trophy the first time out, then you might consider a guided hunt with a reputable outfitter.

As I said at the beginning of this chapter, pronghorns were what I started with, and I've missed very few seasons since then. But in 1984, I took my very first *guided* pronghorn hunt. Texas outfitter Robert Rogers, best known as a whitetail fanatic, has put together a couple of private-land New Mexico pronghorn hunts each season for the past several years. The 1984 season fell over Labor Day weekend, so my wife and I joined Robbie and his partner, Danny Estes, for a hunt near Santa Rosa.

At dawn we were glassing pronghorns, and by noon more than half of the party had filled out on nice bucks, nothing under 14 inches. I held out until Sunday evening, finally taking a decent buck, but I missed the best pronghorn I've ever seen! Monday afternoon we were back in Los Angeles with a duffel bag full of boned-out pronghorn meat. That particular area had a three-day season, but some of New Mexico's seasons are just two days. No matter how choosey you want

With the right planning an antelope hunt can be combined with some excellent sage grouse shooting.

to be, you can't make a long hunt out of it! However, it's a super arrangement for a hunter who is short on time.

In contrast, my typical Wyoming pronghorn hunts have started with a drive of some 1,200 miles, a necessary hassle because hunting vehicles to rent are scarce, and even if you can find one, it will be expensive. Airline connections to that part of the country are also inordinately expensive. So, a Wyoming pronghorn hunt is hardly a weekend affair. Instead, it begins with the tag application period of January 1st through March 15th. Tagholders are notified by midsummer, and plans can begin.

Eventually the season rolls around and you make the gruelling drive. That isn't all bad, of course, because from whichever direction you come there will be enough antelope to see to keep you occupied the

My father took this heavy-horned Wyoming buck near the spot where I took my first antelope years before. When this buck was taken 15-inchers like this one were fairly common. A bad winter came in, and the following year bucks over 12 inches were virtually nonexistent.

last few hundred miles. Of course, you will want to arrive a couple of days ahead of the season to do some scouting. The past couple of years I've been hunting western Wyoming, combining my scouting with some outstanding sage grouse shooting—that alone is worth the trip! If adequate time has been allowed for scouting, then two to four days of actual hunting should be enough. It could be done in a week's time, but not much less.

It's a fairly simple matter to locate areas that traditionally produce topnotch trophy pronghorns; an hour of studying the B&C and Safari Club record books will tell you that. However, unless you're serious about looking for a book head, and unless the season you plan to hunt has been preceded by an abnormally bad winter, you can generally find average, respectable bucks—bucks worth hanging on your wall—

in almost any area. The important thing is to make sure you have a place to hunt long before you head for pronghorn country.

Of course, much of Wyoming and Montana is public land, but many management units, particularly on the east side, are mostly private. When Henry Pohl, Dad and I drove to Wyoming on that first hunt, we had tags in a private land area, but no idea of where we could hunt. It was a big mistake, and that was 20 years ago. We visited the Gillette Chamber of Commerce, got a map, and started knocking on ranchers' doors. Our scouting time was spent just finding a place to hunt, but eventually we found a rancher who took pity on a worried father with an eager youngster. Local Chambers of Commerce are almost always helpful, but the time to start is when you apply for tags, not when the season rolls around! If a guided hunt is your choice, then the normal precautions apply—check all the references you can find, and really grill the outfitter on the kind of bucks he expects to take.

Scouting is one of the most important aspects of pronghorn hunting. Since they are very prolific animals, they are often hunted fairly hard to maintain herd balances. They're territorial animals, until the shooting starts, so the last few days before the season are important because those few days will tell you where to be at dawn on opening day.

I prefer to do as much scouting as possible from a vehicle, using a spotting scope to size up bucks at extreme range. Until badly disturbed they are habitual as well as territorial, so take note of both *when* and *where* you see any promising bucks, and study the terrain to see how you can move in on them on opening day. While scouting, I like to cover as much ground and see as many antelope as possible, hopefully finding one or two that are interesting. But when the season is open, forget the vehicle. Put on a daypack and go after them on foot. All too many pronghorns are shot by chasing after them in a truck. Aside from being illegal and unsportsmanlike, it isn't nearly as much fun as outwitting them on their own ground.

Pronghorns are hard to judge, and trophy judgement is clouded by the fact that many hunters have unreasonable expectations. Pronghorns go into both the Boone and Crockett and Safari Club record books by a combination of factors. The easiest to judge is the simple length of the horns, and that's the figure hunters usually quote. Of equal importance, though, is the mass, the length of the prongs, and for B&C, the symmetry.

In the 1980–82 B&C awards period, only one pronghorn with 18-inch horns was recorded. The Safari Club book, comprised mostly of recent (within the last 20 years) entries, is also a good present day yardstick and it lists only one 18-inch buck. That 18-inch mark seems to be the big barrier, for there have been quite a few 17-inch bucks recorded. It's important to note that by either the B&C or SCI measuring system, bucks with horns as short as 15½ inches place higher than some 17-inch plus bucks due to long prongs and good mass. So length alone isn't everything, but it is the easiest to judge and will continue to be the key element in field judging.

It's obvious that an 18-inch buck is an unrealistic goal. Once in a blue moon a 17-incher may be spotted, and a 17-inch buck will make the book. In a very good year, 16-inch bucks may be seen, and with reasonable mass and prongs most 16-inchers will make the B&C minimum. Generally speaking, a 15-inch buck is a reasonable goal for the serious trophy hunter, and anything over that is pure gravy. The B&C listings are well-sprinkled with 15-inch bucks that had good weight and good prongs, and during the 1980-82 period, eight bucks with length less than 15 inches made the book. So a 15-inch pronghorn is a helluva buck, and anything that is 14 inches or so is certainly of trophy quality. After a tough winter, it can be difficult to find anything over 13 inches, but a 13-inch buck with good weight and a nice shape will look fine on anyone's wall. The idea is to not get all wrapped up in the inches, but rather look at the whole head, and if you like it, go after it.

The ears of a pronghorn are about six inches long, so if a buck's horns appear to double his ears in length, they should be about 12 inches. The amount of hook on the end must also be taken into account, and that is very hard to see. My longest pronghorn came just shy of 16 inches strictly by virtue of a very long hook; I hadn't expected him to be any longer than 14½. Pronghorn tend to appear bigger than they are, perhaps because of the striking jet-black of their horns against a normally drab background. When running, the horns almost always appear much larger than they are. *Never* try to judge a running antelope, and always view the horns from the side as well as from the front or back.

Just supposing that your careful scouting and glassing has revealed the kind of buck you're after, or at least you think he's big enough and you want to get closer to make sure. What next? There are only two choices. You can go to the buck or you can wait until he comes to you.

I'm an impatient hunter, and I much prefer trying a stalk if there is any chance of success. The first thing is to study the terrain. It probably looks flat, but chances are it has little folds, gullies and rises that will offer the concealment you must have. It is important to remain completely out of sight during the entire stalk. Watch the wind, of course, but the pronghorn's sense of smell is a secondary line of defense, likewise his ears. He relies at least 90 percent on his eyes, and if you can stay out of sight and get within range, you should get a shot.

It can mean hours of crawling through cactus and sagebrush, but when you get the drop on a nice buck it will seem worth it.

Sometimes the terrain is simply too open to permit a shot. Then it's time to play the waiting game, either until the buck moves into country where he's stalkable, or until you find a position where he will come in range of you. Most pronghorn country is fairly dry, and the animals will usually drink from the same place at about the same time, usually during midday hours. A rifleman can locate a good ambush position, but a bowhunter or blackpowder hunter may want to consider a blind. It will have to be a good one, too! A fence crossing is another good ambush position since pronghorns don't like to cross fences. If they do, they will generally use the same route.

In the old days they used to "toll up" antelope by waving a white flag. I'm told that the method can still work in lightly hunted areas, but it sounds too risky to attempt on a trophy-size buck. More interesting is the use of life-size pronghorn decoys. I haven't tried it, as I enjoy stalking them too much, but some very successful bowhunters swear by the method.

An important point to keep in mind is the pronghorn's territorial instinct. One time my friend, Tim, and I spotted a nice buck in a

Pronghorn country is often dead flat, with no chance of a natural rest. The Harris Engineering bipod can be a real aid, perhaps making the difference between a buck and no buck.

This New Mexico buck is very typical. About 14 inches in length with reasonable mass, he's the kind of buck a hunter can expect in good country.

sheltered little canyon. It was only an hour before dark, so we tried a risky frontal approach. It didn't work, and dark caught us about four unsuccessful stalks and two miles or so away.

The buck and his does had been bedded when we first saw them, so the next morning just at dawn we looked into that same canyon from a distant ridge. Yep, they had circled back there during the night. This time we did things right, circling all the way around and coming up over a little sagebrush hill behind them. Tim got a good buck with a nice, close shot.

That incident is fairly common. If you lose a buck that's worth going after, the next day go back to where you first saw him and retrace your route. Unless hunting pressure has been fairly heavy, odds are you'll see him again.

Without question, pronghorn hunting involves some of the longest and most difficult shooting in North America—the distance because of the quarry's eyesight and the open country, and the difficulty because of the lack of reference points for judging distance, the usual lack of anything to get a good rest on, the small size of the target, and the constant wind on the plains.

On the open plains it is usual to overestimate distances. Most shots at pronghorns are nowhere near as far as the shooters think they are. Before Dad and I learned how to hunt pronghorns, we used to take long-range pokes at them with some frequency, and even connected on a few. We also used to try to hit them when they were running flat out, and connected a few times there as well. I know now that what I honestly thought was 500 yards when I was a kid was more like 300, or even 250. I will also admit that, as a kid, I made some beautiful running shots on pronghorn—but the antelope that fell wasn't always the one I was shooting at. I've since figured that it's usually possible to get closer, and it's usually possible to wait for a standing shot, but in any case, forget about trying to pull a running buck out of a herd.

Considering the small size of a pronghorn, 250 or even 200 yards is actually quite a long shot, and from what I've seen I wouldn't make bets on the ability of most hunters to connect on such a shot. Most, in my experience, would overestimate and shoot high. In 1982 I made the best shot I've ever made on a pronghorn. I was on a team for the Lander (Wyoming) One Shot Antelope Hunt, an annual event whereby a team of three shooters attempt to take their pronghorns with one shot each. The Shoshone medicine man blesses the single cartridge, and the hunters go forth. There are no prizes for winning, but irrespective of individual performances the losing teams must dance with the Shoshone squaws, while only the winning team dances with the warriors at the victory celebration.

I had rarely been so nervous. I had made up my mind that I'd shoot the first buck that stood still within 100 yards, but ties between teams are broken by time; as the minutes ticked by I mentally began extending that 100-yard range. I finally crawled to within about 225 yards of a nice little buck and managed to uphold our team's honor. Quite a routine shot, actually, but it sure looked to be a long ways off to me!

Pronghorn shots do average longer than for most game, but I'd be surprised if the average distance at which pronghorns are *shot* (not shot at) actually exceeds 200 yards. That 225-yard shot I just mentioned was one of my longer shots in recent years, with 150 yards being more like it.

Since the potential for a long shot does exist, flat-shooting rifles are essential. However, accuracy is perhaps more important than trajectory. A good, clear scope is also essential. Pronghorns are tough for their size, so the cartridge should be adequate, and the bullet designed for relatively quick expansion. The .243 and 6mm Remington are good minimums, with the .25-06 and .270 being nearly ideal. Magnums aren't needed at all, although in accurate rifles the .257 Weatherby and .264 Winchester Magnum take a lot of guesswork out of the longer shots.

Obviously, any rifle suited for open country deer hunting will do just fine for pronghorns, but the need for accuracy and for the rifle to be sighted in properly can't be stressed enough. The vital zone of a pronghorn is small, a badly hit buck can go a long way, and the better bucks simply won't give you more than one standing shot.

Pronghorn country appears flat and featureless, but the country almost always rolls slightly and has hidden folds, rises and depressions. By using the terrain, it is usually possible to stalk fairly close to pronghorns if you size them up before you spook them!

All this was brought home to me most painfully on that recent New Mexico hunt. We did everything perfectly, except for the most basic step of all—making absolutely certain the rifle was "on." It only took a day and a half for Robbie and me to find as nice a buck as I've ever seen, about 16 inches of nicely-shaped horns, outstanding prongs, and good mass. Once spotted, it took us about two hours of crawling on hands and knees and often bellies to close the distance to about 200 yards. And after all that, it probably took me less than 10 seconds to miss a certain shot and watch that great buck trot into a patch of mesquite and seemingly vanish into thin air.

It was good spotting, great stalking, and for all I know perfectly acceptable shooting (though I couldn't swear to the last part). But the 7x57 rifle I was testing had a bedding problem that my range testing hadn't revealed. It seemed that it would group just fine from the bench, but fore-end pressure from shooting with a tight sling, as I usually do, would throw the bullet about eight inches right at 100 yards, or 16 inches right at 200 yards, the distance the buck was standing. Of course I didn't know all that at the time. All I knew was that I'd blown a chance at the best buck I'd seen in 20 years of hunting them, and had also let down a good friend who was mighty anxious to see a photo of that buck in print.

My fault or the gun's? Mine, of course. As oddball as that problem is, I still should have picked it up by firing under field conditions, with a tight sling. But this time I'd done what I suspect most of us do: I'd shot the gun only from the bench, and it cost me.

But that's OK, because I love to hunt pronghorns, and knowing that buck is still out there gives me an excuse to go back. Not that an excuse is really needed. There's something about the lonely splendor of the wide open plains, a special feeling of freedom, perhaps that keeps drawing me back. The pronghorn may not be our most difficult game animal to hunt, but he certainly is one of our most attractive and hunting him on his own terms is without question one of this continent's most pleasant experiences.

Chapter 5
Mountain Game

The wild sheep of the world, including our North American represent-atives, are certainly beautiful creatures. The massive horns of the Rocky Mountain and desert sheep, thick as a man's thigh, are hard to beat for sheer awesomeness, as well as beauty. Of course, the wide curl of a good Dall or Stone comes close, and these two sheep add a lovely pelage into the bargain. All of these sheep live in high, wild country that is without question some of the most rugged and difficult hunting terrain on the continent, and also some of the most beautiful. A sheep hunt may not present the same physical danger as a hunt for brown or grizzly bear—but danger is certainly present. In this case the dangers are from the elements and the sheep's domain, and they're very real. I suspect more hunters are seriously injured on sheep hunts than any other hunting in North America.

The wild sheep has become a cult object, with several associations dedicated solely to sheep and the hunting of sheep. This cult business isn't unusual. Hunters of whitetail deer and wild turkey also have special organizations and special meetings. But the wild sheep was probably America's first game animal to become a cult object, at least in modern times. I think much of this is due to the writings of the great Jack O'Connor. "Mr. Sheep Hunter," as he has been called, was per-haps the most talented outdoor writer of this century, and with a career spanning more than a half-century, certainly one of the most prolific. He was a sheep hunter. Much of his writings were about sheep and sheep hunting, and American hunters listened to him.

Mountain hunting is usually a game of careful glassing. Once something interesting is spotted, it can take as much as a day to get close enough for a better look—so you want to do as much work as you can with the spotting scope and binoculars before making a move.

O'Connor died in 1977, and since then no outdoor writer has taken up the torch for sheep, nor is anyone likely to. There are, of course, a fairly large number of very dedicated sheep hunters; they have a large annual conference, and they raise huge sums of money to aid in sheep management. Sheep hunting is far from dead, but it's a lot more specialized than ever, a lot more expensive, and since 1977, I think it's a lot lower on the average hunter's priority list.

A trophy ram may be gifted with more craftiness than a big moose or caribou, but he is certainly not a more difficult prize on his own merits than a big elk, whitetail, or mule deer. He may live in tougher country but even that is uncertain. Some sheep country is actually fairly easy. Are sheep the most beautiful game? Beauty is in the eye of the beholder, and as lovely as a trophy ram is, I can't say sheep are more beautiful than a big muley, or more impressive than a big elk or caribou. If they are to you, then maybe you're a card-carrying sheep hunter, whether you know it or not.

Sheep are no more expensive to hunt than grizzly or brown bear, but taken collectively, the four wild sheep of North America are our most

Alaskan Master Guide Joe Hendricks "siwashes" on a sheep mountain. You can get fogged in with rams in sight, have rams bedded at nightfall, or be just too far from camp to get back. It's always wise to carry a little food and a tarp or Space Blanket. (Photo by Bob Tatsch)

expensive game animals. Two of them, the bighorn and desert sheep, may be hunted inexpensively *if* you can draw the permits, or at great expense if you cannot. Unless a hunter lives in Canada or Alaska, there is no choice on Dall and Stone sheep; a guided hunt is a must, and costs seem to escalate annually.

The term "Grand Slam," coined years ago, refers to the taking of one specimen each of the four recognized North American sheep species—Dall, Stone, Rocky Mountain bighorn, and desert bighorn. Never an easy task, the Grand Slam is exceedingly difficult today and made more difficult by the laws of supply and demand, driving prices up beyond all reason. Mexico is charging $12,000 for its government-sponsored legal desert sheep hunts, and why not? Desert sheep hunts donated to conservation organizations have brought well over $60,000 at auction. In response, most of the Alberta outfitters, offering the best bighorn hunting today, are now charging more than $10,000, and Stone sheep also approach that figure. Dall sheep, the most numerous, are about half that on the average.

Is sheep hunting a rich man's game? Yes, to pursue steadily and

Sheep camps are rarely lavish; a tent on a boulder-strewn mountain is typical. Some kind of a gasoline stove is usually an essential—there's rarely any firewood in the northern sheep mountains.

consistently. I know a lot of average hunters who hunt sheep, but they do so because they love the game, so they save and sacrifice. The Grand Slam is a worthy goal, but its pursuit has done as much to ruin sheep hunting as it has to further it. Even the great Jack O'Connor, in his later years, wished the term had never been coined and especially, that he hadn't done so much to further the concept!

North America contains the four sheep, plus the Rocky Mountain goat. Wild sheep crossed from Asia when Siberia was joined to Alaska. The wild sheep of the world extend in a broad arc from the Mediterranean across Asia Minor and Asia down through the western U.S. into Mexico. Western Europe had no native wild sheep, nor did the eastern U.S. nor any part of the southern hemisphere. Taxonomically speaking, only two species of wild sheep exist in North America; *Ovis canadensis* (the bighorns) and *Ovis dalli* (the thin-horned sheep). The bighorns arrived in North America first, spreading out throughout the southern mountains and into the badlands of the Dakotas. There are several subspecies of bighorns. Some of them are lumped by hunters in the "Rocky Mountain bighorn" category, while others, smaller subspecies adapted to arid climes, are lumped together as "desert bighorns." There are now considered to be only two subspecies of the thin-horned sheep—*O. d. dalli*, the Dall sheep; and *O. d. stonei*, the Stone sheep. These sheep, ariving on this continent rather late, are actually very similar to the sheep of Siberia. The Rocky Mountain goat, *Oreamnos americanus*, is a totally separate species, unrelated to any other North American or Asian species, but somewhat related to the chamois of Europe.

Dall Sheep

At one time the pure white Dall sheep of the far north was the most difficult sheep to obtain, requiring steamer transportation up the Inland Passage, by rail into the Alaskan interior, packtrip to the foothills, and then a long, arduous hunt in the mountains. It seems the modern world has gone topsy-turvy, for today the Dall sheep is North America's most numerous wild sheep and, thanks to the airplane, our most accessible.

Dall sheep, *O. d. dalli*, are present in most of Alaska's mountain ranges, from the Alaskan Range north to the Brooks. They extend across the Yukon, occurring both in the north-central ranges and the southwest regions surrounding Kluane Park. In this latter area they dip down into British Columbia; there's a small herd located in the extreme northwest corner of B.C. To the east, Dall sheep are widely distributed in Northwest Territories' MacKenzie Mountains. There are estimated to be about 50,000 to 75,000 Dall sheep in total. The latter figure is probably more correct and may well be conservative. As outfitters get deeper into the MacKenzies every year in search of trophy rams, they're finding a lot more sheep than were thought to exist there.

The Dall sheep is hunted across its entire range, including the little herd in B.C., so the opportunities are virtually unlimited. Prices have gone up in response to supply and demand, but a Dall sheep hunt is, to my way of thinking, well worth the cost. A typical 10-day hunt today costs around $5,000, but good sheep hunts can still be found for less than that—and others can be found that are much more.

There are big differences in the sheep mountains across this wide range, and that dictates differences in the hunts. The MacKenzies and most of the Yukon's mountains are fairly gentle, and most hunts are conducted on horseback. The hardy hunter can surely book a backpack hunt in these regions, but horses are in almost universal use. Step

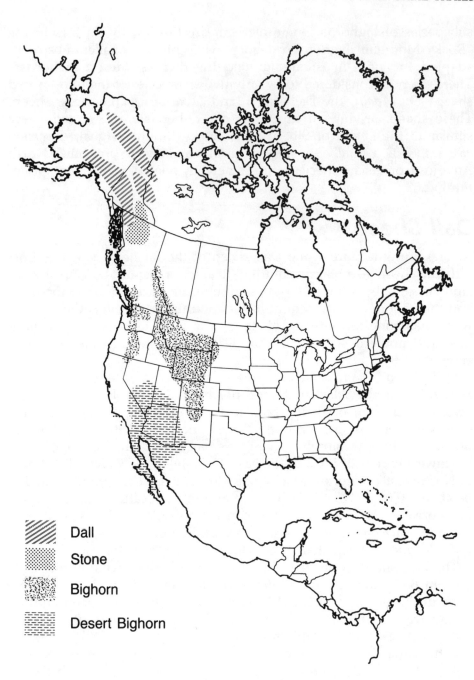

Dall

Stone

Bighorn

Desert Bighorn

NORTH AMERICAN WILD SHEEP RANGE

across the line into Alaska, and it's exactly the opposite! I know of a couple of outfitters who use horses, but 99 percent of Alaska's sheep hunting is done on foot.

Thanks to the Supercub, it isn't a nightmare ordeal these days. The outfitter flies in a guide and a spartan spike camp, landing on a glacier or a convenient flat-topped mountain right in the middle of sheep country. The client is flown in, and the next day he can start hunting sheep. The advantages are obvious; you're landed right in the middle of sheep country and can go right to work.

The disadvantages are less obvious. You're tied to your spike camp, since ultimately it's the pickup point at the end of your hunt. And there are reasons why they don't use horses. Alaska's southern and central sheep mountains, the Wrangells, Chugach and Talkeetna ranges, are steep and rough, covered with loose rocks and scarred by impassable glaciers. The Brooks Range is much more gentle. But even there, there is a limit to how much ground a man can cover on foot. If your spike camp is in a good spot, no problem. But if it isn't, eventually you may have to move.

Few things have revolutionized hunting in the North Country more than the Supercub and its ability to land virtually anywhere. It hasn't necessarily made *hunting* easier, but it's certainly made remote country like these sheep mountains more accessible.

Loose shale slides are typical of much sheep country, only glaciers are potentially more hazardous. With each step you feel the whole mass shift under your feet.

Dall rams on a rockslide—a typical sight in Alaska's rugged southern ranges. The last two rams are definitely legal, and the center one might be pretty good, but unless a ram is really huge you must look at him from several angles to avoid disappointment. (Photo by William D. Phifer)

Horseback hunts are more leisurely. Usually more time-consuming, but horses can cover a lot of ground and lot of country can be looked at. I've hunted sheep both ways, and I'm not sure I have a preference right now since I can still get around the mountains on foot! But give me a couple of years, and I think I'd go for the horses every time.

I hunted the Wrangells in August of 1984 with outfitter Lee Holen, my first time in that mountain range. While it turned out to be a fairly short hunt, it was tough. Those were the roughest mountains I've been in—steep, and every hillside a nightmare of loose rock. I got a nice ram, no record, but a pretty head. We looked around, and I'm fairly certain he was the best ram in that drainage. And on foot, we were pretty much limited to that drainage. At about the same time, only a few miles away, a fellow I know named Sherwin Scott was sheep hunting with a different outfitter. His spike camp must have been located in a bit better spot. On the second day he killed a monster ram, 48 inches with heavy bases, the second largest Dall ram ever taken!

Where can you get the big ones? Literally anywhere. The Brooks Range (and other far north sheep habitat) isn't known for big sheep,

This Alaskan Dall ram shows the classic outswept curl. He looks pretty good, but from this angle it's impossible to be sure; you can't tell how *deep* the curl is. He's probably about 36 inches, a nice ram but no monster. (Photo by Wiliam D. Phifer)

but the occasional 40-inch-plus ram does come out. As hunters get deep into the MacKenzies, bigger and bigger rams are being found. The Wrangells and Chugach mountains and adjacent southwest Yukon have always been considered best for trophy sheep, and these areas are still good. In truth, no Dall sheep country can be ruled out for trophies. And what is a trophy? For the experienced sheep hunter willing to settle for nothing less, a 40-inch ram is a sensible goal. The gent I just mentioned, Sherwin Scott, has gone sheepless on several hunts looking for just that—a 40-inch ram. He finally found one, but he paid his dues.

The first-time sheep hunter might find a 40-incher, but he has no business looking for one unless he is absolutely prepared to go home empty-handed. Most of us, on our first few sheep hunts, are not prepared for that. Depending on how tight they curl, a Dall sheep may be a full curl at 33, 34, or 35 inches. Such a ram may also have some weight to the horns, and could be nine or 10 years old. Not great, true,

Taken in the Wrangells by Sherwin Scott in August of 1984, this is the world record Dall sheep according to the S.C.I. system and the second largest according to Boone and Crockett. It's over 48 inches on the longest horn and carries the mass throughout—a magnificient trophy! (Photo by Sherwin Scott)

but a trophy ram that nobody need be ashamed of. Nobody ever admits to shooting a ram of less than 36 inches, so hunters' expectations become inflated. A 36-inch ram is actually damn good, especially when you consider that a 38-inch Dall sheep has a real fair chance to make the record book. For a trophy to take home, I don't think much of three-quarter- or even seven-eighth-curl Dall rams, but there's really nothing wrong with a full-curl of any dimension, and a ram like that is a reasonable goal for today's beginning sheep hunter.

Stone Sheep

O. d. stonei is a darker-colored subspecies of the pure white Dall. They're named for naturalist A. J. Stone, and are properly Stone or Stone's sheep, not stone sheep! The Stone sheep's primary range is northern B.C.'s mountain ranges from the Peace River north. The Cassiars, Rockies, Skeenas and Ominecas are all Stone sheep range, with the Cassiars the most famed. These sheep range across the line into the

Yukon, where they start to become lighter as they get closer to Dall
sheep habitat.

In some parts of the Yukon, it is possible to find a dark sheep, a pure
white sheep, and virtually anything in between in the same herd. A
classic coloration for these intergrade sheep is gray or white, with a
"saddle patch" of dark hairs. These are the so-called Fannin sheep,
once considered a separate subspecies but now recognized as intergra-
dations between Dall and Stone. Any thinhorn ram with dark hairs is
considered a Stone sheep by the record-keeping organizations.

Including both British Columbia's and Yukon's population, there are
only 14,000 to 20,000 Stone sheep in the world, and they occupy the
most limited range of North America's four wild sheep—from the
Peace River to the northern limits of the Cassiar, Pelly and Selwyn
ranges at the most. Three-fourths of these sheep are in B.C. The Yukon's Stone sheep are generally widely scattered, and while the occasional good ram is taken, hunting is much less reliable there than in
British Columbia.

Stone sheep are gorgeous creatures, typically with gray or salt-and-
pepper on face and neck shading into charcoal gray on the body. This is
a fine ram, just over 40 inches. Top Stone sheep are hard to come by,
but due to a tightly controlled quota system in northern B.C. they seem to
be coming back. (Photo by Bob Tatsch)

This Stone sheep is nearly black, a fairly uncommon coloration. Since Stone sheep and Dall sheep are actually the same species, virtually any color combination between the pure white Dall and a very dark Stone like this is possible. Generally the darkest Stone sheep are in the southern part of their range, with percentage of lighter hairs increasing closer to pure Dall sheep range. (Photo by Leonard Lee Rue III)

About 10 years ago, British Columbia instituted a strict quota system for Stone sheep outfitters. The harvest was reduced substantially and the laws of supply and demand made Stone sheep hunts skyrocket in price. But the quota system works, and, after a decade, some huge Stone sheep are now being taken with much greater frequency. There is a wide variance in costs for Stone sheep hunts today. Some outfitters charge about $6,500 to $7,000 for sheep and goat; others are up to nearly $10,000. The Yukon can be a bargain by comparison. Most Yukon hunts are all-species mixed bag, and a very few outfitters do well on Fannin sheep. But the odds aren't as good as in B.C., and certainly not as good for a really big ram.

Virtually all Stone sheep hunts in both areas are horseback hunts, and they're generally very pleasant. Some of the mountains are rough, others are more gentle, but except for a final stalk the horses can do most of the work most of the time.

Trophy expectations should be about the same for Stone sheep as for Dall sheep. Theoretically Stone sheep average a bit larger, but it's a very, very small amount. Record book minimums are the same for both subspecies, and if anything a record-class Stone ram is harder to find today. To my way of thinking the Stone sheep is the most beautiful wild sheep. The pure white Dall is beautiful, and the drab-colored bighorn impressive. But the iron-gray of the classic Stone ram, with golden-brown horns, is simply gorgeous. The Stone was my first ram, taken on the Kechika drainage in the Cassiars, so perhaps I have a soft spot for them. They're a beautiful animal, almost pretty enough to turn a guy into a sheep hunter.

Rocky Mountain Bighorn

Many sheep hunters still recall the days when the bighorn was easily the most accessible wild sheep, and the first ram sought by a sheep hunter on his way to the Grand Slam. No longer. Today it's nearly a toss-up as to which sheep is harder to come by, the desert sheep or the bighorn.

In the early nineteenth century, bighorns were abundant from the foothills of the Rockies west to the Sierras. Estimates have put the peak population at over a million. The bighorns were hunted unmercifully for meat, it's true, but another factor played even more heavily on the bighorn's decline. Wild sheep are extremely susceptible to domestic sheep diseases, and even in recent years have been reduced drastically by lungworm-produced pneumonia.

Today's bighorn populations have been pushed to the most remote and rugged mountain ranges. Occasional die-offs still occur, despite the utmost efforts of game managers. On the whole, bighorn populations are stable today in most areas, and increasing slowly in some.

About 25,000 bighorns, excluding the desert subspecies, exist today. While most of these are Rocky Mountain bighorns, two present-day subspecies actually comprise this group. The Rocky Mountain bighorn, *Ovis canadensis canadensis*, is found throughout the main Rocky Mountain chain from Colorado to Alberta, and in adjacent mountains. A slightly smaller subspecies, *O. c. californiana*, inhabits the northern Sierras from the northernmost tip of California up through southern British Columbia. A third subspecies, the badlands bighorn (*O. c. auduboni*), became extinct in 1916.

Today the Rocky Moutain bighorn may well be our most difficult wild sheep. Bill Moberly guided John Batten to this fine Alberta bighorn on Copton Creek in 1937. (Photo by John H. Batten)

Game managers, assisted by private groups such as the Foundation for North American Wild Sheep, are making great strides in sheep restoration. Numerous new introductions are made annually, and research is finding ways to inoculate wild sheep against the diseases that have so ravaged them in this century. Every year sees new areas open for sheep hunting, although the hunting remains very limited. It is unlikely that a bighorn will ever become easy to obtain, but the crisis point seems past. It's also unlikely that they'll become more difficult to hunt.

Rocky Mountain sheep have been reintroduced in North and South Dakota to replace the extinct badlands bighorn, and both states offer permits for residents only. New Mexico has several modest herds of bighorns which occasionally offer permits to both residents and non-residents. Colorado has a good herd that residents have hunted for many years, but 1984 was the first year that nonresidents were also offered permits. Both Utah and Nevada have small Rocky Mountain sheep populations; the latter state offered its first permit for this animal in 1984. Both Oregon and Washington have small sheep populations, but they've increased dramatically in both states in the last decade. Hunting is for residents only.

Idaho, Montana, and Wyoming are the traditional bighorn hunting grounds in the U.S. Idaho's herd is fairly small but stable, offering a few permits annually to residents and nonresidents. Montana has vigorously restocked many ranges with sheep, and they're starting to see the population increase by leaps and bounds. New areas are opened every year, and some of the finest bighorns ever taken have come from Montana in just the past few seasons. Wyoming still has the largest U.S. population. The sheep are stable there or increasing gradually, and quite a few permits are available.

Alberta has, at least in modern times, been the Mecca for bighorn hunters. The western part of this province, comprising the spine of the Rockies, holds the largest population of bighorns, and is the traditional home of the biggest rams. A severe die-off hurt Alberta's bighorns badly several years ago, but they seem to have come back; some of the best rams seen in decades were taken in 1984. Nonresidents are required to be guided, and the permits are allocated to Alberta's sheep outfitters. Each receives from two to four permits annually. Southern B.C. has Rocky Mountain bighorns in the east and California bighorns in the west. The populations are small, with a permit quota system similar to Alberta's.

That's bighorn country today. For the hunter who can afford it, Alberta is probably the best bet but plan ahead; the best outfitters are booked some three years in advance. Beyond that, anyplace where a tag can be drawn is a good place to hunt. Wyoming and Montana tend to offer the best chances for success, with the latter offering the biggest rams. Montana also has a couple of unlimited permits areas, the only places left where anyone can simply buy a license and go sheep hunting. But beware, these areas aren't unlimited because they have lots of sheep, but because they're rough, rugged, and the relatively few sheep found there are virtually inaccessible to all but the toughest mountain hunter.

Today the best chance to obtain a bighorn, except Alberta, is to apply every year in every state that offers permits. When the permit is drawn, plan to spend lots of time and to be in the best physical shape of your life. Personally, since those permits are so hard to come by, I would do plenty of research and hire the best guide I could find. Costs are still much less than an Alberta hunt, and well worth spending to fill what might be a once-in-a-lifetime permit.

Getting a bighorn permit is only half the battle. Our present-day bighorn habitat is high, steep and rough. Pressure has pushed the big rams out of the open basins and meadows and into the black timber in many areas. They're harder to catch in the open, and impossible to glass in the timber. It's a tough game. Permits are even more difficult to obtain for desert sheep, but with a permit in hand the odds are on the hunter's side in the desert sheep's more open habitat. Not so the bighorn. Very few "easy" rams are taken today.

A really huge bighorn may have horns of 40 to 45 inches on the curl, but length of horn isn't necessarily the most important thing on bighorns. Instead, it's the massive bases and weight carried clear out to the tips that makes a trophy bighorn. Dall and Stone sheep have horn tips that tend to flare outward, while bighorns typically curl close to the head. In many cases the horn tips grow until they obscure the ram's vision. When this happens he "brooms" them—rubs them off against rocks, trees and such. Rather than detracting, this brooming is highly prized to the trophy sheep hunter as the mark of a mature, trophy ram.

In most cases a three-quarter-curl ram is legal game, but bighorn hunting is made even more difficult by the fact that a legal ram is a long ways short of a representative specimen. To look like a bighorn, a ram must have bases with at least 14 inches circumference; the best

It took Jack Atcheson Sr. 17 days to take this Montana bighorn—but a ram like this is worth whatever it takes! Forty inches on the curl with 16½-inch bases, this ram was taken during the 1984 season. (Photo by Jack Atcheson Sr.)

bighorns often have 16-inch bases. Length isn't important. With good mass, a 32-inch ram might be quite impressive, and anything over 36 inches is very, *very* good. But it takes time to grow the massive horns. A trophy bighorn is usually eight years old at a minimum, and the best rams are usually 10 to 12 which is about as long as a wild sheep normally lives! I don't fault any hunter who fills his tag with a barely-legal ram, for any bighorn is a hard-won prize today. However, it's a sad-but-true fact that a bighorn must be very mature and actually quite a good specimen to be truly representative of his tribe—and that makes him even harder to come by.

Desert Sheep

Most things said about the bighorn apply to his close cousin, the desert sheep. There are four subspecies of *Ovis canadensis* collectively called "desert sheep," and all represent an adaptation of the Rocky Mountain sheep which live in the arid Southwest. They're much smaller in body

The desert sheep is very small in the body, about half the size of a big Rocky Mountain bighorn. However, desert sheep horns average only 15 to 20 percent smaller—if that. Horns like these look completely outsized on so small a sheep. (Photo by Dr. Loren Lutz)

size—an Alberta ram might weight 300 pounds; a Baja ram half that or less. The horns, surprisingly, are only slightly smaller. A trophy desert ram's horns appear out of all proportion to his body size, making him an extremely impressive trophy.

The desert sheep is far and away the most limited of our wild sheep. It occupies a broad range, from the bottom of Mexico's Baja Peninsula up through central Nevada and Utah, but nowhere is it abundant, and throughout this huge area, the desert sheep actually occupies only a few mountain ranges.

Although now on the increase in many areas less than 20,000 desert sheep exist. Permits are available in six areas, but the total number is less than 250. Nevada has overtaken Arizona as the top desert sheep state, with over 100 permits issued in recent years. Arizona is second with around 70. Utah and New Mexico offer but a handful. In all these areas both resident and nonresidents may apply, but of course the permits are very difficult to draw. The government of Mexico conducts a sheep hunting program in both Baja and Sonora. Baja has the largest population of desert sheep on the continent by far, and quite a few permits are issued. Historically Sonora was a sheep hunter's paradise, but the population is much reduced today and only a few permits are issued. The Mexican program consists of a fully outfitted hunt, usually for 10 days, complete with permit. It's a total package deal, and the current price is $12,000. That's a lot of money, but it's the only option not requiring the luck of the draw.

Chihuahua has a very few sheep, and Texas has been working for years to reintroduce sheep to their former range in the extreme southwest. First predators and then disease thwarted attempts, but now progress is being made. I expect to see desert sheep hunting in Texas within a couple of decades. California has the largest desert sheep herd in the States, and also the only herd that is currently declining. Desert sheep have been protected in California for a century, and by an age-old act of legislature, are a non-game species—meaning that normal game department funding, such as license fees, can't be used in their management. In effect, there is virtually no management of California's sheep other than privately funded projects, and the legislature hasn't reclassified them as game animals—not to hunt them, but to manage them. Perhaps it will happen, or perhaps California will run out of sheep first.

The various subspecies of desert sheep are virtually indistinguishable to the hunter, and the man who has a permit could probably care less which desert sheep it's for! But for the sake of completeness, the four desert subspecies of *Ovis canadensis* are: from Nevada and Utah down through most of California and southwestern Arizona, *O. c. nelsoni*,

Bruno Scherrer took this fine desert bighorn in the rugged desert mountains of Mexico's northern Baja Peninsula. Taken during the February 1982 season, it's one of two or three largest desert sheep ever taken by sport hunters. (Photo by Bruno Scherrer)

from southern Arizona down through Sonora, *O. c. mexicana*, from southern California about two-thirds down the Baja Peninsula, *O. c. cremnobates*, and on the southern tip of the Baja, *O. c. weemsi*.

The Boone and Crockett minimum is much lower for desert sheep than for Rocky Mountain, 168 versus 180. This is based on length of both horns, basal circumference, and circumference at the quarters, minus any deductions for lack of symmetry. Time has proven that it's just about as difficult to find a desert sheep of 168 as a bighorn of 180; they are a bit smaller. However, it's interesting to note that at the top end only three points separate the world records; 205⅛ for desert sheep and 208⅛ for Rocky Mountain.

There is no good or bad place to hunt desert sheep; wherever a permit can be drawn is excellent. The best rams have been coming out of the northern Baja, but some real monsters have been taken in both Arizona and Nevada in recent years. Desert sheep live in much more open country than their Rocky Mountain cousins, and are subjected to much lighter hunting pressure. A hunt for them may not be easy—few sheep hunts are—but most desert sheep tags are filled. A resident who draws a permit may be able to scout his area thoroughly before the season and locate some rams, but unless that's the case a permit holder is well-advised to hire the best guide he can find, whether he can afford it or not! That permit is simply too rare an opportunity to leave to chance.

Rocky Mountain Goat

The Rocky Mountain goat isn't a sheep at all, nor is the hunting of it anywhere near as restrictive as it is for the sheep species. In fact, *Oreamnos americanus* is actually quite plentiful across much of its original range, and offers some excellent mountain hunting—as difficult as sheep hunting, often more so, and nowhere near as expensive.

The mountain goat is a slab-sided, stocky animal. Although there is great variation of body size among individuals, big billies can top 300

Mountain goats are often found in steep, rougher terrain than sheep. Trophy billies are usually solitary, making them easier to stalk—but they can be hard to get to, and hard to anchor in a spot where they can be recovered easily. (Photo by Jim Zumbo)

pounds. The coat is white wool with white guard hairs. During the summer, the goats molt, leaving white wool as evidence of their passing. Late in the season the winter coat grows in, making a winter goat one of the world's most attractive trophies. Both males and females grow short, sharp horns. The nannies' horns can actually be longer than a billy's, but the males have much more massive bases. The mass of a male's horns make him a more desirable trophy, usually, but the difficulty in determining sex at long range has dictated that both males and females are legal game wherever goats are hunted. The older billies do tend to have a yellowish cast to their coats, while nannies appear starkly white.

Historic goat range is from southeast Alaska throughout the Cassiar Mountains and down the coastal ranges to Washington, and along the spine of the Rockies from Alberta and B.C. down through Idaho and western Montana. A few reach as far south as northern Utah. Transplanted herds are doing well in several parts of Colorado, the Black Hills, Oregon, and northeastern Wyoming. In the Rocky Mountain states the animals are few in numbers and permits exceedingly difficult to draw. In the Lower 48, Washington offers the most goats, the most permits, and the best chances to draw.

British Columbia has literally thousands of goats, particularly in the northeast. While nonresidents must be guided, a goat hunt is easily arranged either as a short hunt or as part of a hunt for other species. Currently a guided goat hunt will cost about $2,500 and will last about seven days.

Alaska is overlooked as a goat-hunting hotspot, but the animals are actually quite common in the southeastern coastal mountains. The population is around 12,000 and this is confined to a fairly small area. Guided hunts are available, but nonresidents are not required to hire a guide. A word of caution though, the coastal mountains are treacherous, and goat country is almost always suicidally steep. Only an experienced mountain hunter should attempt such a hunt without a guide, and it shouldn't be attempted alone. Alaska's goat season runs quite late, offering a great opportunity for taking them in full winter pelage. Much hunting is done by cruising the bays and fjords in boats, glassing until goats are spotted, then beaching and climbing up after them. Although cold and miserable, the late season is best as the goats come down much lower and are more easily reached from sea level.

Alberta's goat hunting is for residents only, and while both Yukon and the MacKenzie District of Northwest Territories have seasons for goats, the animals are quite uncommon and shouldn't be expected on a normal hunt to either of these areas. But in Alaska, B.C., and anywhere south of Canada where one can draw a tag, a goat hunter can

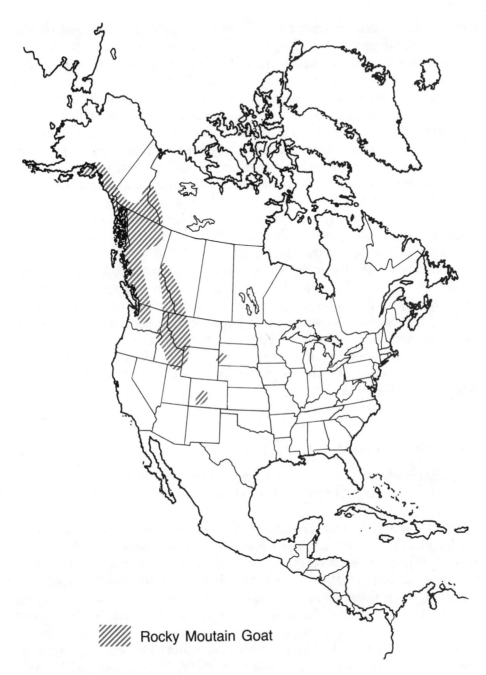

ROCKY MOUNTAIN GOAT RANGE

expect to see good numbers of animals, and have an excellent chance for a nice trophy.

Goats are extremely hard to judge, not only for sex but for quality. Fractions of inches separate good from mediocre, and mass, very hard to judge, is extremely important to a record book score. Only a few goats have ever reached 12 inches, and a billy with 11-inch horns is extremely uncommon. Most hunters reckon that an eight-inch billy is good, nine inches is superb, and few people would hesitate over a billy that approaches 10 inches. Nannies of 10 inches or more are not uncommon, but the lack of horn circumference usually places them out of the running for the books. Of 290 goats placing in the current B&C book, only three are nannies and seven others are listed as "sex unknown." Only two goats are listed with 12-inch horns—the world record billy, and a nanny that places 88th.

Goats are generally more solitary than sheep and definitely more sedentary, both factors making them much easier to approach. On the other hand, they're designed for ease of travel in the steepest, rockiest terrain, and they're generally more agile than sheep. They also tend to prefer rougher, rockier and often steeper country, which tends to balance out their "more huntable" nature. The abundance of goats makes the outcome of a goat hunt more sure than that of a typical sheep hunt, but it won't be easy.

The Mountain Rifle

The requirements for a sheep or goat rifle are simple; it must have enough punch to do the job, it must be accurate, and it must be light enough to carry.

Sheep are not the largest of game, nor are they particularly tough. In theory a .243 or 6mm is quite adequate, but variables come into play. For one thing, the opportunity factor. You need a cartridge that will do the job from any angle and from any distance that you feel capable of shooting. With those things in mind, I'd up the ante a bit and suggest the .25-06 as a sensible minimum. The .270 is, of course, the most famous sheep cartridge, and it's well-nigh perfect for the job. Its bigger brothers, the .280 and .30-06, aren't bad either. The belted magnums are rarely needed, but such numbers as the .257 Weatherby, .264 Winchester, the 7mm magnums, and the .300s are certainly adequate, even nice to have for the occasional long shots. Goats have a well-deserved reputation for being tough. They are, but any of the cartridges mentioned from the .270 on up are quite adequate when matched with a good bullet that will expand properly.

I take a break during a long pack in Alaska's Wrangells. On foot is a good way to hunt sheep if you're in shape for it, but you are limited in the amount of ground you can cover.

Accuracy is really more important. The mountain rifle doesn't have to be a tack-driver, any more than any hunting rifle does, but it should group in about 1½ inches at 100 yards, and it must be *consistent*. The scope should be ultra-reliable and fixed in good, solid, sturdy mounts. I don't have auxiliary iron sights on my mountain rifles, but they're not a bad idea. I've taken several bad falls in sheep country and been left wondering if the scope was ruined or not—and what I could do about it if it was! An extra rifle is a good thing to have in camp, but often inconvenient especially for fly-in hunts. If there is to be no extra rifle in camp, an extra scope with compatible rings *is* a good idea. A collimator is also a smart investment. It actually takes a tremendous rap to knock a good scope in good mounts out of line, but a quick check with a collimator will save lots of worry and unnecessary noise in rechecking a gun.

Gun weight is a big factor in backpack hunts, less for horseback. The new fiberglass stocks, although ugly to my eye, make good sense. Not only do they reduce weight, but they won't warp in damp weather.

Notes on Mountain Hunting

Sheep or goat hunting isn't always a lung-burning, heart-thumping ordeal—but it can be. The altitude can be hard to take, and no two people have the same tolerance for thin air. Being in shape not only makes a successful hunt more likely, but also a safe hunt. Plenty of heart attacks have occurred on a sheep mountain, that's true. But what isn't said often enough is that fatigue is one of the major causes of falls.

Most sheep and goat habitat offers unsteady footing at best—loose rocks and shale slides that must be crossed, streambeds lined with glass-smooth rocks, treacherous snow fields, you name it. When you get tired, your feet become unsteady, and in the mountains a false step can get you into big trouble. You're going to get tired, make no mistake about that. When you do it's time to call a halt, especially if the country is steep. Nobody from flat ground or a desk job can keep up with a sheep guide in *his* mountains, nor should anyone try. But pre-hunt conditioning will help.

Mountain hunting is primarily a game of glassing. Tracks are reassuring, but the mountain hunter looks for the animal itself before making a move. Good binoculars are as important as the rifle itself, and a spotting scope, though heavy, is essential. Glassing can take days, moving from ridge to ridge and scanning and rescanning, trying to see into every fold in every basin. Desert sheep, bighorns, and even Stone sheep can be difficult to spot; their camouflage is nearly perfect for their respective habitats. By comparison, Dall sheep and goats are pushovers to glass, as long as there isn't fresh snow. Then it gets tricky. There's usually old snow in Dall sheep country, and at first you'll eagerly glass each distant white patch. But then you'll realize that the sheep are even whiter than the snow; they literally glisten even from miles away.

Typically, a hunter glasses until a suitable trophy is spotted, then he glasses for a route for a possible stalk. The classic approach is to stay out of sight and get above the game; neither sheep nor goats usually expect or look for trouble from above. Wind is exceedingly important, noise less so since rolling rocks are fairly common in the mountains.

One of the real problems in stalking is that the ground is usually different when you get there than it looked from where you started. Chosen routes may prove impassable, and there are probably little folds and gullies that couldn't be seen. It's common to misplace the object of a stalk when you get to where the animal should be, and that's the time to stay calm, take it easy, and systematically eyeball the situation. It's at this point that many good stalks are blown, or an easy shot at a bedded ram becomes a tough running one.

In the "good old days" of Alberta's bighorn sheep hunting it took a long packtrip just to get into sheep country. In this 1937 photo, outfitter Friday Lonsdale takes a packtrain over Sheep Creek Summit on the Alberta-B.C. line. (Photo by John H. Batten)

And sometimes you make mistakes and things work out anyway. It was about noon, right in the middle of a snow flurry, when my Indian guide and I rode into a little basin. We were cold and wet, and we weren't being careful. The two salt-and-pepper Stone rams looked like stationary snowflakes up on the hillside, but they'd seen us long before we saw them. We eased off our horses, trailing the reins. My guide said simply, "Sheep can't count," and we faded into the low brush, found a cut leading up the hill, and came up to a point that should have been above the rams. It was, but we had "misplaced" them, and it took a few moments of careful shifting around to find them. They were still watching the horses far below. He was right, they couldn't count, and soon I was admiring my first wild sheep. But not my last. Our keepers of the crags may not have the savvy of a big buck, but they're lovely animals that live in some of our finest hunting country. Few of us are fortunate enough to hunt sheep often, but having hunted them, few of us can hunt them only once.

Chapter 6
Bison

The destruction of America's vast herds of bison is one of the most publicized, and most shameful, chapters in this country's natural history. In just a few decades, from 1860 when estimates put bison numbers at around 60 million, to 1900 when only about 541 bison remained, one of the world's most populous animals was virtually destroyed. The truth is, sadly, that the bison wasn't the only species so reduced. Pronghorns once dotted the plains in numbers that might have doubled those of the bison, and by 1900 their existence was also in grave doubt. Gone from the plains, too were elk, and from the foothills and badlands, the mountain sheep. The grizzly were pushed to the most remote mountains, and even the deer were virtually gone from much of their former habitat.

It was the era of Manifest Destiny, when Americans were determined to push their domain to the far corners of the continent and beyond. Nobody was concerned about the cost or what—or who—got in the way. The buffalo was the most vulnerable, and the worst affected, for several reasons. First, it was and is almost exclusively a plains animal. At the very end some remnants moved into the badlands and breaks, even into the foothills, but by then it was too late. It's also a large animal and, worse, a herd animal, not hard to locate, nor particularly elusive. While all game was valued, and killed, for meat, the bison was also assassinated on political grounds. His destruction was viewed as a necessary step in controlling the Plains Indians. The remnants of the

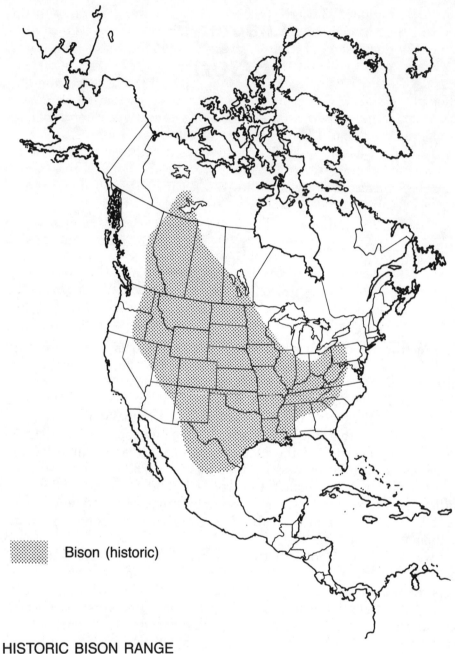

Bison (historic)

HISTORIC BISON RANGE

elk, sheep, grizzly and pronghorn populations were able to retreat far enough into the wilderness to avoid total destruction, but the more vulnerable bison were hunted and killed almost to the last survivors.

The road back has been slow for all these species, and total recovery will never happen. The grizzly is gone forever from the Great Plains, nor will the elk ever return to the wide; open country it once called home. My home state of Kansas, probably the most wide-open state in the Union, was the worst affected; once the heart of bison country, the animals were virtually gone by 1873. The elk went next, then the antelope and deer. Game managers, backed by hunter's dollars, were able to bring most species back after half a century of careful management. But the bison, like the plains grizzly, is gone forever.

However the bison today is not threatened with extinction. The numerous public and private herds scattered across the U.S. and Canada secure his future as a species. But the great herds will never return, and bison hunting today is at best a pale shadow of yesterday.

The last great buffalo hunt was more than a century ago, in the winter of 1882-83. It marked the end of an era that was incredibly short-lived, and equally incredibly destructive and far-reaching in its effects. The destruction of the bison began in earnest in 1865, at the close of the Civil War. A few short years were enough to eradicate the great herds of Kansas and Nebraska. When they were gone the hide hunters turned south, across the Arkansas River into Indian Territory. The southern herds lasted a few seasons, and then only the great northern herds of Montana and Wyoming remained. Though a few hunters stayed in the field through the mid-1880's, by the spring of 1883 it was all over. A few survivors remained in badlands and foothills—Theodore Roosevelt ran across a small herd on the Idaho-Montana border in 1889—and Canada still had a fair number. In spite of laws to protect them, the downhill slide continued until about 1900. The bison is too large, requires too much space, and simply cannot be easily, or cost-effectively, fenced. The great herds are gone forever, and all the modern hunter can expect from a bison hunt is a mere taste of the past.

In spite of all that, there are bison herds today, whether public or private, and they do reproduce. Since the acreage most of these herds roam is limited, there is a huntable surplus in many cases. In fact, many herds are raised strictly for meat, and in some cases hunters are allowed to harvest the animals, with the meat going to the market instead of into the hunter's freezer. There are also a very few public-drawing bison hunts. Arizona offers a few permits on this basis, as does Custer State Park in South Dakota. However, only a few herds currently being hunted can be considered truly free-ranging. These include a couple of transplanted herds in Alaska, the Farewell herd and Delta herd, and a herd in southeastern Utah. Permits aren't easy to draw. The Utah herd offers challenging hunting, and you'll need horses to reach the rough terrain the bison inhabit.

The American bison is an awesome beast. A big bull can weigh as much as a ton—bigger than the largest African Cape buffalo bull. Unfortunately, he's a plains animal and a herd animal, two factors that made him vulnerable to the hide hunters of yesterday. (Photo by Bob Robb)

The bulk of the hunting today is private herds, either on bison ranches or Indian reservations. Either can offer good hunting—or not-so-good hunting—depending on how careful you check around, and on what you're looking for. Bison are simply not as difficult to find and shoot as many other species are. Nothing can give bison hunting the same challenge offered by hunting big bucks. On the other hand, bison hunting doesn't have to be a fish-in-a-barrel situation. However, all too often, it is.

Not too long ago I went on a bison hunt, and wrote a story about it. Like most magazine writers, I get a fair amount of reader mail. Most of it is either complimentary or asks for specific information about a hunt or some piece of equipment I've been pictured using. But the bison story was something else. I got several letters that really castigated me for shooting, or even wanting to shoot, an animal as defenseless as a bison. Perhaps I didn't write that story very well, or perhaps the story of the bison's destruction is so ingrained in hunters today that the idea of hunting them is repugnant to many. Or perhaps it's the general impression that wild bison simply stand there and wait to be shot.

Bison reproduce quickly, and when they overpopulate they're hard to keep fenced and fenced they must be, except in the rare instances of free-ranging herds such as Yellowstone's or the herds mentioned earlier. Because of this a huntable surplus exists, and bison hunting is tightly controlled. It has no relationship whatsoever to the uncontrolled market hunting of a century ago. I wouldn't go so far as to say that a bison offers the same challenge of a trophy whitetail or a big bull elk; some animals are simply not as wary as others. In the same manner, a caribou is not as wary as a big muley but it's still a great game animal. Every animal must be judged on its own merits. If you prefer to confine your hunting only to those animals that offer the utmost challenge, then bison, muskox, caribou, and perhaps even moose should

A midwinter bison is a stunning trophy, offering a thickly-haired "buffalo robe" as well as the horns. Big bulls are hard to judge, as the horns are somewhat in relation to the body size and the long hair may obscure bases, tips, or both.

be crossed off your list. None of these animals can offer the challenge of a trophy deer. But if you enjoy sampling different kinds of hunting, and if you want to take a trip back in time, don't overlook the bison. When you stalk close to a big herd, close your eyes and you'll find it's easy to be transported back in time. The thunder of the hooves will come to you, and instead of the hundred or so animals you're looking at, you'll see bison stretching across the horizon.

But don't close your eyes too long. Bison are not necessarily dangerous, but they are powerful animals and the bulls are extremely unpredictable. Many a bison rancher of today, and bison hunter of yesterday, underestimated them and wound up in the hospital or worse.

I mentioned before that most hunted bison herds are fenced. This is true, but many of them are fenced on very large acreage, large enough that neither you nor they are aware the fence is present. It's important to check around before you arrange a bison hunt. The best situation is to find a large operation that has a breeding herd. There are several

The circumference of a trophy bison's horns often nearly equals the length. A trophy bull will usually be at least 10 years old; such an animal can be difficult to find today.

such bison ranches whose primary purpose is the raising of bison for meat. These herds often have surplus trophy bulls and finding one makes a good hunt. First you have to locate a good bull, then you have to work in and get a shot—rarely an easy task when you're trying to pull one specific animal out of a large herd. If you get the wind wrong or expose yourself within their limited eyesight, they won't stand around. You'll hear the thunder of those hooves, and you'll have to start the selection process all over again.

Some bison "hunting" is available on small acreages, where a few bison have been purchased strictly for hunting. That is unfortunate, both from the standpoint of hunting ethics and for the "hunter" who is robbed of a unique opportunity to relive a bit of the past.

Fortunately, some Indian reservations, bison ranches and private outfitters offer good bison hunts, often on horseback, so the hunter can recapture the feeling of a bygone era. And that's really what bison hunting is all about.

A good tip for having a memorable hunt is to look for a true trophy-class bull. There may not be a huge difference in horn size from cow to young bull to trophy bull, and certainly not much difference in relation of horn to body and head size, but there is a tremendous difference in body size. Leading bison authority Margaret Meagher, research biologist at Yellowstone Park, has written that cow bison average about 1,000 pounds, while bull bison average close to 2,000 pounds. A big bull, aside from having longer beard and topknot and more massive horns, is an incredibly impressive animal—as different to a trophy bull as a cow elk is to a huge six-by-six.

We often interchange "bison" for buffalo. Our bison are only distantly related to the buffalo of Africa (*Cyncerus*) and the buffalo of Asia (*Bubalus* and *Bos*). The nickname "buffalo" has stood for a century, but actually our bison occupies its own genus, *bison*, with only one species, *Bison bison*, and three subspecies are currently recognized. The typical, and most common subspecies is our plains bison, *Bison bison bison*. The wood bison (*Bison bison athabascae*), virtually indistinguishable but slightly larger, was originally found in more wooded or mountainous areas as far east as Pennsylvania. When the bison were nearly gone and efforts were being made to save the species, plains and wood bison were freely mixed, with the result that the MacKenzie Bison Sanctuary in Northwest Territories is thought to hold the last pure wood bison herd. The third bison subspecies, *Bison bison bonasus*, isn't found in North America at all, but is the European bison or wisent of northern Europe. Slightly different in appearance, the wisent was nearly destroyed during War II, but has made somewhat of a comeback in some forest and reserves. It is hunted on a limited basis in Poland.

The common belief seems to be that bison are tame animals. *Herd* animals they are, but not tame. Many an old-time buffalo hunter—and quite a few modern ranchers—have come to grief at the hands of truculent bull bison, occasionally unwounded ones. *Any* animal should be approached with caution, but especially one this big!

Bison hunting today will almost always be a "pay as you go" situation; the only exceptions are the few public-drawing permits. It can be—and usually is—expensive; a trophy bull is worth as much $3,000. However, the cost can often be offset by the value of the meat. Occasionally the cost is reduced substantially if the hunter will take only the skin and horns and some meat, leaving the rest for the outfitter or bison rancher to dispose of. The meat is superb but few hunters have the facilities to store 1,200 pounds of bison!

Wherever you plan to hunt, two things are important. Beware of the operator who tries to pass off a two- or three-year old animal as a mature bull—a trophy bison is usually at least 10 years old—and try to schedule the hunt in the winter. The long, luxurious hair of a midwinter bison is a thing to behold, but in warmer weather the hide becomes patchy and loses its value as a buffalo robe.

It's also important have some respect for the bison, especially the older bulls, and a bit of caution. They can be cantankerous, and even downright dangerous. I feel that their current reputation for being easy to kill comes from the fact that few big bulls are taken these days; it's a great deal easier to knock over a 1,000-pound bison than a 2,000-pound bison. That latter weight puts the bison at about the same size as a very, very large Cape buffalo. If a head shot is possible, then any deer cartridge will do. But if a head shot isn't possible, bison can take some real stopping. A charge is unlikely, but it can happen. It's much in vogue these days to shoot bison with blackpowder arms, and it certainly has a traditional appeal. I consider the .54 caliber as a sensible muzzleloader minimum, and the .45-70 right at the bare minimum for a cartridge gun.

I hunted bison one January on the Oglalla Sioux Reservation in South Dakota. It was something I'd wanted to do for some time, but I didn't expect it to be a really great experience. It wasn't a hunt, in the same terms a sheep, elk, or even caribou hunt, but it was well worth doing. For one thing, seeing the herds of bison at close range, and making a stalk on them, was fascinating. It was easy to feel transported back a century or more, and a mature midwinter bull is one of the most spectacular animals I've ever taken.

I was hunting with Bruno Scherrer, a good friend of mine from Los Angeles who is a trophy hunter's trophy hunter; he will shoot only the very best. We had come to the Oglalla Reservation with Colorado outfitter Alan Baier, one of few modern hunters who has hunted enough bison to be able to make reasonably accurate trophy estimates. After quite a bit of looking with a spotting scope, we located a nice herd with several large bulls. Bruno had the first shot, and I thought he and Alan were going to spend the whole day deciding which was the best bull. Although these weren't the first bison I'd ever seen, until we saw this herd I had figured that one bison was much the same as another.

Wrong! I suspect I had never seen a real record-class bull before. The horns didn't necessarily appear longer than those of lesser bison. Instead they appeared in proportion but the whole animal dwarfed the cows and youngsters. There were four big bulls in this herd, and each seemed at least half again the size of the brownish cows. The big bulls were black, with thick hair rippling in the breeze, a stunning sight as they stood atop a bare knoll.

Two of the bulls were quickly eliminated. They were big, but not of the quality Bruno was looking for. The other two presented a classic bison hunter's choice. One had horns that seemed to have great length,

When you stalk in close to a herd of bison, it's easy for a century or more to slip away and your imagination carry you back to when these great beasts covered the horizon.

rising above the thick topknot; the other appeared to have horns somewhat shorter, but apparently more massive. A good bull will have horns from about 15 to 20 inches in length, but those horns will have a circumstances of 13 to 17 inches. It's very possible to take a bison with horns as big around as they are long.

Bruno and Alan argued endlessly, it seemed, but finally length won out and they moved from our vantage point, maneuvering into shooting position. After the shot I joined them, and we walked up to the first trophy bison Bruno or I had seen up close. What an animal! The hair was nearly a foot long and the horns were incredibly massive.

I hadn't been at all sure that Bruno had made the right choice; I would have preferred the other bull with horns that appeared shorter but more massive. The next day we found him. He turned out to be a little shorter and a little thicker, and the two animals scored just about the same. They were magnificent but I'm not certain that I'd care to take another. I'm glad I did it once. . . .

Chapter 7
Caribou

Hunting the nomads of North America's far North is filled with more inconsistencies than with any other game animal. Caribou are said to be the easiest of all of our big game to find and shoot, but they can also be among the most difficult. Among trophy hunters, much ado is made over divisions between the four, five or six (depending on who you talk to) subspecies, yet in truth almost no one can look at a mounted head and state *for certain* which type the animal belongs to. One hunter with a fair amount of caribou hunting experience under his belt will swear that these animals are easy to kill while another hunter with equal experience will swear that caribou, pound for pound, are tougher to put down than moose or elk. As is the case with most campfire discussions there's a lot of truth in all of these statements.

Unlike almost all other North American big game animals, caribou are first and foremost migratory animals. Hunters speak of migratory mule deer, meaning primarily movement in elevation from summer pasture (high) to winter pasture (low), and of elk migrations. But when one speaks of caribou as migratory animals, one is speaking of migration on the grand scale of waterfowl migration.

Alaska's Porcupine Herd, for example, has a migration route that covers literally hundreds of miles—from the Northwest Territories across the Yukon and into Alaska. And what happens if you plan to hunt this herd in Alaska while it is still in the Yukon? About the same as happens when you try to hunt mallards before the flights come in.

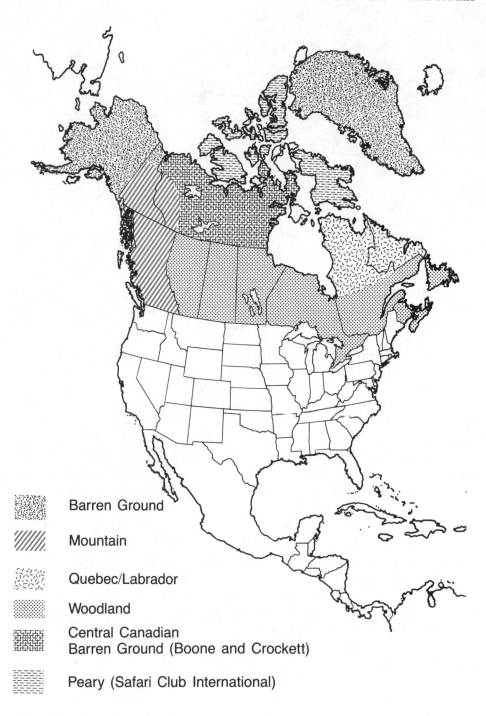

Barren Ground

Mountain

Quebec/Labrador

Woodland

Central Canadian
Barren Ground (Boone and Crockett)

Peary (Safari Club International)

CARIBOU RANGE

Yes, there are such things as resident caribou, just as there are resident ducks and geese. And, as with waterfowl species, some of the caribou groups tend to be more resident than others. Mountain and woodland caribou, for example, are usually hunted as resident rather than migrating herds. But the most common and most commonly hunted caribou, the barren ground and Quebec-Labrador groups, are hunted almost entirely in migratory situations.

Hunting migrating caribou is very much a feast or famine situation. The height of a caribou migration is one of the most spectacular sights in nature, and picking a very good bull is just a matter of being patient. But if you miss the migration, all you can hope for is to encounter stragglers ahead of or behind the main herds, or the few resident caribou that may or may not be present. Caribou country is very big country, and such a search can be a needle in a haystack.

Most caribou hunters, even successful ones, don't actually see a true migration, nor, in many cases, would it be recognizable if they did see it. Herd movement through an area can take weeks, so much of the good hunting will be for the stragglers coming after the main herd, and for the leaders trickling through ahead. Wildlife biologists have classified most of our caribou into "herds," with that term meaning a large group of caribou that occupy a particular region and follow a general migration route. But the herd, sometimes numbering over a quarter million, doesn't migrate all together. The movement consists of thousands of small groups—ten here, a dozen there, perhaps 50 over yonder— spread out over a very broad path of tundra, and all moving in the same general direction. The movement starts slowly and ends slowly. First a trickle of caribou, then an ever-increasing stream until the bulk of the herd is past, and finally a slow trickle of stragglers that can take many more days to pass.

The time of the migration is triggered primarily by weather and within certain parameters it can vary quite a bit from year to year. The route can vary as well, changing as feed conditions and human pressure dictate. The northern tribes who lived off the caribou were masters at guessing the migration patterns. They had to be. No country on earth is as big as the northern tundras, and at a time when no caribou are present, no country is as devoid of wildlife. If the early hunters missed the migration route, starvation faced the tribe.

Today's caribou hunter has long-range weather reports and airplane sightings of herds to aid in guessing the time and exact route of the migration. But the caribou have pipelines, hydroelectric dams, and increasing pressure from native hunters with modern arms and equipment but no modern bag limit. The hunter who lives in caribou country can be flexible and wait until the peak of the migration to hunt.

A true caribou migration is an incredible sight. They rarely move in a tight bunch, but instead in small groups spread out over a vast front—always moving, always feeding, always tacking into the wind. (Photo by William D. Phifer)

Most of us, though, live far from caribou country. When we plan a hunt we must plan for a specific date and hope for the best. If we do our homework well, either planning an unguided hunt, or searching out a good outfitter, we should be able to count on having a few caribou around. But to plan a hunt expecting to hit the height of the migration in a one-week period that was booked months in advance? That's expecting too much.

I've had pretty good luck with caribou, but I've made three specific hunts designed to catch migrating caribou, with vastly different results each time.

The first was an unguided hunt in Alaska in the early Seventies at the height of the pipeline era when caribou were in trouble in several parts of Alaska. I was going through the Army's mountain warfare school near Delta Junction, Alaska. In mid-September we heard that the Fortymile herd, which had a lateral migration between Alaska and the Yukon just south of the Yukon River, was passing the Tok Highway northwest of Chicken, Alaska.

According to the few locals we encountered, a few outriders had come through, but the bulk of the herd was just over the horizon. We tried to walk to them, and I was struck by just how big the barren lands really are. There were a few tracks, but we saw no caribou. We did get very badly turned around when a fog bank rolled in, and I reckon it was a miracle when we reached the highway where we'd left the truck. It convinced me that unguided hunting in the North Country should be undertaken only with plenty of research and the best of equipment.

My last experience with migratory caribou was an outfitted hunt in northern Quebec's Ungava region in 1983. Unlike the shoestring, borrowed-gear Alaskan hunt of a decade before, this was first-class all

The Otter is a great airplane. Those still in service are getting a bit creaky these days, but they're still the bird that keeps much of Canada's hunting industry going.

the way. We flew from Schefferville to a comfortable camp on Lac Dihourse, then worked up and down the lake in canoes. Our host, Jack Hume of Laurentian-Ungava Outfitters, knew how to run a good camp, and the guides were Montagnais Indians, known throughout eastern Canada for their hunting ability. We had also very carefully booked the last hunt of the season, the time which usually catches the great George River herd in some stage of migration.

The key word there is *usually*. A caribou migration is never certain, and sooner or later the law of averages catches up. Jack had been totally honest telling us that the migration was uncertain, and if it came early or late we'd have to hunt hard for stragglers. But the last hunt had been dynamite for years at all the camps along the George River migration route.

Nobody listened, and everybody expected a sure thing. That year it was a warm fall, and the real migration didn't occur until two weeks after all the camps were closed down for the winter. Tough hunting? You bet. I figure I walked 50 miles for the bull I got. But he was a nice bull, and worth the effort. All told we got six caribou out of a camp of nine hunters. Hardly a sure thing, but not bad as big game hunting in general goes.

In between the two previously-mentioned hunts, I did witness a true caribou migration. It was a spectacle unlike any other I've seen in nature, and the sight was worth another dozen tough hunts in the hope of seeing it again.

It was a pioneer hunt, in a manner of speaking. Canada's Northwest Territories were opening up their central caribou herds to nonresidents for the first time, and I was invited to see what the situation was like. We flew into the Courageous Lake region northeast of Great Slave Lake, along the migration route of the Bathurst herd, then about 140,000 strong. Camp was rough, a tarp draped over log poles flown into the treeless tundra. Food was rougher, fresh caribou grilled on a Coleman stove as long as the fuel lasted. The guides were competent hunters, but their primary mission was to secure winter meat for their community and lots of it. Ensuring that Randy Bello, my partner, and I took trophy bulls was a very low second priority. None of that really mattered, though, for the caribou were there.

And how they were there! We made camp by a small lake, the rolling barrens rising to the north behind us to a ridge of some height. Over that ridge, from dawn to dark, trooped endless legions of caribou. Not in a body, but in groups of a dozen or so up to perhaps a hundred. Every few minutes, without fail, a fresh group would skyline on the distant ridge, then descend toward us. With spotting scopes, we could see what they were, and if anything looked interesting we could map

A canoe looks like a great way to hunt, and it is, but once you're out there on a lake in an unstable canoe, perhaps with whitecaps and a storm coming, and you realize that you might last 10 minutes in the near-freezing water, the canoe loses some of its charm.

out a plan to get in their path. They never stopped, nor did they increase their pace. They just moved into the wind, feeding constantly as they went. Each morning found fresh groups close by camp, and others that had passed but were still in sight. Those were best forgotten; no man could catch a migrating caribou in that spongy bog—but we tried a couple of times. Randy and I took good bulls, even excellent bulls, but for serious trophy hunting it was almost a surfeit of caribou. We looked at so many that our judgement became clouded, and it's hard to say if the bulls we took were among the best we saw. It was a sight that will never be forgotten.

Caribou can be relatively easy to come by, as they were on that hunt. It's unusual, and takes unusual luck, to hit the migration as precisely as we did, but anyone who hunts any fringe of a great herd's path would probably come away feeling that caribou country is fascinating and the animals beautiful trophies, but not hard to come by. On the other hand, you can hunt excellent caribou country where there happens to be no caribou at the moment, and you feel like you're hunting dinosaurs. And you can hunt where there are but a few caribou and feel that you have really earned your bull. The best part, of course, is that you're never sure what to expect when you head for a caribou camp. But be it feast or famine, it will be an interesting hunt.

And just which animal will you be hunting? Unlike most North American game species, opinions are sharply divided as to how many subdivisions there should be. The record keeping organizations are not in accord with the biologists, the game departments, or each other! Part of the problem lies in the fact that there is but one species of caribou—*Rangifer tarandus*—and it's spread over a huge expanse of land, with local differences in size and antler conformation. In fact, the caribou is spread over such a large area that the typical subspecies, *Rangifer taran-*

Caribou hunting can be fairly civilized, with permanent camps established across long-standing migration routes. The catch is that migration routes aren't written in stone. Outfitters must be prepared to be flexible in case things change—and sooner or later they will.

dus tarandus, isn't a caribou at all but is instead the reindeer of northern Europe.

Current taxonomical thinking identifies five American caribou subspecies. Boone and Crockett has categories, at present, for five caribou, and the Safari Club recognizes five categories. The problem is that each group's five is different. Confusing? You bet.

The biologists start in the east with *R. t. caribou*, the woodland caribou, and bring it across the continent below treeline to the Mackenzies of Northwest Territories and the mountains of British Columbia and southern Yukon. The caribou of northern Quebec are included, biologically, in this subspecies.

In the barrens of the Northwest Territories, the biologists recognize *R. t. groenlandicus* as being distinct, and above that, on the offshore islands, the small Peary caribou, *R. t. pearyi*. On Greenland itself *R. t. eogroenlandicus* is recognized.

This bull was taken on the "barrens" of central Northwest Territories. These caribou run a bit smaller than the Alaskan barren ground caribou: the Boone and Crockett Club has recently placed them in a separate category for record-keeping purposes under "Central Canadian Barren Ground Caribou."

Lastly, *R. t. granti* is identified as being restricted to Alaska, northern Yukon, and the extreme northern tip of the Northwest Territories above the Mackenzies.

A casual glance at the record books, SCI, B&C and Pope and Young, will tell you that this doesn't work. However, it must be kept in mind that the record books are primarily references for hunters, not for biologists, and the hunter's index is trophy size. If regional differences in trophy size are significant within a subspecies, and if boundaries can be definable, then separate record keeping categories may be called for. With the caribou, that's how we got to five categories.

Traditionally there were just three, the small woodland caribou of eastern Canada, the mountain caribou of B.C., Alberta and southern Yukon, and the barren ground caribou ranging from Northwest Territories westward through Alaska. The "mountain" caribou, you'll notice, is the first category "made up" by hunters. The woodland caribou of the Rockies, Cassiars, Mackenzies, and southern Yukon mountains are much larger in both body and antler than the woodland caribou of eastern Canada, so a separate category was created, and rightfully so. But don't look for mountain caribou, often called "Osborne's", on a biologist's subspecies map. Biologically, they're classed as *R. t. caribou*, the woodland caribou. What confuses hunters is that the game department of Northwest Territories licenses their Mackenzie Mountain caribou as "woodland." That is biologically correct, but all record books class these as mountain caribou, which is also correct for hunters.

In the early Sixties, the great caribou herds on northern Quebec's Ungava Peninsula were opened to outsiders for the first time, and it was discovered that these caribou, though biologically *R. t. caribou*, woodland caribou, had much larger antlers than the caribou of Newfoundland. In fact, they had larger antlers than the mountain caribou, and just perhaps the largest of all. By the B&C system, the largest caribou recorded is from Ungava. Based on antler size, in 1968 B&C created the Quebec-Labrador caribou category. Other record-keeping organizations have followed suit.

At this point, though, opinions have differed. Both SCI and B&C have added a fifth caribou category—but not the same one! SCI was first in recognizing the Peary caribou. These small caribou are perhaps the most distinct of all the caribou subspecies. They're very pale and small, and their population is confined to Northwest Territories' off-shore islands. I suspect B&C will follow suit in recognizing them, and I think it would have been done much sooner except that, until 1983, no sport hunting was ever conducted for this subspecies. Now some of Canada's Inuit (Eskimo) villages have nonresident permits available, either for early fall hunts or later hunts in conjunction with muskox hunting.

While B&C hasn't, at this writing, recognized Peary caribou, they have recognized *R. t. groenlandicus*, calling it the Central Canadian barren ground caribou and identifying it as coming from Northwest Territories' mainland east of the Mackenzies. This subspecies has formerly been lumped in with the larger Grant's subspecies from Alaska, as simply barren ground caribou. The caribou of Northwest Territories' barrens are decidedly smaller, and they've been hunted since 1980; the migration hunt I mentioned earlier was the first modern hunt allowed for nonresidents. B&C now classes barren ground caribou as coming from Alaska and northern Yukon, while SCI still classes these and Northwest Territories' mainland caribou as "barren ground." If it sounds confusing, it's because it is. In truth, unless one is looking at superb specimens of one type or another, there is little difference between any of the caribou groups; only the woodland and Peary are noticeably smaller in trophy size. And with slight differences dictated by local terrain, the hunting of them varies little from coast to coast. If you care to collect them all, be my guest—you'll have four, five or six interesting hunts.

There are vastly differing opinions on whether caribou were hard to put down or not. I think that's a matter of semantics, and also of intent. I don't think they're hard to *kill*, but I think they're hard to put down. I've taken caribou with the 7mm Remington Magnum, the .30-06, and the .375 H&H. I've seen other trophy hunters use a variety of cartridges—.25-06, .270, various .300s, even a .338. Of the 10 caribou I've shot, I've had few one-shot kills, and of the caribou I've seen shot, I've seen few one-shot kills. On the other hand, I've watched native meat hunters shoot caribou with .222s, .30-30s, .308s and .303 Enfields. These guys are strictly meat hunters and they don't have much trouble dropping caribou after caribou with one shot each.

The difference is in intent. The trophy hunter abhors a head or neck shot; the bullet must hit behind the shoulder to preserve the cape. The meat hunter looks for the head or neck shot. He isn't concerned about damage to the cape, and usually is shooting cows or calves in any case. He also isn't concerned about the trophy of a lifetime getting away; he will have picked the time of year when there are plenty of caribou moving through. On the other hand, he is concerned about the cost of ammunition and he'll move as close as possible to try to get that head or neck shot.

Any animal will drop instantly from a brain or spine shot, but different animals do react differently to body hits, whether ultimately fatal

Hip boots are essential in much caribou country, and good raingear a *must* wherever these animals are hunted. Good optics and a flat-shooting rifle round out the essentials for a day's hunt.

or not. I believe caribou have a nervous system that doesn't transmit bullet shock to the same degree that, say, a deer's system does. A heart/lung shot on a caribou will do the trick, but the results may not be immediately apparent. So you shoot again, afraid that the trophy bull you're looking for will slip away. And sometimes yet again. If the first shot was well-placed, it was enough, but caribou take longer to react than a lot of the more familiar Lower 48 animals. No sportsman stands by while a wounded animal remains on its feet and few hunters are so totally confident of shot placement and bullet performance that they'll take a gamble, provided they can get another shot in. So almost invariably caribou are shot more than once, unless the first shot hits heavy bone. Tough? Perhaps, but maybe just too stubborn to know when to give up.

Regardless of which side you take on the caribou arguments, you must admit that a good bull is a stunning trophy. In terms of antler mass versus body weight, the caribou grows antlers larger than any other member of the deer family. Unlike most deer species, cow caribou also grow antlers, though theirs are quite small and spindly. There is no problem telling bulls from cows, or telling a trophy bull from a youngster but it can be a real problem trying to quantify a big bull in the terms of a record-keeping system's measurement.

The problem is that caribou racks have so many aspects, and no two are alike. All you can do is get an initial impression based on the overall size of the whole rack—it should appear as tall as the animal is from ground to shoulder. Then start at the bottom and try to evaluate the shovels, the bez, and finally the crown. Lastly, if you're undecided you can look for back points, but no one caribou has everything.

The shovels are easy to judge. They (or it. Double shovels are rare, and one good shovel is worth two spindly ones) should be broad, and appear to extend to a point even with the bull's nose.

Next look at the bez, the group of points about one-third up the main beam from the shovel. Look for lots of points and plenty of length. The bez should come out farther than the shovel.

Top points, the "crown," are extremely important for record book score, by whatever system. Nothing will add to the aggregate score more quickly than a fan of long top points. Even if the record books aren't your thing, good tops add immeasurably to the overall impressiveness of the rack. Many topnotch caribou have back points on the back of the main beams about halfway up. These points aren't common, but they can be quite long, and they add a lot to the overall score.

Nobody said it better than Jack O'Connor when he wrote that "the big ones look big." But caribou are hard to judge, and at first they all look big. If the first one you see is exceptional, then you'd best take

Wherever there are good concentrations of caribou, wolves are sure to be around. Ultra-wary and extremely difficult to hunt, the wolf is a bonus trophy that's almost impossible to plan on, but it always makes sense to have a license. (Photo by William D. Phifer)

him—but make sure you're absolutely certain what you're looking at.

Caribou aren't large; a huge bull won't weigh as much as a spike elk, nor are they heavy-boned. To my mind a 7mm magnum is about right, with a bullet of decent weight that will give good expansion. The tundra is wide open, and can offer shooting as long as any to be found. For the rifleman, though, the wind is as bad as the potential distance. Flat-shooting rifles and wind-bucking spitzers with good sectional density are the way to go. Good cartridges are anything from the .270 Winchester or Weatherby Magnum up to the various .300s, but the emphasis should be on flat-shooting accuracy and fairly rapid bullet expansion. Good scopes are a must; 6x is fine.

Caribou country can be the soggiest, boggiest, wettest nightmare around in September and October, so both the hunter and his equipment should be waterproofed. Good raingear and hip boots are needed, and this is one hunt where a fiberglass stock makes good sense. On a typical caribou hunt, you will get wet and so will your rifle. There's a good chance you may need all the accuracy your rifle is capable of. Conventional stocks can warp as the wood absorbs water and swells; fiberglass is stable. I'm not crazy about its looks, but it makes sense for this kind of hunting.

Caribou country is the essence of the far North—vast, forbidding, yet amazingly colorful in the fall. The reds and yellows of the lichens and scrub alders march to the far horizon, a horizon that, with luck, will hold the distant silhouette of caribou on the move, and when darkness falls may yield the howl of a wolf. It's exciting country to be in, and the amazing antlers of a good bull are well worth the time and effort of collecting them.

Yet the caribou is easily our most accessible North Country game. In Alaska, he can be hunted on a do-it-yourself basis for those willing to work a bit harder and spend a bit more time. On a fully outfitted basis, there are many areas from Newfoundland to Alaska where a hunter can travel to and from, hunt caribou, and be home in a week's time. Or caribou hunting can be just part of a mixed bag hunt that includes other species.

Alaska is the only place where nonresident hunters can hunt caribou unguided. It's a viable option for serious hunters who are willing to put in the research needed to find a good area, and it's good for a hunter or group of hunters who enjoy "doing their own thing." It is not necessarily the most inexpensive way to get a caribou. Surprised? Think about that incredible-sounding statement. First, depending on where you live, Alaska can be a long way off, and can cost more to get to than Canadian caribou areas that lie closer to home. Second, you must charter a bushplane to get in and out of good caribou country. That can be the case with an outfitted hunt, but in many cases the cost of the flight to and from camp is part of the hunt cost. Bushplanes are expensive, as much as $200 per hour. Third, Alaska's caribou license plus the required nonresident hunting license costs $360, more than double the cost in some Canadian areas. Fourth, you must provide all your food and equipment, and in the Alaskan wilds you must be prepared for any eventuality. And finally, you must accept the fact that you are reducing your chances of success by hunting unguided.

With all that against the idea, it is still very attractive. It's an adventure, and if you pull it off you'll have a special satisfaction. It can be a good way to go for serious bowhunters. Most of the good "sharp stick men" do better working at their own pace, unhampered by a guide who may have hunted only with riflemen in the past. But it won't be a dirt-cheap hunt. A friend of mine went up from California last year and took a superb caribou on his own. His cost analysis showed that the three members of his party spent just over $2,100 apiece.

I'm not sure it would be possible to do a guided caribou hunt, all inclusive, for that figure, in some cases it could be done for $2,500 or less, depending on where you live and the cost of the flight to your jumping-off point.

The Alaskan Game Department is a good place to start making enquiries. Air taxi services in various parts of the state will also help since a good part of their business is ferrying hunters. King Salmon on the Peninsula is a favorite jumping-off point.

Right now the two best bargains in the caribou-hunting world are in Quebec and central Northwest Territories. In both areas hunts can be found that will cost about $2,000 for a week's hunt, including the flights to and from camp. Licenses are very inexpensive; about $150 Canadian, and in northern Quebec that entitles you to two caribou. Yellowknife in NWT is easily accessible from most of the U.S., and either Fort Chimo or Schefferville in Quebec are easily reached from the eastern U.S. Both these regions offer very successful hunts, though

Does velvet itch when it's ready to be peeled? This caribou is a good example of having almost everything a trophy hunter might want. He has exceptional tops, good bez, back points, and long beams—but only one shovel. (Photo by William D. Phifer)

Caribou hunting is a game of glassing carefully and endlessly. The terrain looks flat, but there are innumerable hidden folds and ravines that will hide even a fair-sized herd. (Photo by Bob Tatsch)

the migration has been a bit slow the last couple of years for the camps out of Schefferville.

Newfoundland offers excellent hunting for woodland caribou, with good outfitters charging reasonable prices. Good moose hunting is also easily combined. The drawback is the cost of the caribou license and the fact that it must be applied for a year or so in advance; it runs $600 Canadian.

Most mountain caribou are taken as part of a mixed bag hunt, whether in B.C., Yukon, or the Mackenzies. However, some outfitters do offer caribou only or "antlered game" hunts late in the season, October or so, when it's a bit late for sheep hunting. Wolf predation seems to have hurt the mountain caribou in several parts of northern B.C., so I would expect the Yukon or the Mackenzies to be a better bet.

Alaska, of course, has the largest hunting industry in all the North Country, and hunts for caribou are easily arranged in many areas. Hunting costs in Alaska average a bit higher than in Canada, but

This Alaskan bull has amazing tops, as good as you'll ever see. Is he shootable? At first glance, yes, but the smart hunter would wait until he raises his head; the bez, shovels, or both might not live up to the top. (Photo by William D. Phifer)

camps and services are good and results very good. I did a bit of caribou hunting on the Alaskan Peninsula, and that's one place I'd like to go back to. The caribou are there, and good ones. But there's also plenty of salmon in the streams, emperor geese in the bays, and more ptarmigan than you can shake a stick at.

While this isn't a fishing book, and I'm not much of a fisherman, caribou hunting can't be mentioned without a word about the fishing. In Alaska, depending on where you are, the salmon and grayling fishing is usually fantastic. In the mountains of B.C., the trout practically attacked Dad and me in between spiking out for moose and caribou. And in Northwest Territories hunting barren land caribou is easily combined with fishing for some of the giant lake trout the area is famed for. Caribou hunting is often cold and wet, and can certainly be a feast or famine deal—but it's rarely dull, and it's always a great experience.

Unlike most big game species, the hunting of caribou varies little across their vast range. It's a glassing situation, with animals usually visible at long range—but with the tundra's subtle, unseen folds often hiding whole herds at relatively close range. If the caribou are moving, the best situation is to be positioned along their route; once migrating caribou are past you, they're gone! In Quebec we positioned ourselves at traditional lake crossings, where caribou swim the narrows. When that didn't work, we set out in large circles hoping to find stragglers, and we eventually did. Typical is much glassing, then a mad scramble to get ahead of the herd. In Northwest Territories my partner and I made a bad mistake with a herd of big bulls. They were all good, and we couldn't make a decision. They fed past us, and only then did we figure we'd best do something. Randy took off like a demon, trying to circle around, while I bird-dogged behind them, keeping out of sight. Somehow he managed to get in front of them, and dropped a superb double-shovel. But that's rare. I suspect his being about 22 and a serious runner had something to do with it. When I shot mine a few days later I made sure to make up my mind before the herd got to us, and I shot him as he passed!

My most memorable caribou, though, was my first. It was 1973, in the Cassiars of northern British Columbia. My Indian guide and I had been hunting all day, not seeing much, and we stopped on a high ridge to glass."Big bull caribou," John hissed. I found him in my glasses, skylined on the spine of a knife-edged ridge a mile distant. He was still in velvet, and his antlers were impossibly huge. We watched him bed, then made a long stalk and got him. In truth, he was a fairly average bull, but the sight of that first caribou silhouetted against the blue-green Cassiars remains one of my favorite images.

Chapter 8
Moose

We half-led, half-pulled our horses up the last of the steep grade, passing the uppermost limits of timber a few hundred feet below the grassy saddle. The basins we were heading to were still a couple hours' hard ride away, but we had gained most of the needed altitude. We didn't unlimber either binoculars or spotting scope, but sank down into the soft muskeg to get our breath before mounting up again.

The saddle rose gently on both sides. We were too high for proper trees now, but there were scrub conifers and dwarf willows. Some movement caught my eye in the brush to our right, perhaps a hundred yards uphill. I eased along the sorrel's flank to the saddle scabbard, thinking it might be a grizzly. But before I was half way there, a magnificent bull moose stepped into the clear, followed by two more bulls only slightly smaller. All three were superb trophies, with good palms and lots of points. All were in heavy velvet. I continued my slow movements toward my rifle, mentally calculating the spread on the largest bull. Then I relaxed, and instead of the rifle put my binoculars on them, watching the morning sun glisten on their almost black bodies. We were looking for sheep, and we'd made a long ride to get into this country. A moose simply wasn't part of the game plan right now. With some regret I watched them for a few moments until they'd seen enough and vanished into the low brush without a sound.

Alec, my Indian guide, knew his mountains and the game that lived there, and over the next few days I learned a lot from him. But he

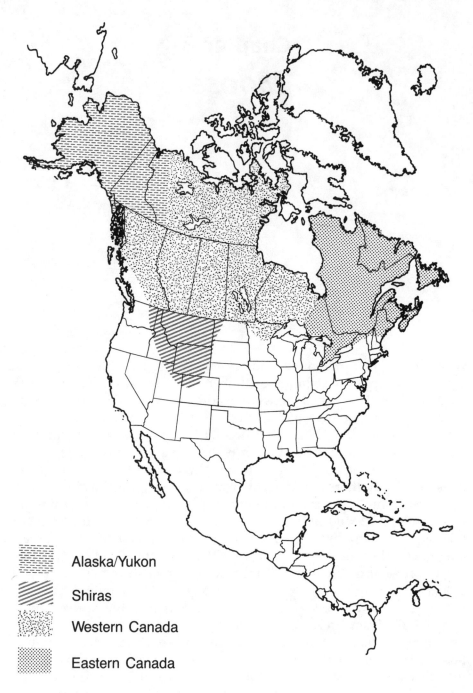

Alaska/Yukon

Shiras

Western Canada

Eastern Canada

MOOSE RANGE

wasn't very talkative. He spoke in short sentences if at all, and he only spoke when he had something worth saying. I knew I wouldn't see a bull like that anytime soon, and he probably did, too. But he also knew we were there to hunt sheep, so he just shrugged and said, "Big bulls go high."

I'm still not totally certain what he meant, but I think I know. Moose aren't creatures of the high mountains; they're primarily denizens of the lakes, rivers and forests. But in even the best country, the big bulls are nearly impossible to find early in the season. They do indeed "go high," or far away to their own private hiding places to grow their huge antlers. In much good moose country the season is open as early as August, but the chances of finding a good bull in traditional moose haunts are slim. Those same spots might be loaded with good bulls a month or six weeks later, but moose have a funny way of simply vanishing, leaving behind plenty of tracks and droppings seemingly designed solely to frustrate hunters.

The problem with moose is that they live in big country. They are one of North America's most populous game species, with something over a million moose ranging between Newfoundland and Alaska—but that's a very big range. Alaska has about 100,000 moose. That sounds like quite a few, and it is, but in real terms, think about it this way; Pennsylvania, just a fraction of Alaska's size, has around 840,000 whitetails. In fact, the density of deer over most of the United States exceeds by far the density of moose over most of their range.

Although there are plenty of moose, they aren't exactly all over the place in any of their range. To successfully hunt moose, any moose, takes proper planning. To successfully hunt trophy moose takes some serious research—you not only must be in the right place, but you must be there at the right time.

Moose are not particularly wary. I've floated within a few yards of bulls on Alaskan rivers while they browsed on underwater plants, but they can be hard to find. A good part of the hard work on a moose hunt involves locating a good bull. Early in the season that means long hours in the saddle or on foot, glassing basins and river valleys. Later it can mean more glassing, or in heavy forests it can mean tracking or cold hours on stand imitating a lovesick cow. The stalk is rarely difficult, nor is the shot; the vital area on a moose gives a fair-sized target. The rest of the work, perhaps the hardest part, depending on location and locomotion, comes when a bull is down and you have about a half-ton of meat to pack out!

The moose is an odd-looking creature. He seems to have been designed by committee, with a huge bulbous nose, the strange pendant-like bell on his neck, an outsized leggy body taller than a horse, and those monstrous palmated antlers. His meat is second to none in the deer family. I once embarrassed myself in a hunting camp when I bit into a moose sirloin and asked my host how he managed to fly beef into camp. But his antlers are what intrigues hunters; the moose is the world's biggest deer with the world's biggest antlers. Unique antlers at that, with their broad palms surrounded by points. A bull moose may be an odd-looking creature, and he may not be mentally gifted by whitetail standards, but a really good bull moose is a showstopper.

We tend to think of the moose as a North American game animal, but actually the moose has close cousins in the forests of northern Asia and Europe. Scientists currently identify just one species of moose worldwide, *Alces alces*, and seven subspecies, four of which are found in North America.

The typical species, *Alces alces alces*, isn't found in the New World at all, but is the moose of Finland, Norway and Sweden. In Europe this animal is traditionally called the *elg* or elk, which leads to much confusion, but it's no relation to our elk or wapiti; it's a moose, very similar in antler size to the moose of eastern Canada. In the northern Soviet Union is found *A. a. pfizenmayeri*, and in southern Russia ranging down into Mongolia *A. a. cameloides*. These last two subspecies are rarely hunted today, but the moose is a popular game animal in Finland, with a harvest of some 15,000 annually.

The moose of North America are not only the world's largest deer, but also grow to the world's largest antler size—all four of our subspecies produce much larger antlers today than their Old World counterparts. While the terrain dictates different hunting techniques across the broad range occupied by our moose, antler size is the primary distinction between our moose subspecies insofar as the hunter is concerned. There are also gradations in body size, and some slight coloration differences.

Based primarily on difference in antler size, hunters have long recognized three categories for North American moose—Alaska-Yukon, Canada, and Shiras or Yellowstone moose.

The largest is of course the Alaska-Yukon moose, *A. a. gigas* to the scientists. Since all moose belong to the same species, there are broad intergrade areas between the subspecies. Since hunters' record-keeping systems must draw boundaries somewhere, the boundaries for moose are drawn on geographic or political boundaries, and are based primarily on antler size. Alaska and the Yukon territory have long been recognized as the range of the Alaska-Yukon moose. More recently, after several outsized trophies were taken in the MacKenzie Mountains of Northwest Territories, the MacKenzie moose were added to the Alaska-Yukon category.

This huge Alaska-Yukon bull is a fine specimen. He has good lower palms, broad upper palms, and plenty of very long points. (Photo by Wiliam D. Phifer)

These moose are truly the king of the deer family. A big bull can stand seven feet at the shoulder and weigh as much as a ton. The antlers, too, are outsized; some spreads are over 80 inches.

The Canada moose category actually comprises two North American subspecies—*A. a. andersoni* from the Great Lakes westward across Canada, including the moose of northern Minnesota and Wisconsin, and *A. a. americana* in eastern Canada, ranging down into New England. There is a difference in antler size between the two. The 1977 edition of B&C's *Records of North American Big Game* lists 327 places for Canada moose; less than 25 come from Ontario and points eastward. The Safari Club's *Record Book of Trophy Animals* (Fourth Edition, 1983), generally with entries of more recent vintage than the B&C book, is even more slanted; of 141 entries, six are from Alberta, five from Saskatchewan, one from Manitoba, and two from western Ontario. All the rest are from British Columbia. Recognizing this disparity, the Safari Club has subdivided Canada moose into two categories, Western Canada Moose

Moose from northern British Columbia are classified as Canadian moose, but actually average only slightly smaller than Alaskan moose. Animals from this region dominate the record book listings for Canadian moose. This one is a particularly fine specimen. (Photo by Bob Tatsch)

for the *andersoni* subspecies and Eastern Canada Moose for the *americanus*. The dividing line is in Ontario, from the southwest shore of James Bay to Nipigon Bay on Lake Superior. Regardless of which system you prefer, it's obvious that the farther west one goes the better the chances for a big Canada moose, with northern B.C. (adjoining Alaska-Yukon moose range, and probably an intergrade area) dominating the listings, followed by Alberta and Saskatchewan. A really nice Canada moose is still a magnificent trophy, with spreads of over 65 inches quite possible. In eastern Canada, spreads of 55 to 60 inches are possible today, and that's a lot of antler!

Our smallest subspecies is the Shiras moose; *A. a shirasi*. Also called the Yellowstone or Wyoming moose, this is the moose of the western Rockies, with its primary range in Wyoming and Montana. In both body and antler size, the Shiras moose averages as much as a third smaller than the Alaskan moose. Its coloration tends to be a bit darker, nearly coal-black, but the most significant difference is size. There is a broad intergrade area between the Shiras moose and the Canada moose, and record-keeping systems have long agonized over where to draw the line.

The true species boundary is somewhere along the Idaho-Montana-Alberta-British Columbia borders, with some moose along the southern Rockies of the latter two provinces unquestionably being Shiras moose. However, the boundary must be drawn somewhere, so the U.S.-Canada border has been the traditional line.

At this writing, Wyoming, Montana, Idaho, North Dakota and Utah are the only places Shiras moose may be hunted according to the B&C boundary. Safari Club includes these states, and adds Washington state's moose as Shiras. Colorado has been actively reintroducing Shiras moose, and chances are that state will offer a few permits in the not too distant future.

The antlers of Shiras moose are significantly smaller than moose from farther north. Spreads of 55 inches have been taken, but a 45-inch bull is quite good and a 40-incher, with good palms and plenty of points, might well make the record books.

In comparing the various moose subspecies I've been speaking primarily in terms of total antler spread. At first glance that's the most significant feature of any moose rack, and it's the figure that hunters generally use in sizing up heads or telling campfire tales. But it's important to note that the greatest spread is only one feature of a trophy moose, and in terms of record book score it's not the most significant.

Both the Safari Club and Boone and Crockett systems use a number of measurements for moose antlers that add up to a total aggregate point tally. For the B&C system, the greatest spread is used as the first measurement. To this is added the number of points on each side (minus any differences), the length and width of each palm (minus any differences), and the circumference of the beam at the *smallest* point (minus any difference between the two beams). The total of all these measurements is the final score.

The Safari Club system differs slightly. The palm width and length on each side is measured, then the circumference of each beam at the *burr*. The total number of points are then tallied. (All of SCI's circumference measurements for antlered animals are taken at the burr, and their system has no deductions for lack of symmetry.) The final measurement is the greatest spread, but taken around the rear of the antlers from the widest notch on one side to the widest notch on the other side. It corresponds to B&C's greatest spread, but cannot be precisely judged in the field since the curvature of the rack adds or detracts from the score.

By either system, the spread is important, but a wide spread alone doesn't make a record-class trophy. In fact, between the two books, with seven categories for North American moose, in no case does the Number One animal have the greatest spread shown in that category. The greatest difference is the Alaska-Yukon category in the Safari Club book. The Number One entry has the greatest spread (around the basket) of 73⅛ inches. The greatest spread shown in that category is a full 90 inches, but that head is clear down in 25th place!

More important in terms of total score and overall quality is long, wide palms. The largest moose, particularly Alaska-Yukon giants, tend to have split palms. The main palm extends upwards from the beam, while a smaller palm, often called the brow palm, extends forward and down from the main beam. The "length of palm" measurements for both systems spans both palms, so the presence of a forward-jutting brow palm adds tremendously to the total score.

Palm width is important, and this can also be judged in the field. The best Alaskan and Canadian moose have palms 15 to 20 inches wide, while the best Shiras moose have palms 10 to 15 inches wide. The points count for one point each, so as long as a rack has an "average" number of points on each side—around 10 to 12—the point total won't be a significant part of the overall score. Obviously, a great number of points adds pure gravy, while few points or a lot of broken points will hurt.

As in the judging of almost all animals, the idea is to take into account as quickly and accurately as possible all the features that make up a top-notch trophy, not just the most obvious. A wide spread will immediately stand out, but the palms mustn't be overlooked. The presence or absence of a brow palm may well be the most significant factor in a record book score, all other things being more or less equal.

Naturally, not all moose are going to make the record books, and one's realistic expectations must be based on what's available in the country one is hunting. Ontario, for example, has a huge moose population, about the same size as Alaska's. It would seem that it's a good place to hunt moose, and it is. But hunting pressure is heavy and management is primarily for quantity rather than quality. That province has produced a fair number of trophy moose over the years, but trophy bulls make up a small percentage of the harvest.

In the East, Newfoundland, with limited nonresident permits and some very competent guides who charge reasonable prices, is an oft-overlooked province with some trophy moose potential. Even more overlooked is northern Manitoba, with a small quota of nonresident moose permits that is consistently undersubscribed. Saskatchewan, too, has some good moose hunting in the northern forests.

Of course, British Columbia remains the top spot for big Canada

A good moose rack is a real load for a strong man—but the rack is just
the beginning. It can take several days to pack out a moose, and if you're
hunting on foot you have to be a little careful about how far from camp
you drop one! (Photo by Wiliam D. Phifer)

moose, with indications that B.C. heads are getting bigger all the time.
A moose taken on the Grayling River in 1980 has been declared the
new World Record according to the B&C system, finally beating Silas
Witherbee's Quebec head, taken in 1914. Another moose taken on the
Teslin River in B.C. in 1982 also beat the Witherbee head.

The Prince George region of British Columbia is excellent moose country. The far north of the province is as good or better, with the Cassiars probably being an intergrade area between Canadian moose and Alaska-Yukon moose.

Athough the far West probably offers the best chance for a big Canada moose, don't overlook the opportunities close to home, if you happen to live in moose country. B&C's *18th Big Game Awards, 1980-1982* recognizes three record Canada moose from Maine and two from Minnesota.

Alaska totally dominates the listings for Alaska-Yukon moose, with just a scattering of entries from the Yukon and MacKenzie Mountains represented. Unchecked wolf predation has had a serious effect on some of Alaska's moose herds in recent years (likewise B.C. and Yukon), so today the hunter in search of a big moose needs to do more homework than ever before. Even so, the big ones are certainly there.

An early fall tent camp in the tundra country of the Far North is an idyllic experience as long as the weather holds. The seasons can vary by as much as a month or more from one year to the next, and the weather can change radically in just a few hours. (Photo by Bob Tatsch)

The current World Record was taken near McGrath, Alaska in 1978, and a new number two was taken in 1981 on the Alagnak River.

The current hotspots for Alaskan moose seem to be the northern portion of the Alaskan Peninsula, the Kuskowim drainage from McGrath to Bethel, and perhaps the Seward Peninsula, where moose have experienced an incredible population explosion. But big moose are where you find them, and at the right time of the year usually later in the season. Most competent outfitters in Alaska, Yukon, and the MacKenzies can give you good odds for a decent moose.

Throughout Canada nonresident hunters must be accompanied by a licensed guide. In Alaska nonresidents may hunt moose unguided. However, I've tried hunting Alaskan moose unguided, and while it can be done, I think an unguided nonresident's chances for moose, especially a good moose, are poor, much poorer than his chances for a good caribou.

Moose hunts have gotten fairly expensive in Alaska these days—the average is around $4,000. In western Canada moose-only hunts average a bit less, something like $3,000. Farther east costs are much lower, generally from $1,500 to $2,500 for a seven to 10-day hunt but east of B.C. the success generally drops off radically, as does the potential size of the antlers.

Moose can be hunted successfully as part of a multi-species hunt, but generally more time is required to do a proper job of things. Moose and grizzly, for example, may well occupy the same range. But moose and sheep are a difficult combination in most areas, requiring a radical change in camps. A combination moose and caribou hunt is quite practical in some areas, but just like trying to combine mule deer and elk, usually potential trophy quality suffers in one species or the other.

Unquestionably, the best chance for a really big moose today is on a specialized hunt for that one trophy. Under those circumstances the outfitter can plan for the best time for a trophy moose, usually late September, October, or even November. Such hunts are usually cold and snowy—pretty miserable—but that's the time for the best heads.

Because of the limited permits, the Shiras moose is a whole different situation. Anywhere you can draw a permit is a great place to hunt. The permits are not as tough to draw as bighorn sheep permits, but they're plenty hard to come by. The best way to hunt Shiras moose is to apply every year in every state that offers permits. When you draw, and you will eventually if you keep on applying, start calling game biologists in the area you're licensed to hunt, and plan to spend the entire season if necessary. That permit is so hard to obtain that you'll want to devote all the time you possibly can to filling it.

Typical hunting techniques for moose vary widely across the huge range of North American moose. They are traditionally animals of forested regions with plenty of water. They spend a good part of their time in water, often feeding on underwater plants with their entire head and neck submerged. Willows are the most important food source in Alaska and the southern Rockies, but quaking aspen, birch and balsam fir are more important across most of Canada.

Where the terrain's relief makes it possible, glassing is the best method for hunting moose. But in much of Canada, the heavy forest and relatively flat terrain makes glassing nearly impossible. Hunting by canoe along lakes and rivers is a pleasant way to hunt under such circumstances. Tracking is also possible and productive, especially in snow.

Like most antlered game, moose are most easily hunted during the rut. Depending on locale, moose generally rut sometime between late September and early November. During this period, bull moose are at the very least incautious—often crazy! They can also be dangerous.

Excessive wolf populations have hurt the moose population in much of Alaska, but even though you have to hunt a bit harder the great bulls are still there. This beauty was taken just 20 minutes by Supercub from Anchorage. (Photo by Bob Boutang)

There are plenty of stories about rutting moose taking on railroad trains. In that case the moose loses, but on the highway in a match between a car and a moose, it's often a draw. And when a bull moose goes for a packhorse, the outcome is uncertain. During the rut, bulls are in the open a great deal more and can more reliably be found in traditional moose-hunting habitat.

In the West, including Alaska, the terrain usually permits glassing to some degree, and that's the method of choice even during the rut. But in the heavy forests of central and eastern Canada, calling is the favorite hunting technique. In some areas, little moose hunting is even attempted until the rut begins!

Moose are fairly vocal during the rut, with cows producing a long, quavering moaning sound that can be heard for as much as two miles. This is the sound imitated by most moose callers, with the sound made in the throat and amplified by some type of tube or megaphone. Like most types of game calling, the hunters find a likely area, call for a while, and if no answering grunts are heard, they'll move quietly to another spot and try again. Often used in conjunction with a canoe, it's a fascinating way to hunt moose and if a rut-crazed bull approaches in heavy cover, it can be a bit dangerous.

In terms of size, moose should rate the heaviest artillery a hunter could carry. However, they're not particularly difficult to kill. On the other hand, they are inordinately hard to put down. They seem to have a phlegmatic disposition that is fairly impervious to bullet shock, and it seems that if the first shot doesn't do the job immediately, the next three or four might not either.

Because of their sheer size, a rifle of adequate caliber with a stout bullet designed to offer good penetration is certainly called for. A .30-06 with 180- or 200-grain bullet is a sensible minimum, and is probably quite adequate. A .300 or .338 magnum might yield quicker results, but I'm not altogether certain about that. The idea should be to place a bullet that will penetrate well into the heart-lung region but don't be surprised if that bullet doesn't take effect immediately, regardless of its caliber or velocity.

Typically a bull hit in that manner will remain where he is or amble off a few yards before dropping over. The hunter should immediately follow up such a shot with another if the moose didn't go down, even though in most cases the first shot would have been enough.

Bullet effect on moose seems to defy all the laws. I've shot moose with a .375 H&H, a pretty decent moose gun, only to see absolutely nothing happen, and have to shoot again. On the other hand, my dad once shot a moose with a 180-grain Silvertip from a .308 Winchester—a bit on the light side. The shot was to the heart, and that moose dropped in his tracks as if struck by lightning. Does that mean the .308 is a better moose gun than the .375? Hardly, but these big deer react to bullets differently than most big game I've encountered, and it's impossible to predict what will happen after you pull the trigger. The best approach is to hit one as hard as you can with a good bullet designed for penetration and controlled expansion. If he starts to go, try to get in another one. And if he vanishes into the brush, sit a spell before you take up the trail. They're not as hard to kill as their size might indicate, but they can sure be hard to stop!

Moose are fascinating creatures. Hardly pretty the way a full-curl ram is, nor as majestic as a six-by-six elk, but a really big bull moose is a magnificent animal all the same. You'll find their huge, cloven-hoofed tracks and distinctive oval droppings across much of the North Country, but you'll usually have to cover a lot of ground and hunt hard to find a good bull.

On a sheep hunt in the Wrangells we were glassing some rams from a steep mountainside of broken shale far above a glacial stream. Timberline was far below us, perhaps a couple thousand feet in elevation and several miles in distance. We packed up and moved around the corner of the mountain to see some new country, carefully picking our way through the treacherous loose rock. We came to a narrow bench of jumbled rock with a spring babbling out and cascading on down the moutainside. Right in the center of that bench was the skeleton of a mature Alaskan moose, antlers whitened with age. No horse or mule could negotiate that slope, nor seemingly could a moose. I don't know what he was doing there, or how he met his end. But like Alec said, "Big bulls go high."

Chapter 9
Black Bear

The black bear is perhaps the most widespread game animal in North America, occurring from Maine to Florida and Alaska to Mexico—and most places in between. He's wary, elusive, and wears a lovely coat. It's quite surprising that he isn't a more highly regarded game animal than he is. But in spite of his availabilty, the black bear takes a decided back seat in hunter popularity, lagging far behind antlered species and even the pronghorn. That's too bad, for the black bear is not only a beautiful trophy, he's also a fascinating animal, and one that has the potential ability to turn the tables on a careless hunter.

Some say that a black bear is a coward, and a hunter has nothing to fear from his tribe. Generally that's true, but bears—all bears—are unpredictable. There are more black bear maulings on record than from grizzly/brown bears, and quite a few deaths. One perfectly healthy male black bear apparently stalked, killed, and partially ate three young fishermen in Ontario's Algonquin Park in 1978. Just the year before this writing a black bear in eastern Canada attacked and killed one fisherman, then attacked his partner, who managed to kill the bear. The report that I read stated that, on autopsying the bear, more human extremities were found than could be accounted for. A careful check of the area revealed another partially eaten body.

This isn't meant to indicate that unwounded black bears are particularly dangerous. Ninety-nine times out of 100 they aren't. But they are extremely powerful and just unpredictable enough to deserve complete

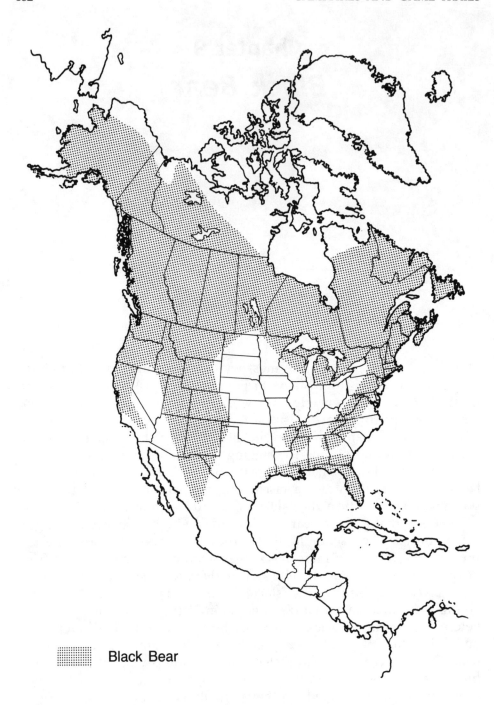

Black Bear

BLACK BEAR RANGE

respect at all times. Wounded, they can most definitely be dangerous. Of the dozen black bears I've taken and several more I've seen taken, there's never been a problem. But two of the guides I've hunted black bear with have scars they'll carry to their graves. Neither bear was particularly large—and it's probably a good thing!

Of course, the danger is greater from bears within a park than at any time while in hunting country. The black bear is by nature shy and retiring, and even in the best bear country chance encounters are unusual. Except, of course, in parks, where signs that read "Don't feed the bears" are interpreted by most people to read "Bear feeding station." Whether through man's carelessness or the bear's lack of fear, most bear problems do occur within some kind of park where no hunting is permitted and the centuries of instinctive fear bears have developed for man have disappeared.

When I was a Boy Scout I made a couple of hiking trips through the Philmont Ranch, a gorgeous piece of northern New Mexico donated to the Scouts by Phillips Petroleum. It was, and still is, great game country with plenty of deer, elk, wild turkey and black bears. We were being as careful as possible, hanging all the food in trees, keeping goodies away from the tents, etc. So far we hadn't seen any bears at all.

Then one night about dark a small cinnamon bear ambled in, scared all of us, and shinnied up the tree our food was in and helped himself. We yelled and banged on pots—standard bear-scaring techniques—but this bear seemed hard of hearing. Finally, either filled up or tired of the game, the bear left. We cleaned up what we could and everybody hit the sack.

A blood-curdling scream brought me from a sound sleep. I tried to sit up, but couldn't. I opened my eyes, looking straight up out of the sleeping bag. Pitch black. Too black. I couldn't see the sky through the open tent flap, but I'd been able to when I went to sleep. Then the blackness moved and more weight shifted to my chest. At about the same time I realized a bear was pushing his way into the tent (no way there would have been room for him, but I didn't want to tell him that!) and had planted one of his paws on my chest, the boy sleeping next to me screamed again. He had awakened a moment before I did, sat up, and had been soundly cuffed across the forehead.

The second scream might have been enough, at least for the moment. The bear backed out the way he had come and commenced to dismantle the camp. Pots, pans, packs, the remains of our food the other bear had been kind enough to leave, whatever this bear could find he tore into with a vengeance. The kid next to me was bleeding like a stuck pig and was convinced he was dying. I wasn't ready to argue the point, either.

Finally the bear left and we crawled out, got a light, and tried to figure how bad it was. Bad enough, a nasty scalp wound, but a long way from fatal. We got a compress on it and somebody headed to the ranger's shack where we could radio for help.

About that time the bear came back. This was a big bear, coal black and bold as brass. I seem to recall having read that if a bear stands on his hind legs, he's ready to turn and run; if he lowers his head he's ready to charge. I've watched a lot of bears since then, and I still don't know if there's any truth to that. But at the time I believed it. I had grabbed a skillet and a pot, and was busy banging them together when the bear eyeballed me, lowered his head and took a couple of steps forward. Those two steps were the extent of it, and then he turned and vanished into the starry New Mexico night. But they were very long steps, and it was a very big bear. In fact, in the 20 years since then I've

Black bears are among the most difficult animals to judge, but a big bear actually *looks* big; it will seem bowlegged and built low to the ground, and will convey a feeling of power.

shot several bears that were probably larger but I guarantee you I'll *never* see a bear that big again!

One of the biggest arguments bear hunters will ever get into is how big a black bear really is or can get. There is a tremendous difference between the outside weight and the average weight. In 1885 a Wisconsin black bear was supposedly scaled at 802 pounds. While that figure seems incredible, there is no reason to disbelieve it. In this century several black bears have weighed over 600 *field dressed*. But bears that come anywhere near that figure are extremely rare anywhere, just as 350-pound people are uncommon and 400-pound people rarer still. A good average for a mature, full-grown black bear is probably closer to 225–250 pounds; a 300-pound bear is getting well into the trophy class, and anything 400 pounds or larger is very big indeed.

Hunters rarely carry accurate scales in the woods, and carting a whole bear to a convenient scale is hardly practical. Hide measurements, too, are unreliable; a wet hide will stretch just about any way you want it to. Partly for these reasons, and partly for sound scientific reasons, bears have always been entered into the record books based strictly on skull size—the skull length plus the skull width for a total measurement. I'm personally not crazy about this method, since it is quite possible to shoot a very large bear that doesn't have a skull commensurate with the body size, and vice versa. However, I certainly agree that there is no other sensible way to measure bears for any kind of official record-keeping system.

Official records aside, it doesn't sound very exciting to say, "My bear measured 21." (The current Boone and Crockett minimum score.) It also doesn't mean much to the average hunter. Weights, most often estimated fairly high, are the most-often quoted figure with black bears. The "square of the hide" is another popular, though unofficial, method for comparing trophy bears. To "square" any hide, the green skin is laid on a flat surface and measured nose to tail *without stretching*, and again measured from one outstretched front paw to another. The sum of these measurements, divided by two, is the "square of the bear." It's possible to take a very large black bear that will square well in excess of seven feet, but a bear that squares around six feet is actually a very, very nice black bear.

In captivity, black bears have lived past 20, but it's believed that 15 years is a fairly long life in the wild. Although black bears are very much omnivorous—they'll eat virtually anything—they must have relatively good food conditions prior to denning up in order to survive the winter. Favored foods vary greatly across the black bear's vast range, but carrion is popular throughout when available. Grasses and clover

This mid-sized bear was taken with Browning's lever action in .358 Winchester, a fine black bear cartridge. The scope is Bushnell's Lite-Sight, featuring a battery-operated lighted reticle. It's another good piece of gear for the bear hunter. Shots are often made just at last light, and positioning the crosshairs on a dark animal in dark timber at near-dark can be tough!

are often one of the first spring foods. In oak country, acorns become extremely important, and in season, berries are favorites. Black bears can be skilled fishermen, and will take advantage of any spawning run in their area.

The tremendous variance in color phases of the black bear is the subject of much confusion and many campfire arguments. There is but one species of black bear worldwide, *Ursus americanus*. Taxonomists do identify as many as 18 subspecies, but it is well beyond the ability of most scientists, let alone hunters, to reliably tell them apart. However, important to hunters is the fact that black bears aren't all black. In some areas, a *black* black bear is somewhat of a rarity! In the East, the black color phase seems to be predominant, but at the midpoint of the continent brown color phases start to become more common. In Manitoba, a bear-guiding friend of mine figures 40 percent of the bears he takes are some shade of brown. In southeastern British Columbia, it might run close to 50-50. However, the genes which determine color phase seem localized to some degree; in Washington state black seems to be the predominant color, while in much of California brown is most common.

The brown black bear can occur in a wide variety of coloration, ranging from honey-blond through reddish browns all the way to chocolate. Color is usually uniform, but I saw a beautiful brown bear taken in Oregon that had a prominent blond stripe down the middle of the back. In both black and brown pelage, a white (or lighter colored) throat patch isn't uncommon.

Black and brown are far and away the most common color phases of the black bear, but hardly the full range. In southeast Alaska, in the glacier country around Yakutat, the so-called "glacier bear" is found. Also called the "blue bear," this color phase of the black bear has pale guard hairs that give the bear an odd blue color, more pronounced at a distance. The glacier bear may be hunted in southeast Alaska on a black bear license, but the coloration is uncommon even in the heart of their range. The blue bear is one of the most prized trophies in all North America.

Rarer still is the Kermode bear—a white black bear. Found only along the central British Columbia coast, mostly on offshore islands in the Queen Charlotte chain, this bear is a pure white color phase of black bear. Not an albino, it has black eyes, nose and claws, but the coat remains white throughout the bear's life. Totally protected for decades, few hunters have heard about this bear and I suspect my mention of it may cause some heated arguments. It does exist. My uncle, Art Popham of Kansas City, took one on a museum permit in the early Sixties, and it may be viewed in a diorama at the Kansas City Museum of Natural History along with a "regular" black bear taken from the same area.

While the various color phases apparently represent gene pools that at some point might have been considered subspecies, it's an established fact that a black sow may have a brown cub, a black cub, or, in the areas where these genes are present, a white cub or a blue cub. Twins might even have different colorations. In Manitoba in the spring of '84 my party and I observed a huge chocolate brown sow who had two cubs—one brown and one black.

Regardless of color phase, they're all black bears. But the trophy hunter does have three basic considerations to keep in mind: color, size, and quality of pelt. Those can be put in any order one wishes, but based on the priorities one places on them, there are some decisions to be made.

If you have a strong preference as to color, then you'll need to hunt somewhere that offers the color phase you fancy. Brown bears are possible across most black bear range, but in many areas they are decidedly uncommon. And in a few areas, black-colored black bears are uncommon.

Life is obviously much simpler if you decide to look for the biggest bear you can find, but you must still keep in mind the quality of the pelt. A record skull is nice, but personally, a well-furred bear rug seems a nicer thing to have than a name in the listings. And unless the bear is unquestionably a huge specimen, there is never any guarantee that the skull will go in the book.

Fortunately, judging the quality of the hide is usually fairly simple, easier than accurately judging a bear's size. Shortly after coming out of hibernation in the spring, a bear's hide seems to itch. The bear's answer to this is to rub against trees, rocks or whatever, and the old winter hair comes off. A rubbed bear usually shows lighter patches

Frank Morales and Duwane Adams of San Manuel are just two of several Arizonans who have had excellent success calling black bears. The arid country doesn't have a large bear population, but it has produced a surprising number of really huge bears.

The cartridge is a 7mm Remington Magnum, making this a very large black bear track. The great size range of black bears dictates carrying a rifle that will be effective on the very largest of bears as well as the average.

through binoculars, places where the skin actually is visible through the pelt. It's possible to take a bear that has been viewed from just one side and find the off-side rubbed, but generally if the rubbing has progressed far enough to be a problem, it's apparent from almost any angle.

The patchy appearance remains through the summer and into the early fall, when the new winter coat comes out. For a good hide, then, it's obvious that the bear must be taken either before he begins to rub in the spring or after the winter coat comes out in the fall.

One of the most-asked bear hunting questions is which is best, fall or spring? There's no pat answer. It depends on the weather—how late the spring or early the fall. It depends on the area and the hunting technique to be used, and of course, it depends on the season, for not all areas offer both fall and spring hunts. Some areas do have very long

Horses are nearly essential for much western black bear hunting, whether spotting and stalking or hunting with hounds. Bear populations are concentrated in some areas, but in many places much ground must be covered to cut bear sign.

bear seasons, sometimes extending through much of the summer. For good hides, late June through early September are usually quite hopeless. But other than that, neither fall nor spring is necessarily the best.

I have a fondness for spring bear hunting, since it comes at a time when little other hunting is available. Also, bears tend to be a bit more predictable in their movements when they're just out of the den; they're hungry and that's the overriding consideration. However, it's hard to say exactly when the rubbing will start, and not all bears in a given area will rub at the same time. It's quite possible that fall bear hunting offers the most consistently good pelts, though the hunting can be a bit more difficult. By and large, fall bears offer the better meat. A spring bear will usually be thin, and may well be feeding on carrion. A fall bear has long since cleaned up the winter-killed carrion and is gorging himself on berries, oak mast, and such. He should be fat and sassy and will offer the best bear meat available, the later in the fall the better.

Judging the color of a bear is simple; you'll rarely get fooled on the basic hue, though dirt (especially in the spring) will often make a brown-colored bear appear darker than he really is. Judging the quality of the hide is only slightly more difficult; it simply requires holding off long enough to get a good look, preferably from both sides.

Judging the size of the bear is another matter. Some antlered and horned animals are more difficult to judge than others, but no animal is as hard to estimate as a bear. If there are hard and fast rules that really work, I'm not aware of them. The important thing to remember is that almost any bear can *look* big at first glance; it's important to study the animal for as long as possible. Nobody said it better than Jack O'Connor when he stated that "the big ones look big." They do, but at a quick glance the little ones can look big as well.

There are some tricks that help. Get a feel for the height of the vegetation in the area you're hunting, and try to picture how a large bear should appear in that setting. Do this long before you see a bear.

The brown color phase of black bear is extremely rare in some areas, yet common in others. Color phases in bears are not fully understood. They are genetic, but a brown sow may have a black cub or vice versa, and if twins, she may have one of each!

Then, when you have a bear in sight, look at him carefully. A big bear conveys a feeling of power. He looks and acts like the boss bear that he is. A younger, smaller bear tends to look leggy and rangy; a big bear is broad, and his body size makes him appear short-legged. He'll walk ponderously and will appear bowlegged. If he's *really* big he probably *is* bowlegged from hauling around all that weight.

With bears, more so than any other animal, it is possible to make a serious mistake in judging trophy size. Fortunately, most common bear-hunting techniques give the hunter some time to size up the trophy. The more time spent before the shot, the more likely you are to be pleased with the trophy. And even then, and even with experience, it's possible to go wrong. I shot a bear from a treestand quite recently, and while it wasn't a small bear, it wasn't the bear I thought it was. No excuses; I was hunting over a bait, and I'd been watching that bear for nearly an hour. Time was running out, and it was a perfectly accept-able bear—but not the bear I'd judged it to be.

The black bear is an amazingly wary animal. He doesn't see particu-larly well, but his hearing is quite good and his nose is outstanding. Excluding the unnatural situations in many of our parks, chance en-counters with black bears are quite rare especially considering how widespread and abundant the animals really are. In situations where the bear is hunted, he manages to stay away from man amazingly well. In many parts of the U.S. and Canada, black bears are legal game during all or part of deer or other big game seasons. But very few black bears are taken by accident while hunting other species. It happens, but considering the numbers of hunters in the woods under these circumstances, it's hardly something one can count on.

Instead, to get a bear rug for your den, you need to hunt bear. Bear hunting is almost as traditional a sport as deer hunting across North America. Four basic techniques are used and each has evolved based on local hunting traditions, terrain, and what works. These methods are spotting and stalking, running with hounds, baiting, and calling. The first one can be used virtually anywhere, but is a viable method only where the country is open enough that glassing is effective. The next two methods are a bit controversial. Some hunters feel that the use of hounds is unsportsmanlike, others feel bait-hunting shouldn't be allowed. Neither method is legal in all parts of the country. Calling is rarely attempted, but in certain parts of the country it's not only *the* method, it's also quite successful. While I'm far from expert at hunting bears by any of these methods, I've used them all with some success.

Spotting and stalking is the classic big game hunting technique. In much of the country, it just isn't practical because there are no open-ings where game can be viewed, or the land doesn't have enough relief

A hunt over bait gives perhaps the best chance to study a bear before making the decision to take it or not, but it's easy to be misled. This bear *looks* large, but the bait she's standing on is a steer, and she's just one-third its size—a mid-sized sow, and the cubs are probably hers. Really large bears almost never share a bait.

to enable the hunter to see the area. Some of our western states and provinces, including such prime black bear country as British Columbia, allow neither baiting nor dogs in taking bear so spotting and stalking is the only way to go. In the spring, bears can be glassed on open hillsides where they're feeding on the new green shoots and grasses. In fall, berry patches are the prime places to look. It's a time-consuming way to hunt, but also quite pleasant. You see a lot of country, and when you see a bear, you have plenty of time to size him up with a spotting scope. And of course, there's much to be said for the excitement and satisfaction of planning and executing a good stalk. This is perhaps not the most successful way to take a bear, but that's weighed against the fact that it's mostly practiced in areas with high bear populations and little hunting pressure.

Black bear hunting with hounds is probably the most successful method of all. Hound hunting in general gets a lot of flak, both from hunters and non-hunters, but I suspect the hunters who knock it haven't tried it. It's a different kind of hunting because the shot is anticlimactic while the chase is everything. A hound hunt begins with a painstaking and often tedious search for fresh tracks, either on foot, horseback, or by four-wheel-drive. It can take days, but has the advantage, usually, of the hunter getting a look at the tracks and making a preliminary judgement as to size of bear before the dogs are released.

Eventually fresh tracks of a good bear are hit, and the chase is on. From there it's as exciting and as physically demanding as any hunt can be. The bear might elude the dogs, or he might turn on the ground and outfight them. Or the chase might simply outdistance the hunters, and days more be spent finding dogs. If all goes well the hunter, by much running, scrambling, climbing and huffing and puffing keeps in earshot of the chase. And when the bear bays or trees, the hunters are able to close in before the bear takes off again. The chase is everything. Once at the tree, the shot is usually at close range and fairly simple, except that the bear, if he's shootable, must be dropped cleanly lest he wreak havoc with a priceless pack of trained bear dogs.

Bait hunters also come in for their share of grief. In many parts of the country, hunting over baits is the preferred method to hunt black bear. But the method is often termed unsporting, perhaps in the belief that it takes unfair advantage of a bear's weakness—his stomach.

True enough, a black bear will bait readily, especially a hungry spring bear, and especially to a particularly smelly bait. But it's hardly that simple. Perhaps bait hunting gets its bad name from the unsportsmanlike practice of shooting bears over refuse dumps. That is done, but it isn't bait hunting, nor is it really hunting at all. Bears will come to dumps, and taking one in that manner is usually illegal as well as unsportsmanlike. But positioning a bait in bear country and getting a bear to take it is a different ballgame, tricky to play and very interesting.

A major problem is to get the bear to come to the bait before dark, and that means careful strategy and some bear know-how in the selection of a bait site and positioning of the blind. Experienced bait hunters also believe that bait itself makes a difference and each successful bait hunter has his own formula for what makes a perfect bait. Some prefer fishheads and such, others use winter-killed steers or horses. A favorite among trappers is beaver carcasses, and apparently that's one bait a bear can't resist. However, I don't think bears are all that picky; material used for the bait seems to be the least critical factor.

More important is the choice of bait site, so the bear has thick cover on the way to the bait and will gain enough confidence to feed before last light. The blind must be positioned so the hunter has a clear shot at the bear, while downwind from the likeliest avenues of approach. Treestands are the most common blinds, preferably in a well-branched tree so the hunter won't be skylined to the bear.

Most bear hunting over bait is done in the evening. Unless the hunter stays in the blind overnight, it's nearly impossible to get into position before daybreak without spooking any bears that might be near the bait. Evening, too, is the customary feeding time for most bears. Hunting over bait can be both exciting and boring, often within moments of one another. It's always exciting as darkness begins to fall and you're certain the bear will appear any moment; boring as you arrive on stand at midafternoon and must while away endless hours, remaining as motionless as possible. It's a solitary sport; the more people, the more noise and the more scent.

In a good camp in good country, the odds are excellent that, over the course of a week's hunt, a bear will make an appearance. When he comes it's usually a total surprise. There may be the sound of a branch breaking, but most often he'll come in silence, suddenly appearing at the edge of

This black bear is an amazing specimen, as big as many grizzlies and easily a record book candidate. Taken in Manitoba in 1983, it's a clear indicator that there are still big bears to be found, but ones this big don't come easy or often! (Photo by Don McCrae)

the forest. If the wind is right, and if the hunter can keep himself under control, this method of hunting offers the best opportunity to properly size up the bear and make sure he's what you want before you shoot. Of course, it's rarely all that easy. The wind can shift, the bear can come in from the wrong direction, or he can lie down behind the bait. On a spring bear hunt in Saskatchewan, a friend of mine waited for the same bear four nights running. He came every night, but every time something happened and no shots were fired until the fourth night, and that made all the frustration worthwhile.

The shot itself is rarely difficult on a bait hunt. It won't be quite as close as on a typical hound hunt, but generally you'll have a good rest and plenty of time. There is tremendous tension, however, and it's tension multiplied by hours and days of waiting for that moment. Bait hunting is usually done in very heavy cover, so there's also the knowledge that there will be but one shot.

Like hound hunting, bait hunting is fairly regional, preferred in some areas and illegal in others. It's widely used in eastern and central Canada and in the upper Midwest and Northeast of the U.S. It is most popular in heavily forested regions where virtually the only way to find a bear is to get him to come to you.

The last method I'll mention is calling, a virtually unknown bear-hunting technique. In Arizona, marginal bear country at best, a number of hunters absolutely swear by it. They use a varmint call, preferably a very loud one, and they "set up" where the sound will carry into a likely-looking canyon. In this locale, at least, bears *will* come to the call. They don't come out of curiosity, either. They come looking for a free meal, and they often practically charge the call. I don't know a lot about this kind of bear hunting—yet—but from what I've seen, a bear that will answer the call is likely to be a "boss bear," a real trophy.

What I do know about the technique I've learned from my two Arizona hunting buddies, Duwane Adams and Frank Morales of San Manuel. They hunt at least in pairs, and when we're calling bears we set up back to back so there are no surprises. More than one call is used. One hunter blows a series as loud as possible and when he gets winded, the next hunter takes over. As in all calling, there has to be a bear around to hear it. Duwane and Frank scour canyons for fresh sign, and don't set up to call unless they've already determined a bear is in the area.

Like I said, the method works at least for these and other hunters in central and southern Arizona. A reasonable theory is that in this harsh, dry climate bears have a tougher time keeping their bellies filled and will readily respond to any possibility of a meal. I'm not prepared to say that you can't call black bears in other parts of their vast range but I'm not ready to say that you can, either.

When attempting to call bears the idea is to make as much noise as possible. Frank Morales calls loud and long, and when he gets tired his partner takes over. The partner is important; black bears may actually charge the call, and it's foolish to use this method alone.

In 1984, 26 states and all the Canadian provinces announced seasons for black bear. The comeback of the black bear has been rather quiet, as opposed to the great fanfare that has accompanied the wild turkey's resurgence. Black bear have been coming back slowly but steadily, reoccupying its former range in such areas as the Ozark Mountains, the Appalachians, and the Deep South. In fact the Great Plains states are virtually the only portion of North America that doesn't have *Ursus americanus*. I've cut his track within an hour of downtown Los Angeles, and once in a while you hear of a bear wandering down Mulholland Drive in the Hollywood Hills. A couple of years ago I was on a reserve training exercise at Marine Corps Base Camp Lejeune, North Carolina. I had taken a patrol out at dusk, and had come back through "friendly" lines about midnight, expecting (though hoping differently) to find the troops asleep. Not that night. The whole perimeter was wide awake.

About an hour before my arrival, our lines were "probed" by a 350-pound bear, judging from the tracks, and he did what no *banzai* charge ever has—he rolled right over the Second Battalion, 23rd Marines!

Obviously, black bears aren't evenly distributed from coast to coast, but there are plenty of places where there are lots of bears, and also places where there are some very large bears.

Alaska has exceptional black bear hunting, with long seasons and a multiple-bear limit in many areas. Nonresidents are not required to hire a guide for black bear. Personally, I wouldn't go that far to hunt black bear; it's a vast land, and one would have to do a lot of research before attempting it unguided. And for a guided hunt, other Alaskan species are more interesting. But the black bear hunting is very good, and of course there's the off-chance for a glacier bear in the Yakutat area.

A bit closer to home is southern British Columbia and southwestern Alberta. This region has an enormous population of black bears, with a good portion of the population some shade of brown. On a spring bear hunt in southern B.C. in 1974 I saw 40 black bears in four days. These provinces offer a two-bear limit, with license fees reasonable. It's very possible to be both size- and color-selective, and take both a brown and a black on one hunt. Nonresidents must be guided in both provinces, and the hunting is spotting and stalking; no bait hunting or hound hunting. Montana also offers outstanding spotting and stalking for black bears, with a high proportion of cinnamon bears. I shot my first black bear there, in the Tobacco Root Mountains east of Dillon.

The northern timber from Saskatchewan to Maine is the stronghold for bait hunting. There are literally dozens of reputable camps in good country, and the better ones offer a high success ratio. A real "sleeper" is Manitoba. In four days in late May, 1984 a hunting partner and I saw 17 different bears on bait.

Northern California, Oregon and Utah are popular spots for hound hunting. Big bears are available, and there are a number of good outfitters with topnotch packs. In some cases horses will be used, and in others logging roads offer a network to stay reasonably abreast of a chase.

The record books are the best source of data about really large bears. The Boone and Crockett listings contain entries from 26 states and provinces, plus one entry from Mexico. Record-class bears (by skull measurement) have been taken in such diverse places as Louisiana, Virginia, Pennsylvania, Alaska, and Newfoundland. However, the record book is very clear as to where the most record book bears have been taken. This is especially striking when you consider that, of the four states with more than 10 B&C entries, only one has what could be considered a large annual bear harvest.

According to the 1981 edition of B&C's *Records of North American Big Game*, Arizona leads the pack with 20 entries.

Colorado is next with 18, then Wisconsin with 17, and finally California with 12. Wisconsin has a much higher bear harvest than the other three, and both California's and Arizona's bear harvests are quite modest.

In the 1980-82 recording period, these trends held more or less firm; Wisconsin, Arizona and Colorado had four entries apiece, more than any other areas. California dropped out, with just one new entry, and Saskatchewan, with only two entries in the past, came up with four new ones. This last could indicate that Saskatchewan's bear population is coming on strong, or it could mean that Saskatchewan hunters are becoming more aware of record-keeping procedures.

For the other areas, the indications are quite clear—they're good places to look for a huge bear. Another interesting sidelight is that Utah, with a total of just five bears in the current book, has three in the top ten, including numbers one and two. Arizona and Colorado have the rest of the top ten, with five and two entries, respectively. However, these areas might not be the best place to fill a tag. British Columbia, Washington, and Oregon, for example, all have much higher bear population densities and higher hunter success.

There are as many different opinions on black bear guns and cartridges as there are good places to hunt them. Some hunters prefer some sort of cannon, while others reckon any deer rifle will do the trick. I've done some hunting with Jess Caswell, a Washington-based outfitter who hunts over much of the West with his dogs. He hunts most of the year, and his hunts probably don't average five days. In other words, he sees a lot of clients a year, and he's been in the business 20 years. But the story he tells about the guy who showed up in camp without a rifle is a classic. Nope, he didn't have a handgun in his duffel, and nope, he wasn't going to borrow one of Jess' guns. Didn't have a bow, either. He was going to get his bear with a baseball bat.

Since the customer is always right, Jess took the gent to a sporting goods store on his request. He thought the gag had gone far enough when his hunter selected and paid for a Louisville Slugger, but after all, it takes all kinds.

The first day out they treed one of the rare bears that you could get within a couple hundred yards of with the truck. It was only when the guy advanced towards the tree with his baseball bat that Jess figured things had gone too far. At some point the sport got a look at the first real bear he'd ever seen, and decided the baseball bat might not be enough gun. Of course, the hunter was the one who backed down. Jess never said exactly how far he would have let things go—and I didn't ask.

Most baited bear hunts use treestands. They offer better visibility, plus, equally important, get the hunter's scent up off the ground.

There's another Jess Caswell story, but it's not funny. In timber country, bears can be a big problem. They tend to eat the bark on newly-planted seedlings, killing them and causing millions of dollars in damage annually. Jess was a professional hunter for the timber companies, and he had an assigned quota of bears he was "taking care of." His gun, for years and years and hundreds of bears, was a .30-30 carbine. Light, handy, and it did the job just fine for bear hunting with hounds. Until a mid-sized bear came out of the tree, badly hurt but not too badly to get even. When Jess got out of the hospital he bought a Remington Model 600 in .350 Remington Magnum, a gun he still uses for backup work with his clients.

There are several unique aspects to gun selection for black bear. First, there's the obvious fact that a wounded bear can hurt someone—you, your hunting partner, your guide, the dogs, or someone who just stumbles on the bear by accident. Black bears aren't usually dangerous, but they can be. Second, most black bears are about the same size as a big deer. Built a bit more heavily and certainly more heavily boned and more stoutly muscled, but still about the same size—mostly. Instead of packing a gun that will do the job on the average 250-pound bear, you must have a gun/load combo that will be adequate for the 500-pound monster you hope to encounter. The common bear-hunting techniques are specific enough that you have some idea of the kind of shot you'll be faced with, and can plan accordingly.

For spotting and stalking, you need a flat-shooting rig that can reach out a couple hundred yards if needed. While the 6mms and .25s will work on an average bear, I think the possibility of encountering a big bear eliminates them. A .300 magnum or .338 isn't required (although they'll work!) but a sensible minimum is a .270 or .280 with controlled expansion bullets. The good old .30-06 with 180-grain bullets is a super choice, as are the 7mm magnums. A good scope is a must.

Hunting over baits moves things a bit closer. One hundred yards is about the max, but shooting will probably be at last light, so a low-

Of the four color phases of black bear—black, brown, blue and white—the white Kermode bear is the rarest. Found only in the Queen Charlotte Islands along British Columbia's northwest coast, it's pure white but has black eyes, nose and claws, definitely not an albino. This one, shown in the museum diorama for which it was harvested, is one of very few ever taken; the bears are totally protected.

powered scope with good light-gathering potential makes sense. It makes sense, too, to use a powerful cartridge, since there will usually be time for just one shot. Again, anything in the deer rifle class from .270 up is fine. My personal favorite for this kind of thing is the old .358 Winchester with a 250-grain Barnes bullet—pure dynamite on bears of any size. Newer cartridges of that ilk, such as the .375 Winchester, .356 Winchester, or .444 Marlin are tops. The old .45-70 is hard to beat, too.

Hound hunting moves things closer still. Scopes aren't essential, but a gun that's light enough to pack during a mad chase is! Powerful handguns are perfectly at home provided the bullet will penetrate and the shooter can be absolutely certain of shot placement. A .41 Magnum is a good minimum, with the powerful single-shot handguns also at home. The bottom line is that the bear must be dead when it hits the ground, and whatever it takes in your hands to accomplish that is what should be used. Some of the best close-range black bear guns aren't around anymore. The .348 Winchester and the .350 Remington were superb. They're gone, and the .358 nearly so, excepting Browning's excellent lever action. But fast-handling carbines in such chamberings as .444 Marlin and .356 and .375 Winchester are ideal.

Calling is a whole 'nother can of worms, since the bear will be adrenalized and he'll be coming your way. I'd suggest the .30-06 as a sensible minimum, and if you shoot a bigger gun well, go for it.

A well-furred black bear is one of our greatest game animals. He's common enough that you can hunt him annually without breaking the bank or feeling guilty about it, and he's good eating as well as a great trophy. I don't think I'm really afraid of bears, but my palms sweat and I have to work to control my breathing when I see one. Any bear provides a special kind of excitement and it really doesn't matter where or by what method you hunt them.

Chapter 10
The Hump-Backed Bears

If we tend to treat black bears with less respect than their track record might deserve, then the opposite is true of their larger cousins, the grizzly and the Alaskan brown bear. No other animal on this continent commands as much respect and out-and-out fear as the great hump-backed bears of the North. Perhaps that's just as well, for these bears are without question among the world's most dangerous game, and this continent's only consistently dangerous game. Smart, tough, strong, plenty big, and with the courage and tenacity to carry a charge through to the finish, these bears mean business, and the hunter who underestimates them or takes the hunting of them lightly is bucking the Fates.

Yet they are among our most majestic animals, a beautiful symbol of wild freedom and one of the most desirable trophy animals. If a survey of American hunters were to rate game animals, I suspect the grizzly and/or Alaskan brown bear would come out on top. There would be some votes for the whitetail deer, a few for the elk, and perhaps some for the sheep but I'd bet money on the grizzly.

The Grizzly

Grizzlies are fascinating to hunters. They are in many ways the ultimate symbol of untamed wilderness, one of few animals that has made no concessions to civilization. And even though most grizzly hunts are

Alaskan Brown Bear

Grizzly Bear

GRIZZLY/BROWN BEAR RANGE

completed without incident, the unquestionable element of danger adds a compelling spice to the hunt.

Sadly, because of the very independence that we respect them for, the grizzly is an anachronism in any but the most remote wilderness. Even in the few parks with grizzly populations there is a periodic hue and cry for the termination of the great bears' lease. Usually this is brought about by the grizzly-caused death of some visitor to the park. The culprit bear, who was, after all, only being a bear, is hunted down and dispatched, and the outcry dies away until the next time.

Unfortunately for the bears, there will be a next time, for grizzlies can't help being grizzlies, and it seems that people, being people, will insist on crowding into their domain. The great bears are secure in the northern wilderness of western Canada and Alaska, at least for the forseeable future, but in the Lower 48 their very existence is precarious at best. That's sad, but it's the nature of the great bears to be as they are—free-roaming and occasionally fierce. It has been their undoing since the days of Lewis and Clark, but I suspect that's why hunters love them so.

Taxonomically, there are two schools of thought, the "lumpers," who place the broadest range of animals possible under one species desig- nation and the "splitters," who subdivide species and subspecies based on the slightest regional deviation. In the case of the humpbacked, dish-faced bears, the "lumpers" seem to have won the day. There was a time when the grizzly and Alaskan brown bear were considered different species. Today they are both classed as *Ursus arctos*. Inciden- tally, this species of bear is now considered to extend across Siberia throughout much of northern Asia, into eastern Europe, and all the way to the Iberian Peninsula. The Old World animals are termed vari- ously as European brown bear, Russian brown bear, or just "brown bear;" the term "grizzly" is reserved for our continent but they're all subspecies of the same bear according to modern thinking.

That same current taxonomical thinking identifies just two *Ursus arctos* subspecies in North America—*U. a. horribilis* over most of North America, and *U. a. middendorffi* on Kodiak, Afognak and Shuyak Is- lands off the Alaskan coasts. In years past, numerous other subspecies have been classified, but today the thinking is that differences in size and regional pelage are primarily caused by climate and diet. Of course, the grizzly has long since vanished from so much of its original range that today it is nearly impossible to determine if the extinct California grizzly is identical to the present grizzly of British Columbia.

All that aside, hunters have long since identified two categories of great bears—the grizzly and the Alaskan brown bear. The grizzly is so named because of the pale guard hairs often found on the hump and shoulders, hence the grizzled or "silvertip" appearance. The Alaskan brown bear rarely has this pelage, but hunters distinguish him primarily because he grows much larger.

The difference in size is believed to be caused by the protein-enriched salmon diet of the coastal Alaskan bears, and also by the milder winters along the Alaskan coast and islands, compared to the winters in the interior. This last is historically consistent, as the long-gone California and plains grizzlies apparently grew to a much larger size than today's grizzlies of the North Country.

The problem for hunters, and those who keep hunters' record books, is that the Alaskan brown bear and the grizzly bear are the same species. Biologically speaking, except for the island bears, they're also the same subspecies. So any division between Alaskan brown and grizzly bears is strictly man-made; wherever the line is drawn, the bears themselves aren't aware of it. Individuals can and do wander across the line at will, classifying themselves as brown bears one moment and grizzlies the next.

However, sound justification does exist for the separate classifications, at least as far as hunters are concerned. There is a tremendous difference in both average size and maximum size between typical coastal bear populations and inland bear populations. The problem has always been where to make the division.

The Boone and Crockett Club basically follows the Canada-Alaska border in southeast Alaska northwest to the Wrangells, then follows the east-west divide of the Wrangells west, the divide of the Mentasta range north, the divide of the Alaska Range west, and finally follows the 62nd Parallel of latitude west to the Bering Sea.

The Alaska Game and Fish Department makes no attempt to establish boundaries between grizzly and brown bear populations, but their coastal game management units do run from the coast inland to the crest of the first range of mountains in most cases. In 1984, the Safari Club Record Book Committee changed their line of demarcation to include as brown bears those bears taken in Management Units 1–9 and 14–18.

Although the size difference between brown bears and grizzly bears is real, the need to draw an abitrary line along some kind of political or geographical boundary has left a couple of inconsistencies. The coastal grizzlies of northern British Columbia, for example, are salmon-feeding bears. They grow large, and bears from this region are quite prominent in the grizzly record book listings. It would be easy to call them "brown bears," but a line has to be drawn somewhere.

Another problem is the fact that *U. a. middendorffi* does exist as a

Ten-year old Brett Boutang took this beauty on Kodiak Island in the fall of '82. One shot through the neck with a 150-grain Nosler Partition from a .30-06 did the job. His father was standing by with a .375 "just in case." (Photo by Bob Boutang)

subspecies. The so-called Kodiak bear is in fact slightly different from the mainland "brown bear," and the primary difference for hunters is that his skull tends to be a bit broader. Since bears enter the book based on skull measurement, island bears have an advantage over mainland brown bears, and bears from Kodiak dominate the record book listings.

Little more than a century ago grizzly bears were common over most of North America. Their original range is believed to cover the entire continent west of the Mississippi, from Mexico to the Arctic Circle. The abundance of these great bears in Kansas, the Dakotas and even California is incomprehensible to us today, but the written record remains.

Lewis and Clark are credited with the first semi-scientific data regarding the great bears, but they were far from the first white men to view him. Those kudos probably belong to the early representative of Hudson's Bay Company. The journal of Henry Kelsey, dating from 1691, has survived the centuries and makes specific reference to a great

A fall bear hunt offers a lot of attractions besides the bear. The fishing is usually excellent, and in many areas there is fine ptarmigan shooting.

bear which was "Bigger then any white Bear & is Neither White nor Black But silver hair'd like our English Rabbit." Apparently Kelsey first encountered the grizzly on the plains of Saskatchewan.

No doubt the fur traders, both English and French, had their share of problems with plains grizzlies, and certainly the early Spanish encountered them in their conquest of the Southwest. But the detailed, scrupulously-kept diary of Meriwether Lewis is literally full of hair-raising encounters with the "white bear." Considering the arms carried on their expedition, it's amazing that none of their party was killed by bears. As Lewis put it, referring to the grizzly, "I must confess that I do not like the gentlemen and had rather fight two Indians than one bear."

Written accounts of grizzlies are fairly sketchy through the nineteenth century, but it's obvious that the mountain men had their share of troubles with grizzlies. In those days, the old saying, "sometimes you eat the bear; sometimes the bear eats you," was fairly accurate. In the case of mountain man Hugh Glass both ends of the saying were true. Though horribly bitten and clawed, Glass managed to finish a wounded grizzly with his knife. His associates, "friends" would be a questionable word, left him for dead, taking his gun, knife, and even his hunting shirt. Somehow he managed to live, eating meat from the slain bear until he regained enough strength to walk out.

After the mountain men came the settlers, hunters, soldiers and prospectors. Encounters with grizzlies were commonplace, but the bears won fewer and fewer rounds. As late as the 1850's grizzlies were incredibly abundant in what is now Los Angeles, but by the end of the Civil War the great bears were already being pushed into the more remote regions. By the 1870's grizzly encounters were more celebrated events than commonplace nuisances. George Armstrong Custer, a dedicated hunter, carefully recorded on both paper and film his first grizzly kill on his Black Hills expedition in 1874. Close to a decade later, Theodore Roosevelt also wrote about his first encounter with a grizzly.

By the turn of the century the grizzly was finished throughout most of the Lower 48, except remnant populations that hung on in the higher mountains. The last Great Plains grizzly was probably killed in North Dakota in 1897. There have been no substantiated reports of grizzlies in California since 1922, nor in New Mexico or Arizona since about 1932. The last Utah grizzly was probably the celebrated Old Ephraim, an outsized bear with a taste for sheep and a distinctive track. Frank Clark hunted him off and on from 1911 to 1923, when he finally put an end to the grand old marauder.

Today the grizzly is just a memory in most of its former range. A few are said to hang on in the remote Sierra Madres of Mexico, but their status is unknown. There are probably a handful in Colorado and Washington, and a few more in Idaho.Wyoming has a small population in and around Yellowstone Park, but in the Lower 48 only Montana has a truly viable population. The majority of the Montana bears are in Glacier Park and the Bob Marshall Wilderness area. Only Montana offers limited grizzly hunting. The harvest is tightly controlled, at this writing a maximum of 25 bears per year.

Fortunately the situation is much brighter north of the U.S.-Canada line. In Canada, the grizzly's main stronghold is British Columbia and the Yukon, with populations stable at an estimated 10,000 to 14,000. The Alberta Rockies and Northwest Territories, primarily the MacKenzies, each have around a thousand grizzlies. Alaska holds about half the world population, estimated between 15,000 and 18,000 (that figure includes both grizzlies and brown bears).

The populations are stable, with hunting controlled so as to have minimal effect. In some areas careful management has resulted in increases not only in numbers but in the average size of bears taken. The real threat to the great bears, as is the case with virtualy all game species, isn't hunting, but rather loss of habitat. While the North Country is still largely wilderness, increased mineral exploration and exploitation poses a real threat to all wildlife, and particularly the non-adaptable grizzly.

For now, though, the great bears are prospering in their last strongholds, and a hunt for either grizzly or Alaskan brown bear is a possible dream. Just as their habitats have made them different, it makes the hunting of the two bears quite different.

Unless you happen to reside in grizzly country, the state and provincial laws will require that you hire a guide to hunt the big bears. Since that decision is made for you, you must decide where you will hunt, and whether you'd prefer a spring or fall hunt.

Today there are five choices for hunting grizzly: Alaska, Yukon, British Columbia, Alberta, and Montana. Northwest Territories has closed the hunting of grizzlies in the MacKenzie Mountains. For nonresidents, Montana would be a poor choice. The bears aren't large, and the season is subject to closure when the harvest quota is reached.

Although some outfitters do well, especially on grizzly-only hunts, the Yukon is generally a poor place to hunt specifically for bear. Of 272 grizzlies listed in the B&C book, only four are from the Yukon. Obviously the chances for a big bear aren't good. Currently the Yukon has a one-bear-per-lifetime limit.

Although Alberta's grizzly population isn't large, the province is well-represented in the record book. The grizzly season is held only in the spring, which gives the hunter an opportunity to concentrate strictly on bear hunting. The harvest is small, but Alberta has some fine outfitters who achieve good success. Black bear can normally be hunted at the same time.

The bulk of all grizzly hunting is done in Alaska and British Columbia. Both areas offer spring and fall hunting. In Alaska, most management units stipulate one grizzly or brown bear every four years. However, the populations have increased enough in some areas that a hunter may take a bear annually. British Columbia operates on a tight quota system for grizzlies, with each outfitter in control of a guiding area which is authorized a certain number of bears. The hunters are further limited to one bear every five years.

Grizzly hunts are quite expensive today. The average is around $4,500 for a 10-day hunt but some outfitters charge a good deal more than that. That's a sizeable chunk of change and it's important that hunters understand that the cost is for the opportunity to hunt the bear; there can be no guarantee of success.

The problem with grizzly hunting is that the animals are thinly spread over a vast region. Some areas have a lot more than others, but nowhere are grizzly bears particularly common. They're wanderers, especially trophy bears and to find one you can usually expect to hunt hard—very hard.

As with black bears, it's a bit of a toss-up as to whether spring hunting or fall hunting is best. It depends a lot on the area, the outfitter, and the weather in that particular year. Baiting is basically illegal for grizzlies, as is the use of dogs.

In the spring, hunting for mountain grizzly, you'll hunt high up in lovely alpine country. You'll glass endless successions of rockslides and greening meadows, and eventually you'll see some bears. In the fall you'll probably hunt a bit farther down. If you're in an area such as coastal British Columbia, where the bears have a fall salmon run, you may have an advantage in the autumn. Then you'll hunt along the streams, and instead of glassing up your bear at a thousand yards, you just might run into him at spitting distance.

Grizzly tracks are distinctive, with long claw marks—absent in black bears—ahead of the pads. A fresh track along a streambed is enough to send chills up any hunter's spine.

I think spring is the better time to hunt grizzly, with the exception of areas with salmon runs. It's not that the hunting is any better, but rather that there is nothing else to hunt, so you concentrate totally on the bear.

As with black bears, spring grizzlies are hungry and are usually on the move during daylight hours, constantly foraging. You'll often see huge excavations in a hillside where grizzlies have thrown aside mounds of dirt and rocks as they attempt to dig up bite-sized marmots and parka squirrels. Fall bears are less concentrated and less dependable, but berry patches are bear magnets.

If a grizzly is the main object of a hunt, then book a hunt specifically for that animal, whether fall or spring. A sensible minimum is 10 days, but 14 is better. Weather will usually preclude hunting for a few days on virtually any North Country hunt, and good grizzlies are just plain hard to find!

Although my preference is spring hunting, there is a great risk of

They say grizzly hunting is a sport for real he-men, but Connie Brooks of Barnes Bullets didn't believe it. This excellent grizzly came from Alaska's Talkeetna Mountains in the fall of '83. Squaring eight feet, it was taken with a fiberglass-stocked .375 H&H. (Photo by Connie Brooks)

scheduling a hunt before the bears come out, or before the thaw will permit access to grizzly country. I made a grizzly hunt into southern British Columbia about 10 years ago. It was late May, theoretically perfect timing. But there had been a record snowfall that year, and the high country was literally choked with deep snow.

We were eight days into a 10-day hunt before we finally staggered into the valley we had come to hunt. The horses had been left behind miles before; the snow was too deep for them. For us, it was the kind of crusted snow that would almost hold you, but just when you shifted your weight to the forward foot you would sink in to mid-thigh.

This valley was in the form of a huge bowl with several likely-looking rockslides and a good southern exposure where a bit of new growth was showing through. We had come as far as we could, so we glassed that bowl the whole day, and the next, fighting our way downtrail to camp just at dark. Late in the afternoon of the second day we saw two bears, but they were way too far off to attempt a stalk that late in the day.

We stepped into the valley about 10:00 a.m. of my last day. By now I knew every tree stump and boulder on the hillsides, but I saw one I didn't recognize. It was a nice silvertip grizzly, sitting up like a big dog, and it was a good 800 yards straight up a steep snowslide. My guide's back was giving him pain, the going was murder. I went up after the bear alone, and managed to get him with a longish shot. As I recall, there were very few bears taken in all of B.C. that spring. The bulk of them weren't out at all until after the season ended. Mine wasn't a big bear, but it was beautifully furred, and to this day I think I value that hide more than any other North American trophy.

There was a lot of luck involved in getting that bear, but also a lot of hard work and a guide who wouldn't quit. It generally takes all three to get a grizzly today. Very few outfitters can honestly say they approach 100 percent success on grizzlies, but 75 percent is damned good, and 50 percent quite respectable. There are some North American animals that, if you're in shape, shoot well, and hunt in a good area with or without a good outfitter, you should expect to obtain a representative specimen of. The grizzly isn't one of them. They're there, but all you can do is try your best, and enjoy the experience—there's no guarantee of success.

There aren't any real hotspots for grizzlies, though some places are better than others. Alaska's Copper River country is traditionally good, as are the upper reaches of the Kuskokwim. The Seward Peninsula is getting better all the time, and although northern Alaska has not been noted for big bears, a couple of outfitters have been pulling out some beauties. Much of northern B.C. is good. Bella Coola is justly famed for big, salmon-eating grizzlies, but virtually all of the Cassiars have a good grizzly population.

Alaskan Brown Bear

Brown bear hunting is a whole different kettle of fish. Obviously their domain has been decreed to be very limited. A hunter in search of a brown bear must hunt southern Alaska or one of the islands. These coastal bears have a much better diet and a much easier life than inland bears, and their populations are much more concentrated. Yes, it's certainly possible to get "skunked out" on a brown bear hunt—nobody can control the weather, or a hunter's physical abilities. But that would be the exception rather than a normal occurrence. Brown bear hunting is far more successful than grizzly hunting, period.

Once again a choice must be made between fall and spring hunting, and there are other regulatory considerations as well. The Alaskan

The Alaskan Peninsula has long been famous for producing the very largest bears, although Kodiak Island bears tend to have slightly larger skulls. This monster was taken near Moller Bay on the Bering Sea side of the Alaskan Peninsula in fall 1981. Since then a couple of bigger bears have come out of the same area.

Peninsula, for example is open only every other year. It will be open in the fall of 1985 and the spring of 1986, but not again until the fall of 1987. In other units, such as Unimak Island at the tip of the Peninsula, a hunter must compete in a public drawing for limited permits. On Kodiak, each outfitter has an exclusive guide area, and is allocated a certain number of bears per season. In some cases it may be only two, but he can allocate those permits to hunters as he sees fit.

The success varies little from fall to spring. Most brown bear outfitters hit at least 75 percent, and some do much better than that year in and year out. However, the hunting is vastly different from spring to fall. In the spring the bears are higher; you'll glass them on the ridges as they look for new growth. You probably won't see as many bears, since many of the females are still denned up with their young. But a bear you do see at long range has a bit better chance to be a shootable trophy when you get close enough to make sure. Physically, it's often a tougher hunt in the spring.

In the fall you'll try to hunt during the salmon run, and you'll spend your time lower down, glassing streams and rivers from a high vantage point, or glassing the surrounding slopes. You may spend time easing along narrow salmon streams, and you might well have a close encounter of the bear kind.

Brown bear country is different from grizzly country. It's generally much lower, but the hills are rugged and there will often be snow, good for tracking but tough going. Much of it is waterlogged, with innumerable streams to cross and valleys of miserable tundra tussocks. Then there are the alders, rarely more than 10 feet tall, but too dense to offer 10 feet of visibility. They're favorite lying-up haunts for brown bear, and they're exactly where you hope you never meet one.

I was stumbling along with my guide on the first day on the Peninsula when we entered my first patch of alders. I was close behind him, as is my custom, and as the trees closed around us Slim stopped me. "Keep some distance between us, so the other can react if one of us gets jumped," he whispered. It's tense stuff, especially if you're on the tracks of a big brownie, or you've just passed a bear's fishing hole and there on the bank is a fresh salmon, still flopping but with broad clawmarks striping its belly.

Virtually all of the brown bear's domain offers good hunting, but of course some areas, and some outfitters, are better than others. In terms of pure body size, the central and southern portions of the Alaskan Peninsula are probably the best. In the old days, when the taxonomic "splitters" held sway (before the "lumpers" took over), the Peninsular bear was considered a separate subspecies based on his size. For a time this bear was accepted as *Ursus gyas*, the giant bear, while the Kodiak

Island bear was termed *Ursus middendorffi*. Now both are lumped under *Ursus arctos*, with the Kodiak bear *U. a. middendorffi* and the *gyas* dropped altogether. It's interesting that well before 1920 the largest bears were recognized as coming from the Peninsula, and the same holds true today especially with the every-other-year management now in effect.

That relates strictly to body size. In terms of record book entries, it's Kodiak Island all the way. I'm also not trying to imply that Kodiak bears, or southeast Alaska bears, are small; no mature brownie is *small*! But the Peninsula does offer a bit better odds for a huge bear. Kodiak also has some very large bears, and in actuality the *average* size from both areas is about the same. Southeast Alaska offers excellent bear hunting, but the average size is a bit smaller than on Kodiak or the Peninsula.

When it comes to brown bears, I like the fall hunt. I think the odds of taking a good trophy are about equal, but in most cases brown bear hunting doesn't require the same intensity of effort as grizzly hunting. And in the fall, a lot of other things are going on in brown bear country. On the Peninsula there's excellent caribou hunting, and on Kodiak the Sitka blacktail hunting is fantastic. In Southeast Alaska there's exceptional mountain goat hunting, plus black bears and in some areas glacier bears. But even if the cost of a multi-species hunt goes above the budget, there's great fishing, plus waterfowl and ptarmigan shooting.

The springtime has its own fascination, too. It's a time of year when you can literally watch the snows recede and the new grass come up, and the days will lengthen dramatically during your stay.

Brown bear hunting is generally a bit more costly than grizzly hunting, partly, I suppose, because of the laws of supply and demand, and partly because it's phenomenally expensive for an Alaskan outfitter to equip and run a camp. Most hunts are for 10 days, and a good average figure is about $6,500.

When discussing trophy size of brown bears or grizzlies, it's difficult to establish any parameters. As with black bears, there are tremendous size variations among individuals, and one must also consider a prime pelt as a key factor in determining trophy quality.

Grizzlies are substantially smaller than Alaskan brown bears, but also substantially larger than black bears. Weights are difficult to establish since scales are rarely available. However, about 800 pounds seems to be the maximum outside weight for a really large grizzly. Such a bear would probably have a hide that squared nine feet, and that is one huge grizzly bear. Also an unrealistic goal for a hunter.

Most grizzly hunters try to find a bear that will square eight feet.

Hunting the big bears is largely a matter of glassing—high on the slopes in the spring, and lower along the salmon streams in the fall. With snow, a bear can be tracked, but it's better to get a look at the bear before shooting.

That's also a very large grizzly in most areas, and such a bear should weigh around 600 pounds. Most grizzlies taken today probably square about seven feet. And if the hide is good and the animal well-taken, that's a fine trophy. Grizzlies squaring eight feet are possible in most grizzly areas, excluding the tundra grizzlies of the northernmost areas, and nine-footers are certainly taken every now and again but you might have to look for a long time.

Brown bears have the potential to be at least a third larger than grizzlies. The brown bear hunter's Holy Grail is a bear whose hide will square 10 feet, but that's a most unusual bear today. A nine-footer is quite good, and many hunters settle quite happily for a bear that squares under eight feet. In a recent spring season on the Alaskan Peninsula, of 150 bears taken the average squared hide for males was 7.9 feet, the average age seven years. In the same season the averages were about the same on Kodiak. No doubt there were a few 10-foot-plus bears thrown into the average, but that gives some idea of the realistic expectations. A mature male brown bear that squares an honest 10 feet should weigh close to 1,200 pounds if he's in good shape, and that's a lot of bear.

Though considered a "typical" bear pose, it's actually unusual to see a big bear stand on his back legs. They aren't menacing in this pose; actually they're quite unbalanced and fairly helpless. They'll stand up to get the wind better or locate other bears. (Photo by William D. Phifer)

Judging grizzlies and brown bears is even more difficult than with black bears. One doesn't often see enough of them to gain any level of skill, and they're usually hunted in unfamiliar country where it's difficult to judge size relations. Again, look for the feeling of power that a mature male bear conveys. A big bear will never look "leggy," but will appear ponderous and bowlegged. A fellow told me to look for a bear with a small head. The reasoning went like this: They've *all* got big heads. If you find one whose head looks small, the body must be huge." I don't know if that holds true or not, but it's worth considering.

I don't know how the experienced guides can accurately judge bears, but they can do it. It was very early in a hunt on the Alaskan Peninsula when my guide and I glassed a bear about 1,000 yards off, peacefully working his way up a ridge. It was good bear country, and the one thing a friend who had hunted this area before advised was not to be in a hurry to shoot a bear. So I was acting nonchalant while Slim stripped off his pack and prepared for an end run to head off the bear. He looked up and said, "We'd best get after him." So I asked him if he thought the bear was big enough.

I guess Slim thought so. "Man, that's at least a 10-foot bear. Let's go!" he snapped.

That put me in a hurry, too. Slim was close; the bear squared 10'8"x11'2". I've seen quite a few bears, and I can (I think) reliably tell a big one from a little one, but I honestly don't know how those guys can put fairly accurate squared-hide figures on a live bear at a distance. They can, though. Find an honest guide and trust his judgement.

When it comes to rifles and cartridges for the big bears, there isn't a lot of argument. Most hunters are in agreement that the best gun is the biggest you can shoot well. That's true enough, but the hunting of the two bears is different enough that the ideal grizzly rifle may not be the ideal brown bear rifle.

In either case, the .30-06 or the 7mm magnums are the absolute minimum, but I feel they're on the light side. For grizzly hunting in the

Horseback grizzly (or brown bear) hunts are uncommon in Alaska, but are the method of choice in Alberta, British Columbia and Yukon. From the back of a horse is a fine way to see the country, and you often have to see a lot of it to find a hump-backed bear! (Photo by Bob Tatsch)

mountains, you do need a gun/load that will put down the largest possible grizzly, but you also need a rifle that will reach out a bit. It isn't wise to take a particularly long shot at a big bear, but shots from 200 to 250 yards are occasionally all that are offered. For this kind of work the .300 Magnums with good 200-grain bullets are fine, and the .338 Winchester or .340 Weatherby Magnums are even better. A low-powered scope, no more than 4X, or a low-range variable such as 1¾-5X, makes a nice rig.

The ranges are a bit closer for brown bears, and the bears can run a good deal larger. The cover is generally thicker and there is a much greater likelihood of a close-range confrontation. I'll leave the minimums the same, but personally I'd not care to hunt brown bear with anything less than a .338 or .340. The scope requirements are the same, but a detachable mount with auxiliary iron sights makes sense in the event you have to follow up a wounded bear in the alders.

You might note that I haven't mentioned one of the all-time great bear

Veteran hunter Jack Atcheson Sr. took this exceptional grizzly on British Columbia Stikine River in 1982. Easily meeting the Boone and Crockett minimum, this bear was 23 years old and squared 9'3"—but look at those claws! It wasn't all that easy: in 10 days of hard hunting Atcheson saw a total of one bear—this one! (Photo by Jack Atcheson Sr.)

rifles, the .375 H&H. That has been my personal choice, and I don't see any reason to switch. It has the trajectory to connect easily from a long distance and it offers the stopping power up close. I would have expected it to be the odds-on guide's choice as a backup rifle. It might be, considering the North Country as a whole. But it's worthwhile mentioning that, in my brown bear camp on the Peninsula, every guide carried a .338 for backup, and all were pleased with the results. So take your choice, but don't skimp on the caliber. You might need all you've got.

I also haven't mentioned handguns. Now, brown bear and grizzlies have been successfully taken with handguns, and will be again. It's not my cup of tea, but there's no reason to believe that some of the modern single-shot pistols firing wildcat cartridges won't do the job. For that matter, the .44 Magnum can do the job, given perfect shot placement. However, for those who insist on carrying a handgun for "insurance," or for those who feel the .44 Magnum, definitely a potent handgun, is perfect bear medicine, let me share a statistic with you. A study was made of bear maulings in Alaska. Since records have been kept, it appears that no one who responded to a bear attack with a pistol has lived to tell about it. In some cases the bear died as well, but if a man carrying a pistol was attacked by a bear, and if he used that pistol, he died.

That doesn't mean bears haven't been taken sucessfully with handguns, of course they have. We're talking about an adrenalized bear who initiates the attack. What it tells me is to forget about packing the extra weight of an "insurance" handgun—pack a big enough rifle and carry it everywhere.

A good friend of mine was hunting on Kodiak one fall, and before getting serious about brown bear he shot a nice Sitka blacktail. He and the outfitter climbed a little knoll to glass and eat a sandwich, while a young fellow who was helping out climbed down to gather up the deer and pack it up. He didn't take a rifle, and he nearly died. A big sow with two cubs decided the meat was hers. His metal packframe saved his life. When the bear tried to bite his head the rear extension of his packframe prevented her from getting a good grip. A tooth did go into his eyesocket, and he was bitten through the thigh and arms. He survived and kept his eye. He also kept some of the scars. In a letter about a year after the incident, he mentioned that he was getting a .375 and, like the American Express card, wasn't planning to leave home without it.

Chapter 11
Arctic Game

No game is found on the north polar cap itself, likewise with the southern polar region. However, the sub-polar northern region, from the Arctic Circle to Ellesmere Island, a mere 500 miles from the true North Pole and somewhat north of the magnetic north pole, teems with wildlife, including several unique big game species. Strangely, the very similar regions of Antarctica are rich in bird life, but devoid of the large mammals found in the northern hemisphere.

The Arctic region is a barren, desolate land, but considering the nature of the climate and the terrain, our Far North is amazingly rich in game. Alaska's entire Brooks Range lies well above the Arctic Circle, and of course that mountain range is home to a large number of Dall sheep, some grizzly, and quite a few moose. Many of North America's great caribou herds summer well above the Arctic Circle along the northern coasts of Alaska and Canada, and some never migrate below that magic parallel.

Just three big game species inhabit the high Arctic, although any animals at all seem like a lot once you've seen the country! They are the polar bear, the muskox, and the walrus. Also confined to the northern region is the small Peary caribou subspecies of Canada's offshore islands. Although not considered trophy game, seals are an important food source throughout this region, and are eagerly hunted by man and polar bear alike. Wolves are widely distributed on the mainland north of the Arctic Circle and are found on some islands. Arctic

The Arctic is a lonely place, beautiful in its way but also deadly for the outsider. On a calm day, there is total absence of sound. On a windy day, presence of *all* sound.

foxes and hares, ptarmigan, and a few other small mammals and quite a few birds round out the fauna of the Arctic.

Hunting in the Arctic is primarily a "good news and bad news" situation, and has been for the past decade or so. The premier game animal is the great white bear, *Ursus maritimus maritimus*, and its populations are in good shape. The Marine Mammal Protection Act of 1972 has prevented polar bear hunting in Alaska and has prohibited Americans hunting the bear elsewhere, from bringing back the skins. The walrus is also covered by the MMPA. The good news is that the muskox has been brought back from the brink of extinction and is today more available to the sportsman than ever before. The Arctic is a fascinating region, and its game has a unique way of captivating the imagination.

Polar Bear

The polar bear is without question one of the most magnificent creatures on the globe. He is perfectly adapted to his environment, an environment in which, even today, man is at best an unwelcome guest faced with a struggle for survival not dissimilar from that of the bear. The great white bear is very possibly the only large mammal on Earth that has never learned to fear man, but instead continues to view him as a prey species; another meal in a world in which every other creature is a source of protein.

The polar bear is not exclusively a North American animal. Its range extends across the entire northern polar region, and in years past he has been hunted in the northern portions of the Soviet Union, Norway, Canada, Alaska and Greenland.

The polar bear is a very large bear, and it can be argued endlessly which is the larger—the polar or Alaskan brown bear. The polar bear is much rangier and more streamlined, adapted to his semiaquatic environment. His skull is narrower than that of the brown bear, hence the record book minimums totalling length and width are smaller for polar bear than for brown bear.

Regardless of skull measurements, the trophy hunter's yardstick—the squared hide—is about the same for the two bears. In the heyday of Alaskan hunting, a hunter could hold out for a 10-foot polar bear with a reasonable hope of finding one. Today, though, with the limited ground (ice, actually) that can be covered by dogsled, a hunter can't be quite that selective. A few 10-footers have been taken, but a hunter who turns down an eight-foot bear should have his sanity questioned.

Over the years most polar bear hunting has been done for skins, either for the market or subsistence hunting by native peoples. Sport hunting has never been a significant portion of the polar bear harvest. However, sport hunting of polar bears was popular, particularly in Alaska, through the Fifties and Sixties. The problem was that unchecked hunting for hides, particularly in the Soviet Union, started the hue and cry that we were running out of polar bears on a global basis. In 1955 Russia banned all hunting of polar bears. Although their own bear populations was in serious trouble, there was no hard scientific evidence that anyone else's polar bear populations were depleted.

In 1965 the first international convention on the status of polar bears was held in Fairbanks. Even at that meeting the only "experts" who thought the polar bear was in trouble were the Russians. The peak polar bear harvest was about 1965, when a total of some 300 bears were

Polar Bear

Walrus

WALRUS AND POLAR BEAR RANGE

taken in Alaska by sportsmen and subsistence hunters alike. In the same year Canada's harvest was about 600, all by Inuit (Eskimo) hunters. Norway's harvest was about 325, with about 20 of those taken by sportsmen. Greenland's harvest was probably close to 100. With the Marine Mammal Protection Act of 1972, sport hunting is virtually non-existant today, but subsistence hunting continues nearly unchecked.

Is the polar bear really in trouble today? Probably not. In the vastness of the Arctic, bear numbers are impossible to judge accurately, but conservative estimates place the population at about 20,000, certainly enough to justify limited sport hunting especially considering the revenue that a polar bear hunt can generate.

In Norway, most of the polar bear hunting was done from boats. As a youngster I recall seeing brochures from booking agents that advertised such hunts. The costs were certainly far less than Alaskan polar

It may well be a toss-up as to which is larger, the polar bear or the Alaskan brown. The polar bear is much more streamlined, probably due to adaptation to life in a semiaquatic environment. However, the two are very closely related; they can mate and the offspring will not be sterile! (Photo by Leonard Lee Rue IV)

bear hunts from the same period. However, since the boats were limited to the very edges of the pack ice, selective hunting was not possible—if you wanted a bear, you took what was available.

Alaska was the real center of sport hunting for polar bears, and in the "good old days" it was accomplished with the aid of the airplane. Working in pairs for safety, two ski-mounted planes searched the ice for fresh tracks or, better yet, a bear. Most of the hunting was in late winter or early spring before the breakup, and the idea was to find a bear, determine his course, land the plane on the ice and intercept him.

However, it wasn't that easy. Weather played a big factor; just being out there over the ice was dangerous, and landing the plane tremendously risky. Every polar bear guide who survived—and some didn't—has a tale of losing a plane on the ice, of leads (open rivers in the ice pack) that opened up, and of storms that closed in while they were flying somewhere between the U.S. and Russia.

Currents and winds create leads—open rivers in the pack ice. These leads are followed by the Inuits and Eskimos for hunting seals, and they're followed by the polar bears as well. Once a seal is shot, tiny sled-carried boats are used to retrieve. It's a deadly business. A man wouldn't last five minutes in the near-freezing water.

Lee Holen, one of the best-known of the old-time polar bear guides and the best pilot I've ever flown with, once lost a plane way out on the ice pack. He and his client, apparently a fairly tough gent himself, waited a couple of days for help, but none came. Lee saw search planes on the horizon, but saved his flare for fear it couldn't be seen. He's still kicking himself, for he later discovered that type of flare was visible for miles. But he didn't know that, so he saved it for a plane he was sure could see it. That plane never arrived. He and his client, without food or proper gear, *walked* back to the Alaskan coast. They arrived several days after they'd been given up as lost.

Of course, once the plane was landed the encounter with the bear differed little from the traditional hunt of the Eskimo or Inuit peoples, except for the more powerful rifle of the sportsmen as opposed to the Eskimo's traditional .222 or .30-30. Close calls were common, and serious frostbite part of the game.

It is unlikely that the airplane hunting will ever return but it did offer a great advantage. It's probably the only polar bear hunting technique that allows the hunter to be truly selective, taking only the older, trophy-size bears. The pack ice is simply too vast for the dogsled hunter to be as selective, and in any case the largest bears are generally not found as close to land as the younger bears and the sows.

The only sport hunting for polar bears currently available is Canada's limited permit dogsled hunts, conducted by several Inuit villages along Canada's north coast and offshore islands. This is a relatively new program, in effect since the late Seventies. Subsistence hunting continues and has always been authorized, but the Inuit peoples and the Canadian government felt that a "cottage industry" could be built around sport hunts for polar bear, conducted in the traditional manner.

American hunters cannot legally import polar bear hides into the U.S. even though they are legally taken in Canada. The Safari Club International and other sportsmen's groups have been fighting hard against this unfair legislation, and I suspect will win eventually. But in the meantime the interest in polar bear hunting seems undeterred. Canada is offering few permits, perhaps two dozen annually, and the prices for the hunts are high, in 1985 about $12,000 to $14,000. There's a waiting list of a couple of years for the permits in the best areas.

This is probably the most physically demanding hunt in the world today. Using dog teams to carry a camp and supplies, most hunts are at least of 14 days duration out on the ice, where temperatures will average far below zero and wind chill is life-threatening.

In February and March, the prime months, daylight is short and hours spent in tents out on the ice are long. The polar bear's prime food source is the ringed seal, and the hunters follow open leads

The Arctic nights are very long, 18 hours or more on some polar bear or muskox hunts. During that time the tent is home and it's a great deal more pleasant inside than outside. Drinking water is obtained by melting ice.

containing known seal concentrations. With luck, fresh tracks are spotted and followed until the bear is found.

The hunting is quite successful on the whole, but depends somewhat on the ice conditions from year to year. A few villages have achieved 100 percent success for their sport hunters, but 60 to 75 percent is closer to the average.

What does the future hold? Who knows? Eventually I believe Americans will be able to bring in legally-taken Canadian polar bear trophies, but I'm not certain whether we'll see sport hunting in Alaska anytime soon. Right now it's a political ballgame, with the native peoples wanting unlimited subsistence hunting and total control over sport hunting. The non-native resident Alaskans want the right to sport hunt polar bears, and the outfitting industry wants the right to guide nonresident hunters. These groups must reach a mutual understanding before polar bear hunting can return to Alaska. If it does return, it's a sure thing that it will return without the airplane, and that in itself is a problem. Unlike northern Canada's more protected waters, the Bering Sea is rougher and more treacherous, more subject to leads opening and

A gruelling dogsled hunt onto the pack ice in Canada's Far North is the only way to obtain a polar bear today. The hunts are quite successful, but probably the most physically demanding hunts on Earth. (Photo courtesy Canada North Outfitting)

more subject to storms. Dogsled hunts, dangerous enough anyway, will be more dangerous in Alaska, and it will be even more difficult to reach the really large bears. But I hope it happens, for that's one hunt I'd like to make but not until I can legally have the rug in front of my fireplace.

Walrus

Sad as the situation is with the polar bear, it's even worse with the walrus. This huge marine mammal has been a mainstay of the Eskimo for centuries, and was (and is) hunted for tusks, meat and blubber. In recent decades sport hunting had a limited popularity off Alaska's coastline, but, as with the polar bear, it was never a significant part of the harvest. Hunting in Alaska was curtailed in 1972 under the same MMPA that eliminated polar bear hunting, but limited hunting was

One of the real tricks to walrus hunting is to anchor a big bull with one shot. They weigh over a ton and a body shot is almost certain to allow the animal to get in the water and be lost. Head shots with heavy rifles—often .458s—were standard, but from a bobbing skin boat tough to make. (Photo by Leonard Lee Rue III)

again conducted in 1977-79. It is possible that walrus hunting will open again in Alaska, but the problems are essentially the same as with polar bear and must be solved first.

The walrus is a huge animal, ungainly and clumsy on land but extremely agile in the water. A big bull may weigh a ton and a half, and grows magnificent tusks up to 40 inches long and 10 to 13 inches in diameter. The walrus ranges from Greenland's coast across Canada's northern waters to the Bering Sea. The Boone and Crockett book actually recognizes two walrus subspecies, the Atlantic walrus (*Odobenus rosmarus rosmarus*) off Greenland and Canada, and the Pacific walrus (*Odobenus rosmarus divergens*) off the Alaskan coast.

A serious sportsmen might well ask the question, "Why would anyone want to shoot a walrus?" On the surface that's a good question, but actually it is, or was, a very interesting hunt. Usually conducted in the late spring after the breakup, the hunters ventured out into the

Bering Sea in traditional skin boats. St. Lawrence Island and Little Diomede Island were favored spots. Walrus would be located on ice floes or rocky islands where they had climbed out of the water to rest, and if a suitable bull was found the hunter had to make a head shot or other instant kill. A wounded walrus would get into the water and surely be lost. Every hunter I've spoken to who made such a hunt had the same comment, "It sounded crazy, but it turned out to be interesting, exciting, and well worth doing."

What are the chances of doing it again? As with polar bear, who knows? At one time walrus populations were badly depleted, but the Pacific population now numbers over a quarter of a million, and the Atlantic walrus has also recovered to some degree. A huntable surplus does exist, and as long as that's a fact there's room for hope. The most positive note is that Canada's Inuit peoples are interested in, and are lobbying for, limited permit sport hunting for walrus on the same basis

This outstanding Pacific walrus was taken by C. J. McElroy, Chairman of the Board of Safari Club International, prior to the Marine Mammal Act which closed walrus hunting. (Photo by C.J. McElroy)

that their polar bear and muskox hunts are being conducted. If that happens, it will be the first time the Atlantic walrus has ever been available to sportsmen. But unless the law changes, Americans would be prohibited from bringing home their trophies.

Muskox

The only real bright spot on the northern horizon is the muskox, and that unique North American animal is now more available to hunters than ever before. The muskox were hunted by the early Arctic explorers around the turn of the century, but were virtually unavailable to hunters for nearly 50 years. A quick look at the Boone and Crockett muskox listings is fascinating. A few heads from the 1890's and 1900's are still listed; Admiral Peary took two in Greenland for the American Museum of Natural History in 1909. That is virtually the end of the listings until the mid-Seventies! In the ensuing 50-odd years a very few were taken in Greenland, but obtaining a permit was a Herculean task requiring much political influence.

In 1935 and 1936 some muskoxen from Greenland were introduced on Alaska's Nunivak Island. They flourished there, and have in turn provided transplants to several other sites. In the mid-Seventies, hunting was opened on Nunivak on a limited-permit basis, and that's where the record book listings pick up again. Today permits are still available in Alaska on a drawing basis, and the hunting is extremely successful.

More recently, around 1980, Canada's Northwest Territories began offering muskox hunts from Inuit villages on Victoria Island, Banks Island, and later in the eastern Arctic. The Canadian permits are limited in number, but are on a first-come, first-served basis. Canadian muskox hunts average around $4,400 at this writing. Like the polar bear hunts, everything required to survive in the Arctic is supplied, including the traditional caribou-skin mukluks, parka, trousers and mittens. The Canadian heads seem to average a bit larger than those from Nunivak, and the muskox record book listings are literally being rewritten after remaining static for so many decades.

The muskox is a unique animal. His Latin name, *Ovibos moschatus*, means musky sheep-ox. While similar to the bison in appearance, he has some characteristics similar to the sheep and goat family. These include hooves that are well-adapted to climbing in his rugged, often rocky habitat, and also the layer of fine wool underneath his coarse, shaggy coat. This wool, *quiviut* to the Inuits, was prized for knitting in earlier times. The "musk" portion of the name comes from preorbital

Muskox

Muskox (introduced)

MUSKOX RANGE

scent glands just under the eyes; a muskox may rub these glands with a foreleg when under stress, releasing a strong musk odor.

Although a fairly large animal, the muskox's incredibly shaggy coat—with hair as long as 24 inches—makes him seem much larger than he actually is. Six hundred to 700 pounds is about right for a mature bull, less than half the weight of a bull bison. The horns are quite fascinating, growing out of the skull with a thick boss, coming straight down along the skull, and turning sharply up at the tips. Both males and females have horns, and the females' horns can equal the males in length but they won't grow the bull's massive boss. Both the Safari Club and Boone and Crockett systems measure the boss and length of horn, but the B&C system also takes into account circumference at the horns' quarter, minus deductions for lack of symmetry.

Taxonomy of the muskox is in some dispute, both for the scientists and the hunters. Formerly the Boone and Crockett book recognized two categories for muskox—the Barren Ground subspecies (*Ovibos moschatus moschatus*) from Canada and the Greenland subspecies (*O. m. wardi*) from the high Arctic and Greenland. In 1977 the two categories were lumped together. The Safari Club record book still has both categories. The scientists originally identified both these subspecies, plus a third, *O. m. niphoecus*, the Hudson's Bay muskox. This last subspecies is no longer recognized by most authorities, and the *wardi* subspecies is questioned. However, the Nunivak muskox are of pure Greenland stock, and they are definitely slightly smaller.

The muskox were market-hunted close to extinction by the turn of the century, but their comeback has been remarkable. As late as 1978, 25,000 was the total world population, but today Canada believes its own population to be as high as 50,000. The limited polar bear hunting may be well beyond the means of most of us, and walrus hunting may or may not be available again, but muskox hunting is exceedingly available, and offers an excellent taste of the Arctic region.

After just one just muskox hunt I'm hardly an expert on the species, and I'm unlikely to become one; it was a great hunt, but I doubt if I'll do it again. Its chief value was in seeing the country and hunting with the Inuits and listening to their stories of polar bear hunting and close calls in their harsh land. The muskox is a fascinating animal, and the mounted head of the bull I shot is perhaps the most striking trophy I own. The backskin, with silky hair over two feet long, makes a great bedspread. But the muskox is certainly not the most difficult animal to find or to stalk and shoot.

A couple of things worth noting, though. The classic muskox defensive circle does exist; it's their traditional defense against their only traditional enemy, the wolf. But it's not a static circle. The way it actually works is for them to form the circle when endangered, but from that circle individual animals charge the threat, then retreat.

It seems to be the widely held opinion that muskox form their circle when pressured by men, and all that's required is to walk up and shoot one. That can happen, but as muskox get more and more hunter-educated, they're using their feet and running more. They *can* run, and they can also climb extremely well in those wind-swept icy hills.

I found judging trophy quality to be a real problem as well. It's quite easy to tell the bulls from the cows, as the boss really stands out. But making a truly accurate qualitative judgement is beyond me. Case in point—I agonized over the decision as to whether or not to shoot the bull that I did take for some time. The Inuits are good hunters, but at that time trophy judgement was new to them—*omingmak*, as he is known, is historically just a source of meat and *quiviut*. The guides are now a lot better at trophy judging, but at that time all that my guides could tell me was that it was a nice bull. I already knew that, but I wanted an opinion as to whether I could do better.

Muskox are well-adapted to climbing and running in their rugged habitat. Their defensive circle, traditional against wolves, is becoming more uncommon as a defense against hunters.

Taken on Victoria Island, one of Canada's largest northern islands, this muskox is a world record according to S.C.I.'s scoring system. Horn length is good, but the boss is exceptional.

After much indecision, I decided to pass. When John and Eddie realized I was not going to shoot, they gave me the judgement I'd been looking for. "Mebbe storm come, mebbe not see 'nother muskox. Pretty big bull." So I shot him, and after two editions he's still the world record according to the Safari Club measuring system. So I'm no great shakes at judging muskox, but I would suggest that a good, heavy boss is an extremely important part of the score, perhaps as important as length of horn.

It's a lonely, inhospitable land, surprisingly rugged and rocky, and even more surprisingly arid. The snowfall is rarely heavy, but it's plenty cold. I hunted on Victoria Island off Canada's north coast in mid-November. We left the Inuit village of Holman Island, travelling over the pack ice until we reached a range of hills that were supposed to hold muskoxen.

The days were short, half-light at 10:00 a.m., and a tiny sliver of sun at 11. By 3:30 the sun would set again, and by 4:00 p.m. it was full dark, and the Arctic nights are long and cold. The first night was dead calm, and I walked away from the tent for a distance to watch the northern lights, a sweep of color across the sky like a giant gone mad with a huge paintbrush.

The northern lights are my most vivid impression from that hunt, but there's yet another that I'll not forget. After a successful muskox hunt I went out on the ice to hunt seals and check a trapline with one of the villagers. It was a perfectly calm day, but the lead we were hunting looked treacherous and the whole affair scared me. We had shot a seal when it came up for air. It was a perfect head shot and the seal floated as it was supposed to. Isaac went back to the sled to drag up his small boat since the ice was too thin to bring the sled close to the lead. I stayed there with the little .222 Remington, a favored gun in that region, hoping for another seal to come up. After a few moments I heard a sound, sort of like the thumping of a distant train. I listened, but couldn't make it out. With a shock I realized it was my heart, not pounding frantically but just doing its normal job—rather noisily in the complete absence of sound that marks a calm day in the Arctic.

Chapter 12
The Great Cats

North American hunters may not be blessed with magnificent predators like the great cats of Africa and Asia, but we do have our big bears, ranking among the most dangerous game in the world by anyone's standards. And while we don't have the world's largest cat, the tiger, nor the second largest, the lion, we do have both the third and fourth largest of the world's cats—both significantly larger than the leopard.

These two cats are the jaguar and the mountain lion. Both occupy an incredibly broad range, spanning the Central American isthmus and thereby being simultaneously North and South American animals.

Jaguar

The jaguar, *felis onca*, is easily our least-known game species. Thought of as a creature of the deepest Amazon jungles, he is actually an adaptable cat that ranges across much of South America, savannah as well as jungle. Although the United States was always the northern fringe of jaguar habitat, historically jaguars ranged into the U.S. with some frequency. *El tigre*, as he is better known south of the U.S., is still widely distributed in Mexico and Central America, although certainly not as common as he once was.

The jaguar is the largest spotted cat, nearly twice the size of the leopard and much more stockily built. A big male may attain a weight

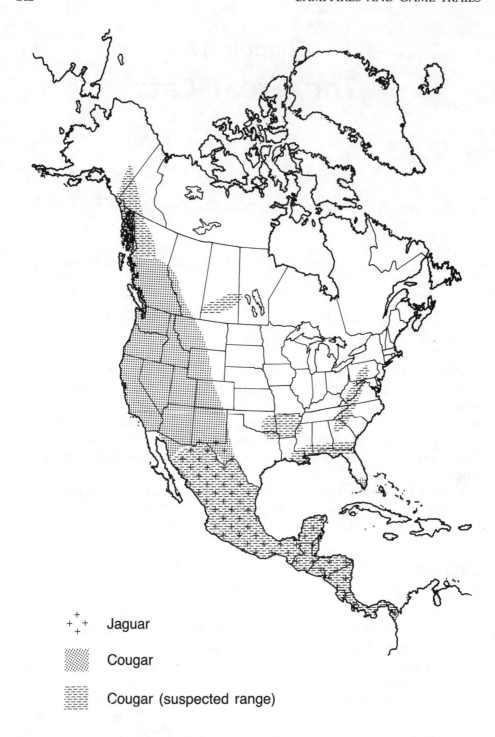

+ +
+ +   Jaguar

░░░   Cougar

▒▒▒   Cougar (suspected range)

JAGUAR AND COUGAR RANGE

of 300 pounds, perhaps 350. The blocky build is easily distinguished from the more streamlined leopard, but the rosettes on the hide are also different; the jaguar's generally a have black spot in the center, lacking on a leopard.

The U.S. Endangered Species Act of 1973 lists the jaguar as endangered, and while it is possible to hunt them today, an American may not bring the hide back into the United States regardless of whether or not the cat was legally taken in Mexico or points south. In truth, the jaguar is most certainly endangered, nonexistent would be a better term, in the United States, but he is doing quite well in the more remote regions of Mexico, and his populations are essentially the same as they always were in such countries as Belize, Honduras, and the Amazon region of Brazil, Peru and Colombia.

The leopard was similarly classified as endangered, but years of lobbying by the Safari Club International finally got the leopard downlisted from "endangered" to "threatened" in 1982, thereby allowing import of sport-hunted skins by special permit. Though it was a long fight, it was made easier by the fact that there was much scientific evidence proving that the leopard was far from endangered over much of his range. In the case of the jaguar, the governments of Central and South America have more pressing concerns than determining the status of their fauna. The jaguar issue will be tackled by hunters' groups eventually, but not much hope is given for the import of jaguar hides until the Endangered Species Act is repealed altogether—if ever.

The Boone and Crockett Club is not currently accepting entries for jaguars, but the category is still carried in *Records of North American Big Game*. Since the book is concerned strictly with North American trophies, only jaguars from the U.S. and Mexico appear therein. The Safari Club record book accepts entries for jaguars under two categories, North American and South American. Their cutoff between the two is the Panama Canal. The minimums for the South American category are much higher, recognizing that the bigger cats have always come from the interior of South America.

Although the southwestern U.S. forms the northern extremity of the jaguar's range, there were once a fair number of jaguars within our borders and it hasn't been so long ago. The jaguar received protection only recently, and the Boone and Crockett book lists several jaguars taken in the U.S. easily within living memory. One came from Big Bend, Texas in 1962, and between 1958 and 1965 five record-size cats are listed from Arizona. Chances are that these were old males, wanderers that ambled in from Mexico, but historically jaguars have been much farther north. Around the turn of the century one was killed near Fort Tejon, 60 miles north of Los Angeles, and in 1854 James

Capen Adams, "Grizzly Adams," claimed he encountered two adults with two cubs in southern Colorado.

Are there still jaguars in the U.S.? Perhaps the occasional wanderer, but probably not a resident population. They do occur in Tamaulipas, Chihuahua and Sonora, right across the border, and some of the border country in Texas, Arizona, and New Mexico is wild country.

But the hunter interested in collecting a jaguar today must look farther south, and he must do so with the understanding that he can't bring the hide back at present. He should also understand that he's letting himself in for a tough hunt, and the chances of success are very slim.

As recently as 1984 the Mexican states of Campeche, Jalisco, Nayarit, Quintana Roo, San Luis Potosi, and Sinaloa had open seasons for jaguar, generally in the late winter. However, permits are difficult to

This lovely jaguar came from a savannah region of central Mexico. Although Americans are prohibited from importing jaguars under the Endangered Species Act, the great cats are actually fairly plentiful in many areas.

obtain and good outfitters scarce. I know one man who got a fine jaguar in Jalisco on his first try, but I know several others who have tried up to five times with no luck. I'll admit that I've not hunted the jaguar. I'd dearly love to, but it's too much work and too much money for a hide that I can't bring home!

There is some good jaguar hunting in South America, primarily in Brazil and in the jungle region of Peru. Again, a shortage of competent guides and lack of good communications makes arranging a hunt difficult at best.

In Mexico jaguar are generally hunted with dogs; with a good pack of hounds they're not hard to tree, but reports indicate that good hounds are scarce. An outfitter friend of mine with an excellent track record on cougars fought all the red tape and took some of his dogs to Peru a couple of years ago. Although hunting conditions were miserable in the jungles near the headwaters of the Amazon, his dogs were able to tree jaguar with little difficulty.

Other methods include baiting or, when possible, waiting up over a kill. Calls are also used, the traditional jaguar call being a *pujandera*, or drum-like device emitting a grunt like that of a male jaguar. Farther south, jaguar calls are made from hollow gourds, and a typical technique is to float down jungle rivers at night, calling until an answer is heard.

The jaguar is easily one of the world's greatest game animals, and quite a dangerous one at that. But he's difficult to obtain and impossible to keep, and none of that is likely to change anytime soon.

Cougar

Fortunately our other great cat, the cougar, is doing much better. In fact, he's in excellent shape across western North America.

If the jaguar is our least-known game animal, then the cougar is surely our least understood. Feared, hated and persecuted for generations, the fact that the cougar is faring as well as he is today is strictly a tribute to his adaptability and cunning. The cougar's original range extended from northern British Columbia to the tip of South America, and from the Atlantic to the Pacific. His Latin name is *Felis concolor*, meaning simply "cat of one color," but he is known variously as cougar, mountain lion, panther, catamount, painter and several dozen other titles.

Over the years there have been a few—very few—documented cases of cougars attacking man, and even a couple of confirmed maneaters. However, such instances are very rare, and in general the cougar is no threat to man. He is a threat to man's domestic stock, though, and

A mountain lion is plenty big enough and has the equipment to be dangerous, but the animal's shy nature renders him almost no threat to man unless cornered, and then all cautions must be taken. (Photo by Gwyn Shannon Weaver)

there have been many, many instances of cougars killing sheep and cattle. That's probably the basis for man's centuries-long war against the cougar. Until fairly recently the cougar not only received no protection, but bounties were paid for cougar scalps and government hunters were employed strictly to hunt them down.

By the early part of this century the cougar had vanished from most of the eastern U.S., leaving only a remnant population of Florida cougars in the Everglades region. The western mountains were the cougar's last stronghold, but he had learned to evade man well enough that his population changed little from the 1920s to the mid-Sixties. By about 1965 things were beginning to change. Sportsmen had begun to appreciate the cougar as the great game animal he is, and instead of bounties there were seasons and regulations in states with stable populations, and total protection in most states with few cougars.

Today the cougar is in great shape, with populations stable or expanding across much of the West. The Florida cougar is still rare and
totally protected, and east of the Rockies there cannot be considered
any truly viable populations. However, cougar sightings in the East,
usually unconfirmed, are becoming more common all the time. The
Ozark Mountains of Arkansas are believed to have a few, likewise the
Black Hills. There are also a few along the Gulf Coast in Louisiana and
Mississippi. More interesting yet are the random reports across a broad
swath of the eastern U.S.—Maine, North Carolina, Missouri, Kansas,
Tennessee, North Dakota, and most surprising of all, several sightings
in Alaska and the Yukon—neither of which is historic cougar habitat.

Cougar *hunting* is still confined to the western U.S. and Canada, and
that's unlikely to change. In general, cougar hunting today is a midwinter season, with December through February being the most popu-

In cougar hunting with hounds, the chase is everything and the shot
anticlimactic. Ranges are close, making handguns very suitable.

lar months. However, several western states open cougar hunting in September and two, Colorado and Arizona, have an open season all year but a special license is required in both states, with an annual limit of one.

The extremes are represented by Texas and California. Texas has no season, no bag limit, and no protection for cougars at this writing. Not surprisingly, there are few cougars in the state—a few in west Texas, and a few more in the Brush Country along the Rio Grande. On the opposite end, California, with perhaps the largest cougar population in the West, enacted a moratorium on cougar hunting in the early Seventies. The result is a rapidly expanding population, with cougars now present virtually statewide, including within Los Angeles County. Many California hunters are convinced that the state is giving the deer herd to the cats. Running across cougar kills is commonplace in many deer ranges. With total protection, it's interesting to note that stock predation has escalated dramatically also.

Fortunately the rest of the West has recognized the cougar as a game animal, offering him not only the protection that status carries with it, but also the management to maintain his population at sensible levels.

Twenty-thousand cougars are believed to live in the U.S. and Canada but because of the animal's shy nature, this is probably a very conservative estimate. *Felis concolor* has 14 subspecies identified in the U.S., Canada and Mexico, but for the hunter they are virtually indistinguishable. The fourth largest cat in the world, the cougar averages significantly smaller than the jaguar and quite a bit bigger than the African leopard. A mature male will average about 140 to 150 pounds, but the occasional 200-pound tom is taken. The heaviest recorded is believed to be a monster that weight 276 pounds—field-dressed! Obviously, that weight would put the cat well into the jaguar-size category. Nose-to-tail length can range from 7½ feet for an average male to over nine. Females are much lighter, with a big tabby rarely weighing over 110 pounds or so. In most circumstances a female without cubs is legal game, but most hunters look for a nice tom because of the extreme size difference.

Cougars, like all cats and bears, enter the record books based on skull measurements. A quick study of the record books indicates no real preference in hunting area. Record cats have come from all over the West. However, the northern part of their range, British Columbia, Alberta, Washington, Idaho and Montana, has historically produced somewhat larger cats. For the 18th Big Game Awards, 1980 to 1982, the Boone and Crockett Club recognized 26 record-book cougars. Five came from B.C., including a new World Record. Three came from Idaho, but only one each from Montana and Alberta. Oregon had

I took this cat in the rugged Chiricahua Mountains of southeast Arizona. Riding mules are preferred by many outfitters in tough country such as this because they are more sure-footed than horses.

three, and Washington did very well with four. In the southern areas, Colorado had two and Utah just one. But surprisingly, New Mexico topped the listings with *six* record cats in a four-year period. I can't explain that except to note that big cougars are where you find them, and are quite possible anywhere in the West.

It's interesting to note that the long-standing world record cougar was taken by Theodore Roosevelt near Meeker, Colorado in 1901. A record animal of that vintage would seem nearly impossible to unseat, but it's now happened twice—in 1964 with a Utah cat, and in 1979 with a B.C. cat. That's a clear indication that the cougar is in good shape as a game species, and that big ones are still out there.

Perhaps one of the reasons why the cougar has been so misunderstood is his shy, almost mysterious nature. He's surprisingly common in many areas, yet relatively few hunters ever lay eyes on one. Tracks, scratches, and the occasional kill, yes, but the animal himself is rarely seen. In 20 years of serious hunting in the West, I've laid eyes on cougars twice while just out in the backcountry. Once was when I was a kid in central Kansas, a cougar crossed a field where there were supposed to be no cougars for several hundred miles. The other time was in California, where cougar sightings are now commonplace after more than a decade of total protection. But two sightings in 20 years are, I suspect, well over the average. One just doesn't *see* cougars even though they're often nearby.

If you want a cougar for your den you must enlist the aid of a good pack of hounds. Unlike all other North American game, including the jaguar, there are no other viable options.

Regardless of where you hunt them, cougar hunting is primarily a matter of finding fresh tracks, then getting the hounds on the trail and following their music until the cat trees. It sounds simple, but it's rarely that. Finding the track of a good cat usually means days on horseback in tough country, or, worse, endless freezing hours on snow machines or snowshoes. And that's the easy part.

They say cats are short-winded, and that might be true in relative terms but a cat with a pack of dogs behind him will head for the steepest, toughest, most miserable country in his territory. He can and often will, lead a chase that goes for miles. Sometimes a horse can make it, but often it becomes a foot chase, and that can mean snowshoes for much cougar hunting. There's a time element, too, for a cat, particularly a trophy tom that's probably been chased before, may tree long enough to get his wind, but he may not stay put for long. Sometimes a good cat comes easy, but usually it's a physically demanding hunt. And it's an exciting one, with the din of the hounds echoing through the canyons.

Houndsmen are a different breed. To them the chase and the music of the hounds are what make a hunt. They aren't "hardware men." Choice of gun makes little difference since the shot is the least important part of the hunt. Many houndsmen turn to guiding from sheer practicality. It gives them more opportunity to work—and show off— their prized dogs, and it can help subsidize the cost of a good pack of lion hounds. But in the off-season, or between hunts, the dedicated houndsmen are often still out there, following their dogs. The difference is that, when an animal is treed, the hunt is over. Dogs are called off, or leashed and dragged off, with no shots fired.

Currently a guided cougar hunt with a top pack costs somewhere between $1,500 and about $2,250—very reasonable as guided hunts go these days. Because of the nature of this kind of hunting, an outfitter's terms vary a great deal and they must be clarified well in advance. Hound hunting is about the only situation, except non-native game, where you might see a "guaranteed hunt." Usually it's so many dollars as a deposit, then so much more when the animal is taken. The outfitter is banking on the country he hunts and the ability of his hounds.

These dogs have momentarily lost the scent in Arizona's arid mountains. Dry-ground trailing is difficult, and it's difficult to locate a fresh track. Strike dogs are usually used to find a fresh trail—a chore that can take several days of hard hunting.

However, the hunter is often obligated to take the first mature cat treed. Other common arrangements are a flat rate for the hunt, and the hunter understands the first mature cat is his. Or, for a higher price, a trophy hunt can often be booked, whereby the hunter has the "right of refusal" on lesser cats until a trophy tom is treed. Still other outfitters simply book a seven or 10-day hunt for a flat rate, with no guarantee, as is customary for most types of hunting.

This all makes cougar hunting sound very commercial, but it must be kept in mind that a trained cougar hound is literally beyond price. It takes years to train a good one, and thousands more than the outfitter's fee to buy one. Few houndsmen make any money in the business. If they're lucky, they manage to subsidize their addiction to the cry of their hounds on a hot trail.

I've hunted cougar at both extremes of their North American range—British Columbia and Arizona. The difference between the two situations summarizes the great distinction in types of cougar hunting—snow and dry ground.

In the northern areas, most outfitters come to depend on a good tracking snow. It generally makes life easier, and they can reliably depend on a good snowfall for winter hunting. The key to any cougar hunt is fresh tracks, and snow obviously makes the search easier. In snow, the search is for actual tracks, as fresh as possible. The men do this searching, using 4WDs on logging roads, snow machines and, if necessary, horses and snowshoes. Sometimes several fruitless days are spent, but if all goes well there will eventually be a good skiff of new snow, and then you're in business. In fresh snow, the size of the track can reliably be evaluated, and if a track looks good, only then are the dogs put on the trail.

It's not an easy hunt. I spent several days on snowshoes in the rugged Kootenay region near Cranbrook and Fernie in southern B.C., and for a man unaccustomed to snowshoes, it's pure murder. But on the whole, snow hunting is generally a bit easier than dry-ground cougar hunting.

In the southern part of the cougar's range—Arizona, Nevada, Utah and New Mexico—snow isn't a sure thing. It may happen, but it's a gift the outfitters can't rely on. So they don't wait on the snow, but look for sign on dry ground.

I've also hunted cougar in the rugged, arid Chiricahua Mountains of southern Arizona, lovely country that almost never receives a tracking snow. Here snowshoes and snowmobiles are unheard of, and 4WDs only useful to get to road's end. I hunted with Marvin and Warner Glenn, who have hunted cougar in the rough Arizona mountains since the Thirties. Their method is simple—they attack the heart of the cougar's domain on tough riding mules. Watercourses, low spots and dusty trails are checked for tracks, but the strike dog is the key. On dry ground any scent their strike dog cuts is likely to be fairly fresh. When he hollers, they try to find a track to evaluate the size and get the direction, if possible. Sometimes a chase goes all the way to the tree without being certain if the cat is shootable or not.

It's tough hunting, and the Glenns make no guarantee. It's also extremely rewarding hunting, and those Arizona mountains are my

Scratches like these are left by cougars marking their territory. If fresh they're a clear sign that there's a cat in the area. It might be possible to call him in with a varmint call, but generally the only way you'll find him is with a good pack of hounds.

favorite hunting country. My Arizona cougar came surprisingly easy; some trappers gave us a tip about a javelina freshly killed by a cougar. We trailered the mules as far as we could, rode in to the designated place and Jaws, their big black-and-tan strike dog, found the scent. The lion was laid up nearby. The pack jumped him, and after a couple of miles of pell-mell chase, he treed in a big pine. He was a good cat, especially good for southern Arizona; he weighed about 150 pounds and his skull was just a sixteenth or so off the B&C minimum. That was the Glenns' 451st lion out of the same range of mountains. I'd guess they're well over 500 by now, and they've seen no diminishing of the cats' numbers.

Depending on the country, there may be other game available on a cougar hunt. Bobcats share the same range throughout, and depending on your arrangement with the houndsmen, bobcats can often be picked up on a cougar hunt. In the North, lynx are occasionally run and treed, and in the extreme south, coati mundi occur. Sort of like a big possum with a furry tail, the *chula*, as they're called, make an interesting trophy but their razor-sharp teeth probably tear up more dogs in that country than cougar ever thought of.

Two other long-shot techniques for bagging a mountain lion should be mentioned. They can be called, but because they're thinly scattered over a wide area, the difficulty is finding a calling site where you have some assurance that a cat will hear you. Odds are poor, but a cougar might respond to a varmint call. The other hunting method sounds like a campfire yarn, but I've heard it enough times to believe it. On the other hand, I've never talked first-hand to anyone who has done it. It's said that a *good* man on snowshoes can *walk* a cougar up a tree in heavy snow. I couldn't do it, but it's been done . . . or so the story goes. Personally, if I wanted a cougar, I'd find a good houndsman.

Almost any type of trailing hound will work for cougars. Black and tans, Walkers, blueticks, redbones—you name it. A good nose, plenty of stamina, and a good voice are essentials, plus the common sense to

Hunting in snow isn't easy. It's tough to get around and tougher still during a hard chase. But in fresh snow you have a better chance of sizing up a track before committing to a chase. This nice tom was taken in central Utah. (Photo by Ludo J. Wurfbain)

stay alive in close quarters with a big cat. Similarly, practically any gun will work for this kind of hunting. The bowhunter, handgun hunter or muzzleloader is at no real disadvantage—the shot is nothing, the chase everything.

Cougars are soft-skinned and not heavily-boned; many experienced houndsmen prefer a .22 Hornet or .22 Magnum to reduce pelt damage. In B.C. I carried an old Colt Lightning slide action in .25-20, the preferred caliber among those hunters. In Arizona I used a Thompson/Center handgun. Any centerfire rifle will also work just fine, but the risk of undue damage to the hide becomes great with high-powered, high-velocity rifles.

It is important to place the shot carefully. A wounded cougar isn't to be taken lightly even if he poses no great threat to you—and that isn't a certainty. He can do a lot of damage to a prized pack of hounds, and do it very quickly.

I will have to admit that I'm not a houndsman at heart. There are many kinds of hunting that I'd love to do every year if I had time and wherewithal, and cougar hunting isn't one of them. But the cry of the hounds in a distant canyon and the excitement of a hard chase are unforgettable thrills, and the sight of a big cougar up close—a sight few hunters ever experience—is a memory I'll carry forever.

Chapter 13
Wild Boar and Javelina

If someone says they're "going pig hunting," they might be referring to either the collared peccary, better known as javelina, or the European wild boar, also called wild hogs and razorbacks, it just depends on which part of the country the speaker is from. "Pig hunting" both types, is popular across a surprising portion of North America, and it's getting more popular. That's odd, since this continent has no native wild pigs.

The wild hog *Sus scrofa*, is a native of Europe and Asia—an exotic species, although recognized as a big game animal in an increasing number of states. The javelina is, of course, a native game species but it's not a pig. The collared peccary, *Dicotyles tajacu*, resembles a true swine in general appearance, but the two families are only remotely related. Differences include number of teeth (38 for peccaries and 44 for swine), gall bladders in swine and none in peccaries, significant difference in legbone structures, and scent glands on the javelina, lacking in swine.

In spite of the misnomers, "pig hunting" for both species is exciting sport that's avidly pursued by large numbers of American hunters, enough that no book on North American big game could be complete without them. The hunting for these two species is as different as the animals themselves. In fact, the only things the two have in common is a general similarity in appearance and the common nickname of "pigs."

Collared Peccary

White-Lipped Peccary

JAVELINA (PECCARY) RANGE

It could be reasonably argued that the javelina is our biggest small game rather than our smallest big game. In truth, they're quite small. Very rarely javelinas are reported with a live weight of over 60 pounds, but 50 pounds is big and 40 pounds about average. However they're hunted as big game across their range, and they're an interesting trophy.

The peccaries are strictly American animals. Current taxonomical thinking identifies three subspecies. Our collared peccary or javelina ranges from southern Mexico up through the southwest third of Texas and the southern third of Arizona. New Mexico has a fairly small population in both the southeast and southwest corners. This subspecies gets its name from a collar of paler hairs around the neck just in front of the shoulders. Farther south, the white-lipped peccary ranges through the jungle regions of Central and South America, while the Chacoan peccary is found in parts of Argentina, Bolivia, and Paraguay.

Javelina

Although small, the javelina is a wicked-looking creature, with elongated canine teeth that fit together straight up and down, with the upper "tusks" sharpening the lower ones. The upper tusks on a good trophy are two inches or longer. These weapons plus the bristly hair and stiff mane make the javelina appear quite dangerous, and there are plenty of stories of javelina "treeing" hunters for hours, even charging. While javelina fight among themselves and can, in a group, give a good account against predators, they're hardly any danger to man. They can smell and hear fairly well, but their eyesight is poor. When a hunter shoots at a javelina in a herd, it isn't unusual for some of them to come toward him as they explode in all directions but that's not a charge—they're just running away in the wrong direction!

Collared peccary typically are found in small herds of a half-dozen or so to perhaps 20. The white-lipped peccary are often seen in herds of 100 or more, but groups of this size are unusual for javelina. However, large herds, often called packs, are occasionally seen. On a Coues deer hunt in Arizona in 1984 a buddy of mine counted 47 in one group—and that's a lot of javelina!

The southwestern United States is just the fringe of javelina range, with most of the animals located in Mexico. However, it is conservatively estimated that there are 70,000 javelina in the U.S. New Mexico has the smallest population and issues a limited number of permits on a drawing basis. Arizona has a great deal more javelina and offers many more permits, but they are still on a drawing basis. Arizona's

Javelina have good senses of smell and hearing, but poor eyesight. The careful stalker can get in fairly close if he moves quietly and has the right wind.

rifle permits are fairly hard to obtain in some areas, but special drawings are also offered for bowhunters, handgun hunters and muzzleloaders; at this writing these permits are much easier to obtain.

The bulk of the population is found in Texas. There are no special licenses or permits required, just a state hunting license. Texas' javelinas are managed on a by-county basis. Most counties open javelina hunting only during deer season and establish a season limit of one or two animals. However, a few counties in the South Texas Brush Country still allow year 'round javelina hunting with no bag limit and if that seems an indicator of how plentiful the javelinas are, it is!

Surprisingly, the difference between javelina hunting in the arid hills of Arizona and New Mexico and the dense brush of south Texas is about like the difference between night and day. In Arizona it's a glassing game. Typically, the animals will lie up under mesquite trees or in oak thickets during the midday hours, but mornings and evenings they'll be out feeding. In most areas the heavy cover is sparse and the terrain offers some relief. Hunters scout for sign, and when a likely area is found, they'll hike up to a vantage point and glass until a band is spotted. Then it's a question of making a stalk to shooting range.

Most of Texas' prime javelina country is wall-to-wall brush, and hunters rarely have the luxury of either a vantage point or sufficient open area to glass. They are obliged to hunt the edges, check feeding areas or find well-used trails and sit—preferably on an elevated stand.

The pads and fruit of the prickly pear cactus is the javelina's preferred food. Across their range, patches of prickly pear are among the best places to look for sign. Freshly chewed pads and the tiny, distinctive tracks indicate that javelina have been there, and probably will return.

Baiting for javelina is legal in Texas, and is quite successful but not nearly as much fun as other methods. It is also possible to run them with dogs, but is practiced little. Even less common, but also effective, is calling with a varmint call. A friend of mine once called up a pack of 20, and after that he was willing to believe the stories of hunters put up trees by javelina!

This javelina was taken out of a herd of 25 in Arizona's Galiuro Mountains. The pistol is a customized Remington XP-100 in 6mm Benchrest. My partner, Duwane Adams, and I "lost" the herd in a series of rough canyons, but after an hour of glassing found them when a "pig" squealed in some brush just below our lookout—typical in javelina hunting.

Most javelina taken in Texas are incidental to deer hunting, while Arizona and New Mexico offer special licenses and separate seasons, so a hunter goes javelina hunting on purpose. I've taken a number of javelina while deer hunting in Texas, but I actually prefer the latter approach. They're interesting little animals and offer a nice hunt on their own merits. Of course, there's nothing to stop anyone from making a javelina hunt to one of Texas' open counties at any time of the year; I've done that, too, and it's a lot of fun.

The Boone and Crockett Club does not recognize javelina as a big game animal, but the Safari Club does and accepts entries for their record book based on skull measurement. Obviously, it's pretty near impossible to look at a javelina on the hoof and tell if he has a big skull

Arizona's javelina seasons, usually held in February and March, offer extremely pleasant hunting. The weather is mild, and while javelina aren't tremendously difficult to locate and stalk, Arizona's herds are scattered and the mountains are tough, all the makings for a challenging and enjoyable hunt!

The prickly pear is perhaps the single most important food source for javelina across much of their range. In season the fruit is eagerly devoured, but when the fruit isn't available the little "pigs" go after the pads themselves—and they don't seem to worry about the thorns!

The bristly hair and sharp tusks give the javelina a fierce appearance, but they actually pose no threat to man. Stalking them does offer great sport, especially with an open-sighted handgun.

or not. Hunters after a nice trophy are best advised to pick the biggest javelina in a group and hope for the best. Of course, if you have the opportunity to observe them for some time, you might be able to pick one with a particularly nice set of tusks. But even that is often difficult, especially in brush of any kind. One word of caution. If you're looking for a trophy rather than just a meat animal, don't shoot a lone javelina unless you've had plenty of time to observe it. In a pack it's easy to pick out a big one, but a lone animal can fool you. It might be a monster, but chances are it's smaller than you think!

Javelina meat isn't the greatest, but it's not all that bad, especially from younger animals. Much ado is made over the musk or scent glands, located on the midline of the back near the rump. They do give the javelina a strong, musky odor which you'll surely scent if you stalk close to a herd. But these glands will not taint the meat unless the meat actually touches the gland. Normal skinning, done quickly, will take care of any potential problem.

Javelina are fairly tough for their size, but they aren't large enough to be hard to put down. Practically any centerfire from the .22 Hornet on up will do the trick if the bullet is placed right, but actually you should decide if you want to *snipe* javelina or *stalk* them. They're a small target, and can be the rifleman's game for exact shot placement. On the other hand, they're fun to stalk in close, and are great game for handgunners, bowhunters and blackpowder shooters. Any accurate handgun from .38 Special on up is adequate, and any muzzleloader from .45 caliber on up will work nicely.

Wild Boar

As much fun as the javelina is to hunt, his adopted big brother, the wild hog, is even more exciting. He can be as much as 10 times bigger, and while the javelina *looks* dangerous, the wild hog *is* dangerous.

Swine are prolific breeders and fairly adaptable, requiring year round water, fairly mild winters, and little else. They have established wild populations in many parts of the U.S., including Arkansas, Tennessee, North Carolina, Texas, much of the Gulf Coast and California. They are also well established in breeding populations on many private preserves throughout the U.S.

There are many names for this animal—wild boar, wild hog, Russian boar, European wild hog, razorback—you name it. Our domestic hogs are descendants of the European (or Russian) wild boar, and all belong to the same species, *Sus scrofa*. In years gone by domestic hogs were left to fend for themselves, and escapees started some of the wild populations we have today. There have also been several releases of

Wild hogs in California, and many other parts of the country, are a grab bag in terms of color. Very few herds have a predominance of pure European blood and many individuals show clear traces of feral domestic stock.

pure European wild boars over the years. The first known was on the Corbin estate in New Hampshire in 1893 and probably the best known was by George Gordon Moore in the Hooper's Bald area of North Carolina in 1910 and 1912. Since then there have been local releases in several areas designed to improve the bloodlines of existing feral populations. It is possible, though unlikely, that some private preserves actually have pure European wild boars, but the truth is that virtually all of America's wild hogs are just that—feral domestic pigs with some degree of wild European blood in them.

All of that is just to set the record straight; it doesn't make them less of a game animal. Actually, the wild strain is present in all domestic hogs, and it doesn't take many generations of free ranging for the whole appearance of the pig to change. Hogs that have lived in the wild for several generations will have a longer snout and heavier shoulders in place of the huge, meaty hams you see in a barnyard. They appear leggier, the tail is straighter and the ears aren't floppy. They develop a thicker, woollier coat, and of course the boars develop nice tusks.

They do come in all shades and colors. I've seen white, black, red, spotted and belted hogs here in California. The black hogs come closer to the appearance of true European wild boars, but the actual European boar has vari-colored hairs, dark with a lighter tip that gives a grizzled appearance. This is seen in some feral populations, and is a sure sign of purebred influence.

Wild hogs, whether feral or true European, are also not as large as domestic swine. They store fat, but they have to work harder for a living and simply don't get as big. I've heard stories about wild hogs that topped 600 pounds, and I've even heard a "told as the truth" story about a 900-pounder. Pigs like that are usually taken on guided hunts, and I suspect those hogs weren't long out of a stock auction somewhere. Size does vary greatly from area to area, depending on feed conditions, but a 350-pound boar is truly huge. In our northern California pig range, very few boars ever top 250 pounds. Farther south, around King City and Paso Robles, 300 pounders are occasionally encountered. I've seen enough wild pigs in Texas to believe that they grow a little bigger there, and I'm told they get bigger still in Florida but even there, 400 pounds is a lot of pig, and I doubt if anything over 500 pounds is remotely possible. Even in eastern Europe, Turkey and Russia, where the largest wild boars are taken, a 400-pound boar is huge.

Surprisingly, body size doesn't have all that much to do with size of tusk. The lower tusks flare up and out, making contact with the shorter upper tusks, which keep them sharp. The tusks continue to grow throughout the boar's life, but the sharpening process plus using them to root and dig continues to wear them down—if one or both tusks doesn't break off, which is common. A pig with two to 2½ inches of lower tusk showing above the gumline is quite good, three inches excellent, and four inches about as big as they come, and that's true in Europe as well as North America. The Safari Club accepts entries for North American wild boars in the exotics category, and places European boars under the Europe section of their book. Their measurements are based on length and circumference of each tusk when removed from the skull; both tusks are added together. It's interesting to note that the S.C.I. book lists three U.S. pigs, one from North Carolina and two from California, that are larger than the biggest European tusker, that one taken in Poland in 1936.

Pigs are one of the more difficult animals to judge in the field. The head is usually held low, rooting and digging, and when awake pigs are usually moving a bit as they feed. Worse, while they're feeding they often have grass in their mouths that obscures the teeth. In spotting and stalking situations, if you're patient you can usually get some kind of a look at the tusks, but remember, two to three inches is good, and that isn't much to look for. A good indicator is a lip that seems to curl out; the pig will usually have good teeth. For a trophy mount, hunters also like to shoot for color. The black boars make a better-looking mount than light or multi-colored pigs, but color doesn't dictate tusk size, so sometimes a choice must be made. With hound hunting, trophy estimation is next to impossible. It certainly is totally impossible until you get to the bayed pig. Tracks may indicate size, but

Fresh "rootings" are a sure sign wild pigs are in the area. Unless disturbed, pigs will customarily return to these feeding areas during late evening or early morning.

Don Pine, game biologist for the California Fish and Game Department, is one of the nation's leading authorities on wild hogs. This boar, weighing perhaps 175 pounds, is very average in size. Pigs weighing 300 pounds are possible but unusual, and much over that is very, very rare. (Photo by Durwood Hollis)

that says little about tusks and nothing about color. Of course, not all pig hunting is for trophies. A non-lactating sow provides some of the best wild meat going, in my opinion far superior to domestic pork. The boars aren't bad, either but if you don't care about big tusks or a trophy mount, go for a nice sow. Your family will love it!

Regulations concerning wild hog hunting vary considerably across the U.S. Some states, such as North Carolina and Tennessee, establish hunting seasons. Some, such as Texas, consider them exotics with no regulations whatsoever. My own state of California classes them as a game animal—our second-most popular behind deer—having a year round season and a bag limit of one per day, one in possession.

I've hunted pigs in such diverse areas as Vermont, Texas and Ten-

In more open country, wild hogs can be hunted successfully by spotting and stalking. They will customarily feed in the morning, then lay up in brush until evening. However, on cool or overcast days they may be active throughout the day.

nessee as well as California, and they're the same animal but local vegetation and hunting conditions dictate how you hunt them. Hunting with dogs is popular in many areas, and in extremely heavy cover is the only sensible way to go about it. In more open terrain, spotting and stalking is practical and, unless you're a houndsman, a lot more interesting.

Like most species, pigs are active early and late, preferring to lie up in heavy cover during the heat of the day. In very open country, a hunter will glass clearings and abandoned barley fields for sight of the actual animals. In heavier cover, look for sign—wallows and rubs, fresh scat, and well-used trails going into the thick stuff. If water is fairly scarce, a pond or other water source with a wallow nearby makes a great place to wait mornings and evenings.

The houndsman, of course, looks for sign fresh enough to get the dogs on. Hound hunting is exciting. It's usually a wild chase through dense cover, and you need to stay close. When the boar turns to bay, he can literally unzip a careless or too-brave dog in a hurry.

And he can also unzip a man. This is one animal that really mustn't be taken lightly. He isn't particularly hard to kill, but the bullet must be placed right and it must be from an adequate rifle. The boars have a thick gristle plate over their neck and shoulders, probably armor against fights with other pigs. It's not steel, and it won't turn an adequate bullet, but it will cause an inadequate bullet to mushroom prematurely and fail to penetrate.

A good friend of mine, Mike Ballew, is hunting manager for Dye Creek Preserve, a northern California cattle ranch with a large pig population. Over the years he's guided hunters to over 1,500 pigs, making him much more of an authority on them than I am. He sees no reason to carry a cannon, but he feels the .243 and similar cartridges

This California wild pig has it all—long, thick tusks, plus good color.

are too light for pigs. He likes to see hunters use a normal deer rifle—
.308, .270, .30-06, with a good controlled-expansion bullet. He generally uses a 7x57 for backup work, and although he has to go in after
several wounded pigs each year, he hasn't yet had a problem. However, his hunting is all spotting and stalking in fairly open country,
with most shots from 40 to 100 yards. Under those circumstances, he
hasn't had much success with handguns in the .41-.44 Magnum class.
I'd have to agree. I've seen .44 softpoints from both rifle and handgun
fail to penetrate the gristle plate.

For hound hunting, the story is a bit different. There the shooting is
in close and one can usually get a good head or neck shot. Bill Richter,
owner and operator of Wild Hill Preserve in Vermont, hunts wild boar
almost exclusively with dogs in the thick Vermont woods. He uses a
.44 revolver for backup and finds it satisfactory, but unlike Mike, he's
got a couple of scars from pigs.

I hunt hogs a lot. They're great to eat, available year 'round in my
area, and lots of fun. So I don't intend to make them sound more
dangerous than they are. On the other hand, you can't get careless. I
was waiting on a deer trail in south Texas one evening. I'd seen several
pigs, but was waiting for a big buck. Twilight finally deepened enough
that I knew I'd have trouble judging antlers, and about that time I saw
a big boar step out of the treeline 100 yards away. I got up and made a
quick stalk and angled a 160-grain bullet from a 7mm Remington Magnum into his shoulder as he stood quarter-on. He got into the trees like
a shot, long before I could fire again. I *knew* he was dead, and it was
getting dark fast. So I followed, too quickly. I didn't find him, but he
found me. He lumbered at me out of some shadows, but fortunately he
wasn't quite steady enough or fast enough with one shoulder broken. I
jumped out of his way and practically touched his side with the gun
barrel as I pulled the trigger. He went down, and before I dragged him
out of the gloom I sat down to count up all the rules I'd broken and
gotten away with—that time.

Chapter 14
The Exotics

American hunters are blessed with an incredible variety of native game species—species that span the continent and offer some kind of hunting opportunity at practically any time of the year. But no picture of North American hunting can be complete without a brief look at our non-native game—the so-called "exotics."

Although their availability to hunters varies widely, at present there are at least 30 non-native big game species found either free-ranging or on game ranches in the United States. Many of these are strictly experimental and may never be available for hunting, but at least 15 of these immigrants are sufficiently established to offer huntable surpluses. What it all adds up to is opportunity—expanded hunting opportunity for American hunters, and for the species themselves, the opportunity to establish populations and flourish in suitable habitat. This last is extremely important, for many of our commonly-hunted non-native species are truly endangered on their native ranges.

The term "exotics" is commonly applied to all of our non-native species. It's a good word, and it aptly describes the situation. According to the dictionary, one of the preferred meanings of the word "exotic" is "introduced from a foreign country; not native to the place where found." Well, that fits perfectly, for our exotic game is exactly that—non-native species transplanted from a foreign land.

Unfortunately, the word "exotics" and exotics hunting has gotten some bad press in recent years. The word has come to mean fenced hunting and "fish in a barrel" situations far removed from sportsman-like hunting and fair chase ethics. This is unfortunate, as it condemns a tremendous range of hunting opportunities for the abuses of a few. The truth is that most exotics hunting today is conducted on large acre-age with natural habitat. Game fencing might be used to protect that property, but on a game ranch with suitable habitat and sufficient acreage to develop a breeding population, the game fencing should not interfere with a quality hunting experience. There are also substantial free-ranging populations of several exotic species, and these are found in a surprising number of areas. When free-ranging, most exotics are subject to some form of game regulation, and some have achieved the ultimate status of naturalized citizens—legal big game animals man-aged by set seasons and sometimes requiring special licenses and per-mits.

Obviously not all of our exotics are big game. The ring-necked pheas-ant, chukar partridge, and Hungarian partridge are three popular game birds that are exotics by any definition of the word. In suitable habitat and with breeding populations established, these birds offer sporty hunting that has made generations of American gunners all the richer for the experience. The same can be said of our big game exotic species.

"Fair chase" is a subjective concept. It was created by hunters as a sort of code of honor. It is subject to individual interpretation, and each of us has our own ideas. Some of the hunting methods discussed in previous chapters, use of dogs in hunting big game, baiting for bears, and perhaps even treestand hunting or driving, are considered un-sportsmanlike and not in fair chase by many hunters who don't use the methods and have no experience with them. But the Boone and Crock-ett Club, perhaps the most rigid of all hunting organizations in its concepts of hunting ethics and fair chase, has no problems with any of the above hunting methods so long as they were legal where the hunting took place.

However, for any entry to be accepted into the B&C book, a hunter must sign a "fair chase" affidavit affirming that there was no spotting or herding from the air, that no motor-powered vehicle was used in herding or pursuing game, that no electronic communications were used to locate game or guide the hunter to game, and that the game was not confined by escape-proof barriers, including escape-proof fenc-ing, and the game was not transplanted solely for hunting.

Now, that's a mouthful, but it's a good code of ethics which any sportsman worth his salt would agree to in theory, but that last stipula-tion regarding fencing causes problems for exotics hunting. As I men-tioned, much exotics hunting is done behind game-proof fencing. Does that mean the hunting is not "fair chase?" According to the Boone and Crockett Club, yes. But in actuality the answer isn't so clear-cut.

We all are somewhat familiar with the whitetail deer and his ability to make fools of us. Given a prime chunk of Texas whitetail country—brushy, thorny, maybe with some relief—if you had a 5,000-acre tract game-fenced, would it really make it any easier for you to hunt a trophy buck within the fencing? How about 1,000 acres, or even 500? Most whitetails live and die within a square mile, 640 acres, so what difference would a fence make?

To the Boone and Crockett Club, who must adhere to the strictest code to prevent possible abuses, a whitetail taken within a game-proof fence is not taken in fair chase. But the hunter must decide for himself, and it's *his* concept of fair chase, and his ability to look at himself in the mirror that's most important.

Exotic species are no different from our native species. Each has different preferred habitats, and in that habitat each uses its natural abilities and senses to whatever degree it possesses to escape danger. In 500 acres of suitable habitat, a mature whitetail buck is at no disadvantage. In the same acreage, with habitat suitable to the species, a pronghorn would be at a severe disadvantage. He uses his eyes and legs, not the cover and terrain, and he would need much more room to be on an even footing with hunters. Exotics are the same. Brush-loving deer, like the Asian sika, need relatively small acreage to be quite secure; plains game such as the blackbuck need much more space to provide a quality hunting experience. Somewhere between those two, all of the exotic species can provide quality hunting that will meet any hunter's personal "fair chase" yardstick.

The Exotic Wildlife Association, based in Texas but with game ranchers, breeders and professional hunters nationwide among their membership, defines "fair chase" as follows: "Hunting in an area, by any method, which provides the hunted animal with a reasonable chance and opportunity to avoid being found by the hunter, and having once been found by the hunter, to escape." Some of America's exotic hunting today is for totally unfenced, completely free-ranging animals, and there the question of "fair chase" never comes up—it's usually damn tough hunting. But on private land, a large number of ranchers and outfitters are living up to their organization's concept of ethical hunting, and under those circumstances, you can have a great hunt and neither you nor the game will be aware of the fences.

While the exotic hunting industry is fairly new, the idea of introducing foreign species is quite old, nor is it confined to the United States. The palmated-antlered fallow deer is a classic example. A European deer, the fallow has been transplanted and domestically bred for so many centuries that its original range is uncertain. I recently shot a nice fallow buck in Spain. It's a European deer, and since I was hunting in Europe I assumed it was native to that region. Not so. I asked about the fallow's origins, and was told that the first fallow deer were brought to the Iberian Peninsula by the Romans some 2,000 years ago! A popular exotic, fallow deer have also been transplanted to New Zealand and Australia, South Africa and India. They were probably America's first big game immigrant. It's said that George Washington himself brought in the first ones for the grounds of his Mount Vernon estate!

Old George probably brought them in simply because they were pretty to look at, and that's how a lot of our exotics got started. The first Texas import is believed to be Indian nilgai antelope (blue bull), released on the King Ranch in 1930. Blackbuck antelope and axis deer, also from India, soon followed. They were nice to look at, totally different from native species, and in those days fencing was cheap and range cheaper. Other imports followed, most notably mouflon sheep from Europe and aoudad, or Barbary sheep, from North Africa. These species did well, but the spread was slow. The purpose was whimsical, and the idea of hunting these animals on a commercial, paying basis was decades away.

The great Y.O. Ranch near Mountain Home, Texas must get the credit for really getting exotics hunting going. The Schreiner family, owners of the Y.O. since the region was settled, had experimented with several exotic species and had quite a few on their spread. They had deer hunters on the place during the fall, and once in a while one of them wanted to take a blackbuck or axis deer home as a trophy. It didn't take a good businessman long to figure out that these grass and browse-eating lawn ornaments might well be able to pay their way! They were, and before long the demand for exotic breeding stock sky-rocketed.

It was a good idea, too. The exotic game competed little with cattle (and in many cases they proved more profitable than cattle!), and less with native deer. Today Texas is easily the heart and soul of the exotics industry, with thriving populations on private land and quite a few free-ranging populations that wander back and forth at will. Most of the Texas hunting is at the landowner's discretion, with fees charged for animals taken but no state jurisdiction.

The big exception is the Palo Duro Canyon region, where the state funded releases of aoudad and controls the hunting. The Palo Duro aoudad release represents another purpose behind the introduction of a non-native species—to fill an "ecological niche." An ecological niche, simply stated, is a piece of habitat that is suited only to highly specialized species. In some cases, suitable species might not exist naturally. The Palo Duro was a prime example. Rough, rocky and dry, it has always been very marginal deer range. But it's actually fairly similar to North Africa's desolate Atlas Mountains, home to the Barbary sheep or aoudad. The Texas Parks and Wildlife folks reasoned that aoudad would do well in the Palo Duro, and probably not adversely affect the few deer that were there. They were right. This area now hosts a good herd of aoudad, and offers some of the country's toughest sheep hunting.

New Mexico, though, not Texas, deserves the laurels for furthering the "ecological niche" concept. Under the chairmanship of well-known hunter-naturalist Frank C. Hibben, the New Mexico Department of Fish and Game conducted a program of some 20 years' duration to "fill" some ecological niches within that state. Gemsbok from the Kalahari Desert of Africa were released in the desolate White Sands region, Persian ibex into the rugged Florida Mountains, Siberian ibex and aoudad into the Canadian River Canyon. While the New Mexico game department is presently planning no further species introductions, it's obvious that the program was a total success. All four species are full-fledged game animals, with permits for all four available by drawing. With Iran currently closed, and with most Texas ibex of mixed blood, New Mexico is the only place where the Persian ibex may currently be hunted, and it's worth noting that an ibex taken there in 1981 is several inches larger than the Iranian record listed in the S.C.I. record book.

The New Mexico transplants were largely a grand ecological experiment, with a by-product of increased opportunity for New Mexico hunters. Most of the other American transplants were, and are, conducted for less altruistic reasons, either for the animals' aesthetic value, or for profit either from hunting or sale of breeding stock. But few things are free in this world, and the dollars hunters are willing to spend for the experience of hunting these animals has resulted in the preservation and proliferation in America of species that are quite endangered on their home ranges. Several of our most common exotics— aoudad, blackbuck and axis deer, to name three—are much more numerous in the United States than on their home ranges. The addax and white or scimitar-horned oryx, desert antelope from the Saharan region, have become increasingly popular with trophy hunters and are being found on more and more Texas game ranches. However their very survival in North Africa is in question. Several authorities now believe them to be extinct in the wild. As is always the case, hunters' dollars contribute the most to the conservation, management and preservation of wildlife, and in the case of our exotics, hunters can literally be the salvation of an entire species.

A word about costs. Many (though hardly all) of our native species can be hunted simply by purchasing a license and going hunting. That is rarely the case with exotics. In some situations a license may be purchased or drawn, and there's no difference between that and native hunting. Rarely, free-ranging populations may simply be hunted, if you know where they're located and can obtain landowner permission. But the bulk of the exotics hunting is for privately-owned animals on private land. This hunting is controlled by the laws of supply and demand. Sometimes a guide—and a guide fee—are obligatory, and sometimes just a simple trophy fee is payable for animals actually taken. Obviously, the more desirable the animal, the higher the trophy fee. The "ultra-rare" exotics fetch a pretty fancy price, sometimes into the thousands. At this writing the most popular exotics are axis deer, blackbuck and aoudad; average costs seem to be somewhere between $1,000 and $1,500 for these species. Mouflon, sika and fallow deer average about half that or less. Is it worth it? That's a personal decision, but they are lovely trophies!

The wild boar (*Sus scrofa*) is our most popular and most common exotic. Because he has achieved legal game status in so many states, he has been covered separately.

Figures are extremely sketchy on the number of exotics within the United States, but it's likely that, after the wild boar, the mouflon and mouflon-type sheep are the most numerous. The true mouflon (*Ovis musimon*) is a wild sheep originally native to Corsica and Sardinia. He's a very small wild sheep, almost never exceeding 100 pounds, and typically has a distinctive pale "saddle patch" on his back. In truth, 100 percent pure mouflon are very rare in the United States. Most have been crossed with some type of domestic sheep, usually barbados. These crosses have been generically termed "Corsican sheep," which is not and never has been a true wild sheep. The Corsican sheep are generally a bit larger with a longer tail, but the real truth-teller is the horns. A true mouflon has horns that curl back and out, then pinch forward toward the jaw. A ram whose greatest spread is his tip-to-tip is *not* a pure mouflon. On the other hand, the various crosses do grow spectacular horns, often curling outward and growing to quite incredible length. Horns over 40 inches have been recorded.

Mouflon, mouflon-type, and Corsican rams are found and hunted on private preserves and game ranches in several parts of the country, and they can offer excellent hunting. Typically these are not sheep of high

The mouflon sheep were originally native to Corsica and Sardinia. They're the smallest of the world's wild sheep, beautifully marked with a distinctive saddle patch.

elevation, preferring wooded or brushy habitat with some relief. There are a number of free-ranging populations, including parts of the Texas Hill Country, west Texas, and some of California's Channel Islands, particularly Santa Cruz. They are not particularly wary, but in tough terrain can offer challenging hunting. I spent several very pleasant, but tough, days hunting them near Llano, Texas, and they aren't push-overs.

The beautiful Axis deer (*Cervus axis*), native to India, is perhaps the world's prettiest deer, and certainly one of the most popular exotics. A semi-tropical deer, transplants have been successful only in Texas and Florida. At least 20,000 axis deer are estimated to be in Texas, including several thousand that are free-ranging.

The axis deer retains its spotted coat throughout its life. A large buck weighs about 175 pounds and sports fine three-tined antlers consisting of a heavy main beam, a forward-jutting brow tine, and a rear or inward-pointing second tine. While the mass and point lengths are

The axis deer, a native of India, may well be the world's most beautiful deer. The three-tined antlers and "beer barrel" curve to the main beams are typical of the better axis stags.

important to overall quality, main beam length is the single most important feature. Anything 30 inches or better is superb, with 33 inches possible.

Axis deer are edge animals. Primarily grazers, they prefer semi-open terrain with shaded glades to lie up in. Since they're a tropical deer species, their antler growth cycle is not in synch with our domestic deer. In fact, a few axis bucks can be found in hard antler at any time of the year. However, the majority of the bucks will be in hard antler from mid-May through November, making these the most popular months.

Axis deer can be wary, but since they prefer more open terrain they can be hunted by glassing or still-hunting slowly through likely areas. They're a marvelous animal, and a hunt for them not only offers a stunning trophy, but a pleasant off-season experience. I once took a fine axis deer on a combination turkey-axis deer hunt in May, just exactly half-way between regular deer seasons!

In terms of beauty, it's probably a toss-up between the axis deer and the blackbuck antelope (*Antelope tragocamelus*) of India and Pakistan. Another tropical species, the blackbuck has done well only in Texas and Florida in the U.S., although there's also a good herd in Argentina. Even in Texas, severe storms or cold winters have periodically decimated the blackbuck herds.

The blackbuck is a small antelope, with males usually weighing from 80 to 90 pounds. Their horns grow in corkscrew fashion with prominent rings or ridges. A mature blackbuck horns might make up to five complete turns; three or four is normal. Two different systems are used to measure blackbuck. They are *Records of Exotics*, which follows the length of the horn, and the Safari Club system, which goes around the spiral. Texas outfitter Thompson Temple and I just took an excellent buck which measured 22½ inches on the straight and 30 inches on the spiral, so it's important to know which measurement is being quoted!

The Indian blackbuck antelope is a tiny creature, but every inch is pure class. Cold winters are terribly hard on them, but by and large they do well in Texas and Florida. A trophy like this one, taken in Texas, exceeds the best heads taken in India and Pakistan.

On the straight, blackbuck are quite shootable at 18 inches; around the spiral about 25 is quite good. White eye-rings, chin underparts and ear markings accentuate the black body. Because of its sheer beauty, a trophy blackbuck is one animal that really deserves a life-size mount. The females and younger males are tan to medium brown in color, with only the dominant males exhibiting the striking black coat.

These are open-country animals, using eyesight and speed in much the same manner as our pronghorns. When alarmed, they'll cover a lot of ground without stopping. Virtually all of America's blackbuck are found behind fences, but they're extremely spooky. On adequate acreage they can offer a good hunt, especially if one stalks them on foot.

Of them all, the one exotic that almost never offers an easy hunt is the aoudad, or Barbary sheep. Scientifically termed *Ammotragus lervia*, the aoudad is actually neither a sheep nor a goat, but possesses some characteristics of both animals. His native habitat is the rugged desert mountains of North Africa, and he has adapted well to life in some of North America's roughest terrain. Although some populations are theoretically fenced, most exotic ranchers feel that no fence can effectively hold an aoudad. In addition to New Mexico's Canadian River canyon, Texas' Palo Duro and the Texas Hill Country, aoudad are established in several other areas, including Colorado's Chalk Bluffs and California's coastal mountains near Hearst's Castle.

Aoudad are very large animals, with a big male often weighing 300 pounds. Coloration is tawny, unbelievably difficult to spot in the rocky country these animals prefer. Aoudad have a neck mane typical to the goat species, but the mane extends all the way down the chest and there are also long tufts of hair on the forelegs, called chaps. Both males and females have horns, but mane, chaps and horns are much more impressive on the males. Aoudad have produced much better trophies here in the U.S. than were ever taken in North Africa, probably because of the better (comparatively!) feed and water conditions. *Any* mature aoudad taken in fair chase is a fine trophy, but horns of 27 inches or so with 12-inch bases are good, and horns up to 35 inches have been taken in the U.S.

Aoudad hunting is a sheep hunter's game. Trophies taken from areas like the Palo Duro and the Canadian River Canyon are prized by their owners as much as any of our native sheep, and may well have come much harder. Even in the more gentle Texas Hill Country, aoudad hunting means days of hiking rugged hills and countless hours of glassing. They might be exotic, but you'll earn them. If you are under the impression that hunting our non-native game is so easy that it isn't worth the time and money, then start with aoudad. But be ready to

Former Kenya professional hunter Finn Aagaard guided me to this aoudad, or Barbary sheep. A native of North Africa, the aoudad is consistently the most challenging of all the exotics to hunt.

wear out some shoe leather. An outdoor writer I know has now hunted aoudad four times without firing a shot.

The fallow deer (*Dama dama*) is one of the most widespread exotics, though not one of the more numerous. As a European deer, he is suited to a wide variety of North American climates and is found literally from coast to coast, though not necessarily all points in between. There are free-ranging populations in Texas, California, the East and the Deep South, and of course private herds on numerous ranches. Fallow deer are found in various color phases from nearly black to pure white. The white fallow seem to be the most popular with hunters, perhaps because of their unusual appearance. Personally I've always preferred the darker colorations, but whatever the color, the antlers are of the greatest interest to hunters.

The palms are the most important part of a fallow rack. Fallow antlers have a main beam, usually with brow tines and perhaps one or more additional points. About halfway up the main beam widens into

The fallow deer originated in Europe, but the species has been ranched for so many centuries its original range is uncertain. Fallow deer have distinctive palmated antlers and an "Adam's apple." They occur in several color phases from nearly black to pure white, including spotted.

a broad palm, often (and hopefully!) with numerous additional points off the palm. No two fallow racks are alike, but a good buck is sure to be an interesting and unusual trophy.

Fallow deer are generally less wary than most deer species because they have been "ranched" in Europe for centuries. However, they do have the good senses common to most deer species, and when subjected to hunting pressure often learn to use them. I've seen fallow deer in both Texas and Spain that were wild as March hares and as difficult to hunt as any deer. Usually, though, they are less challenging than most exotic species.

Sika deer (*Cervus nippon*) are Asian deer with subspecies from China, Formosa and Japan being intermixed here in the U.S. The Japanese subspecies is the smallest, averaging about 125 pounds; the large Manchurian sika can weigh up to 275 pounds. U.S. sika average somewhere in between, depending on the bloodlines.

Sika deer are close relatives to our elk, similar in overall appearance and with elk-like antlers that typically have four points per side. Sika are shy, secretive animals; if anything they love heavy cover even more than whitetails. I have seen sika on Texas ranches where the owner swore he had no idea how they'd gotten there! They can be difficult to hunt, but during the October rut the bucks lose some of their caution. At this time they bugle much like elk, and can be bugled in. They also fight viciously during the rut, and after it's over most mature bucks will have broken tines, another good reason to hunt them early.

These are the most popular exotic species, but of course there are many others. The various ibex species—Siberian and Iranian ibex, and the ibex-goat crosses—offer some excellent hunting, especially in traditional ibex habitat such as New Mexico's Florida Mountains and Colorado's Chalk Bluffs. While not truly a game species, it should also be mentioned that Spanish goats, also called Catalina Island goats, offer some challenging, and often tough, hunting in several parts of the country.

The Indian nilgai, a huge antelope weighing up to 600 pounds, is actually quite plentiful on some large Texas ranches. But its small

This fallow buck was taken in Vermont. These exotic deer occur in several parts of the U.S., including some free-ranging populations. It is believed that the first fallow deer in North America were imported by George Washington for his Mount Vernon estate.

straight horns—only nine inches on a real monster—are unimpressive and probably account for the animal's lack of popularity with hunters.

European red deer are becoming more popular. These animals are very close relatives of the elk; they're only slightly smaller and will interbreed freely with our elk. Aside from size, the principal difference is that red deer tend to have additional "crown" points near the tip of each antler. I expect there to be more red deer available in the U.S., but, unlike most exotics, so far trophy quality in this country doesn't approach that available on the species' home turf.

Most of the other exotic species are termed "super exotics" by the game ranchers, breeders and outfitters. Most of these species are more or less experimental, but the occasional surplus male may be available. Eland, addax, red sheep, scimitar oryx, Himalayan tahr and perhaps a dozen or more other species fall into this category. Of these, addax and scimitar oryx are proving to be very successful exotics, and are becoming much more available every year. I expect that they'll eventually become very common exotics. Since they are no longer hunted, and may not exist, in the wild, this could be a really good thing.

What is exotic hunting like? It's really up to the hunter. Unfortunately, it's true that "fish in a barrel" exotic hunting is available. The

The sika deer is an Asian member of the *Cervus* genus, round-antlered deer and thereby a close relative to our elk. The sika deer prefer heavy cover much like our whitetail, and can be among our most difficult exotic deer to hunt.

Ibex are increasing in popularity as an exotic. Many of the North American herds have been crossed with some feral goat blood, but ranchers are breeding back to repurify the strain. This huge male, photographed on a Texas ranch, appears to be of pure Iranian stock.

same can be said for many of our native game species. But whether in a free-ranging situation or on private land, many exotic ranchers and outfitters today are striving to provide a quality hunting experience, and they're succeeding. The animals themselves aren't pushovers. They're wild animals just like our native species, and when transplanted to suitable habitat will react just like they do on their native ranges. They provide unique, interesting trophies, and offer the added bonus of hunting when most native game seasons are closed.

Two considerations are of prime importance when planning an exotics hunt. First, if, like most of us, part of the enjoyment of hunting is the challenge it offers, you need to shop around and check references before arranging a hunt. Make sure the habitat is natural, and if it's a private-land hunt, make sure the acreage is suitable to the animal. Second, take the exotic species on their own merits. An axis, fallow, or sika deer isn't the same as a whitetail—just like a whitetail isn't the same as a mule deer. The hunting won't be the same, and there's no point in making critical comparisons. Enjoy them for what they are. I've made a number of exotic hunts, and have enjoyed all of them. And

I'll probably make quite a few more. It can be a long time between one fall season and another, and we're fortunate to have these fabulous foreigners to fill the gap!

Author's Note

Ours is a vast continent, and no mortal can lay claim to having hunted all of it. Some hunters, and likewise some hunting writers, are specialists, devoting the bulk of their time afield in pursuit of trophy rams, mossyhorned whitetails or muleys, outsized bull elk, or some other particular animal or type of hunting that strikes a chord in their imagination. I'm no specialist; I like it all, and over the past couple of decades I've been fortunate to have sampled a wide assortment of the incredibly varied hunting North America has to offer.

I lay no claim to being an expert on any of our hunting. Instead I've rambled from one end of the continent to other, and am truly a jack-of-all-trades and master of none. But I've enjoyed it, and I doubt if my hunting habits will change; we have too many great game animals in too much beautiful country. These lines might be the conclusion to a book—hopefully an enjoyable and informative one—on hunting North American big game, but they're far, far from a conclusion to my North American hunting. I'm struck by the mountains that remain to be climbed and the deserts, plains, forests and marshes waiting to be crossed. They're out there, all across this huge land. None of us will tread on all of it, but it's there, and the game is there—not only undiminished, but in most cases increasing. North American hunting has changed radically in the past 20 or 30 years, and this book has been written to present as accurate a picture as possible of what it's like today. It will continue to change. The hunting will not become easier, more accessible, or less expensive, and ultimately some of the information herein will become dated. But unlike so much of the world, the wildlife and the land to hunt will still be available here in North America and the hunters of this continent, teamed with the game managers, will continue to make it all possible.

This book is about the country and the game of this continent, and the way it is hunted today. I have, hopefully, provided information that will aid in planning a hunting trip anywhere on this continent, but I have avoided providing the addresses of game departments, outfitters, and hunters' agents. These can be obtained on a more up-to-date basis from the "where to go" sections in the outdoor and hunting magazines or, in the case of state game departments, from Directory Assistance in the respective state capitols. That doesn't mean that I'm not grateful to the many fine professional hunters whose campfires I've shared and who have led me along so many game trails. To Finn Aagaard, Duwane Adams, Jack Atcheson, Sr., Alan Baier, Mike Ballew, Jess Caswell, Frank Cook, Danny Estes, Mike Freeland, Marvin and Warner Glenn, Lee Holen, Jerry Hughes, Jack Hume, Don and Warren Johnson, Arlys Kanseah, Ed Langlands, Cameron Lee, Frank Morales, Don McCrae, Bill Richter, Robert Rogers, Thompson Temple, John Ward, Lester Wright, a fine brown bear guide who preferred to be called "Slim," and so many others, my thanks for showing me the way.

And to all my good friends—for hunters who share campfires, if only briefly and never again, *are* good friends—my thanks for good times shared, and my hopes that our paths cross on another game trail.

This book has been many years in the making. Special acknowledgement is due Ken Elliott, Publisher of *Petersen's Hunting* magazine, for putting up with my occasional absences "doing research," and to Bob Elman, a most competent editor who oversaw the project from start to finish. But if the background was a matter of years, the actual writing was compressed into weekends, late evenings and early mornings of a very few harried months—and for her support, patience amd understanding, my thanks to my lovely wife Paula.

Craig Boddington
Los Angeles, California

Index